D1461616

Androgyny in Modern Literature

Androgyny in Modern Literature

Tracy Hargreaves
School of English
University of Leeds

palgrave
macmillan

First published 2005 by
PALGRAVE MACMILLAN
Houndmills, Basingstoke, Hampshire RG21 6XS and
175 Fifth Avenue, New York, N. Y. 10010
Companies and representatives throughout the world

PALGRAVE MACMILLAN is the global academic imprint of the Palgrave Macmillan division of St. Martin's Press, LLC and of Palgrave Macmillan Ltd. Macmillan® is a registered trademark in the United States, United Kingdom and other countries. Palgrave is a registered trademark in the European Union and other countries.

ISBN 1–4039–0200–3

This book is printed on paper suitable for recycling and made from fully managed and sustained forest sources.

Logging, pulping and manufacturing processes are expected to conform to the environmental regulations of the country of origin.

A catalogue record for this book is available from the British Library.

Library of Congress Cataloging-in-Publication Data

Hargreaves, Tracy.
    Androgyny in modern literature / Tracy Hargreaves.
        p. cm.
    Includes bibliographical references and index.
    ISBN 1-4039-0200-3
    1. Androgyny (Psychology) in literature. 2. Literature, Modern–
20th century–History and criticism. I. Title.

PN56.A57H37 2005
809'.93353–dc22   2004054299

Transferred to digital print 2007
Printed and bound by CPI Antony Rowe, Eastbourne

This is for my mum – for teaching me to read

Contents

Acknowledgements

I owe an important debt of thanks to Suzanne Raitt who taught me a great deal, and acknowledge with very grateful thanks Morag Shiach, Alan Stewart, Andrew Penman and Emily Hamer, and especially, and for all kinds of reasons, Liz Maslen. Thanks, too, to Adriana Craciun, John Logan, Sarah Graham, Emma Parker and Gill Plain for listening and commenting on drafts of the typescript. At Leeds, I am particularly grateful to my colleagues whose intellectual generosity and social largesse is never less than impressive and always more than expected. So thanks to Fiona Becket, Mark Batty, Viv Jones, Ed Larissy, Katy Mullin, Catherine Packham, Pam Rhodes, Juliette Taylor and John Whale for all kinds of support and reassurance, and particularly to John McLeod, Francis O'Gorman and Gail Marshall for being so totally affirming and generous. Thanks, too, to Andy, Lily and Rosa, and to Mike, Caroline and Florence. I also owe a special – and very warm – thanks to my MA students who studied 'Representations of Androgyny in the Twentieth Century' for making teaching – and learning from them – so utterly pleasurable and rewarding. I am also grateful to Helen Trompeteler at the National Portrait Gallery. The jacket illustration of Gluck's self-portrait is reproduced by courtesy of the National Portrait Gallery. The best and biggest thanks are to Máire for being so astute, and for her monumental patience in listening, reading, commenting, suggesting and generally making it possible for me to write.

Introduction

Cal, the narrator of Jeffrey Eugenides' *Middlesex*, sets the record straight at the beginning of his narrative:[1] 'Something you should understand: I'm not androgynous in the least' (p. 41).[2] Cal rejects androgyny in favour of scientific exactitude: '5-alpha-reductase deficiency syndrome allows for normal biosynthesis and peripheral action of testosterone, in utero, neonatally, and at puberty' (p. 41), There is no ambiguity: 'I operate in society as a man' (p. 41). His repudiation of androgyny is a refusal to live with gender or sexual ambiguity, and once his hermaphrodite status has been revoked, his (masculine) femininity can be sloughed off. Cal, as Calliope, *was* biologically hermaphrodite, and towards the conclusion of his story, Plato's *Symposium* is cited by Cal's new friend, Zora, who offers him an alternative explanatory narrative to the scientific category '5-Alpha-Reductase Pseudohermaphrodites':

> There have been hermaphrodites around forever, Cal. Forever. Plato said that the original human being was a hermaphrodite. Did you know that? The original person was two halves, one male, one female. Then these got separated. That's why everybody's always searching for their other half. Except for us. We've got both halves already.[3]

This equation, in which sexual difference is always already transcended, is offered as a consolatory narrative at a particularly low point in Cal's life. Having run away from home, Cal makes a living as Ovid's Hermaphroditus, swimming in a water tank to better display a patent hermaphrodite body, a living fetish for paying customers to ogle. Two significant, but different, myths of a violent metamorphosis sit side-by-side – one of complement, one of competition.[4] One is Aristophanes' story as it is told in Plato's *Symposium*. Originally, there were three sexes, not two, and we were doubly formed, not individual: male and male, female and female, and male and female. Zeus split the spherical creatures in two as punishment for their arrogance, causing each to experience the loss of the other – a loss that we long to redeem through sexual union, as the once androgynous couple become the procreative heterosexual couple. The other myth is Ovid's story of the female nymph Salmacis and Hermaphroditus, son of Hermes and Aphrodite. Salmacis forces and welds herself to the unwilling male body of Hermaphroditus, a suture that suggests the violent and unusual rape of a man by a woman, leaving him weakened by an unsought, and unwanted, femininity, 'a fantasy of unity', as Hélène Cixous described it: 'Two within one, and not even two wholes.'[5] Neither myth entirely fits Cal, raised as a girl, biologically hermaphrodite, surgically reassigned to maleness in adulthood: '[t]he idea,' Eugenides has said, 'was to write a fictional book about a hermaphrodite, and I wanted it to be medically accurate – to be the story of a real hermaphrodite, rather than a fanciful creature like Tiresias or Orlando who could shift in a paragraph; to avail myself of the mythological connections without making the character a myth.'[6] What the 'real' hermaphrodite demonstrates in *Middlesex* is the cultural and psychic necessity to have one gendered and sexual identity, not two, rather than an exploratory fantasy of speculating what it might be like to have or be both.

The inclusion of Plato's and Ovid's foundational myths in *Middlesex* reinforces their status as explanatory narratives, invoked by Eugenides, as by many of the writers included in this book, in accounting for the intersexed, intermediate body. Less obviously, it speaks to the ways in which they may be appropriated to meet the requirements of the storyteller. Whether the original human beings were hermaphrodites or androgynes depends on which translation of the *Symposium* you read, though the difference between them amounts to more than a matter of lexical choice.[7] As signifiers, and in the history of their representations, the androgyne and the hermaphrodite have twinned and shadowed each other (reviewing *Middlesex*, Mark Lawson makes the familiar slippage, referring to 'the possibility of androgyny' rather than hermaphroditism).[8] Darwin (*Descent of Man*), Freud ('The Sexual Aberrations', 'Leonardo da Vinci'), Havelock Ellis (*Studies in the Psychology of Sex*) and Richard von Krafft-Ebing (*Psychopathia Sexualis*), as well as Earl Lind (*Autobiography of an Androgyne*) all made the terms interchangeable and synonymous, and though they all have different issues at stake in their various representations of androgyny (or the androgyne) and the hermaphrodite, there is agreement[9] that the dual-sexed figure is atavistic, a throwback to an earlier age when vertebrates appeared to be a mixture of both anatomical sexes.

Cal's certainty about himself ('I'm not androgynous in the least') is unusual – at least, in the long history of androgynous representation. The cumulative, prismatic effect of that history suggests that 'androgyny' belongs to, or indicates, no secure or transcendent ontology, but is always in the process of being made in relation to the various requirements of history, culture and the literary imagination. Androgyny is not a stable or a transcendent category, but is subject to historical and cultural change. Foucault's insights suggest to us that the emergence of a homosexual identity was a product of Victorian taxonomies of sexual and criminal behaviour, never an immanent identity, and whilst representations of androgyny also emerge from intricate sexological taxonomies, they are never limited to those categorisations. From the late nineteenth to the twentieth century, androgyny has been produced as a shifting category, mobilised in different discourses – literary, sexological, psychoanalytic, sociological, feminist. The meaning of androgyny depends on its function in a given discourse. It can appear in many forms: a sensibility, a pathology, as symptomatic of a repressed desire (as Freud argued in his psychoanalytic biography of Leonardo da Vinci), the embodiment of an identity defined through usually same-sex sexual orientation and/or cross-gender identification, an emblem (or fantasy) of a behaviour where positive traits, identified as masculine and feminine, work harmoniously in a single individual. Even as androgyny was revised during the late 1960s and 1970s in feminism's second wave, it still remained a problematic symbol, one that eschewed femininity in prioritising masculinity. More recently, androgyny has been criticised, by Judith Halberstam in *Female Masculinity* and Chris Straayer in *Deviant Eyes, Deviant Bodies*, as a too generalised identity that effaces the sexual politics of specific embodied female-masculine identities. When Judith Butler argued (in *Gender Trouble*) that 'Gender is the repeated stylisation of the body, a set of repeated acts within a highly regulatory frame that congeal over time to produce the appearance of substance, of a natural sort of being', the reifying principles of masculinity and femininity that secure androgyny as the balanced equation of binary gender constructions come to seem naive and misconceived.

'Aristophanes' playful recounting of the story of primordial union and its collapse into fragmentation ... sets in motion a powerful cultural narrative about the origins of human sexuality.'[10] Catriona MacLeod's observation is borne out by the evidence offered by early twentieth-century literature. Aristophanes' account of androgyny in

Plato's *Symposium* has been influential in representations of androgynous unity and sexuality throughout the twentieth century, from
Freud's (mis)reading of Aristophanes' story to account for pathological
models of sexual behaviour in 'The Sexual Aberrations' (1905), to John
Cameron Mitchell's rock musical *Hedwig and the Angry Inch* in 2001
(Hedwig's song, 'Origin of Love', is a faithful re-telling of Aristophanes'
story of androgyny; the film itself follows Hedwig's quest to find
his/her other half)[11] and Eugenides' *Middlesex* in 2002. When 5-alpha-
reductase deficiency syndrome fails to explain Cal's biology, Plato and
Ovid (though they offer such different accounts of desire and its
embodiment) provide reassuring explanations. The *Symposium* in particular has proved an important resource in literary imagination. James
Joyce is said to have kept a copy of Shelley's translation of the *Banquet*
(as the *Symposium* was then translated) on his bookshelves. In *Woman
and Labour* Olive Schreiner directed her readers to Benjamin Jowett's
translation (1871) to underline her point about the natural compatibil-
ity of men and women, which, she argued, had been corrupted by the
organisation of labour: 'The two sexes are not distinct species but two
halves of one whole, always acting and interacting on each other
through inheritance and reproducing and blending with each other in
each generation.'[12] Diana Collecott has argued that 'Aristophanes'
fantasy in the *Symposium* offers models for the heterosexually inflected
notion of bisexuality that we encounter in HD's *Bid Me To Live*, as
well as the homosexual coupling of Midget and Josepha into a "perfect
whole" in *Paint It Today*.'[13] For Havelock Ellis and for Freud,
Aristophanes' speech functioned as an explanatory narrative that
might enable an understanding of humanity's latent bisexuality, a
bisexuality which, for Ellis, was somatic rather than erotic:

> The conception of the latent bisexuality of all males and females
> cannot fail to be fairly obvious to intelligent observers of the human
> body. It emerges at an early period of philosophic thought, and from
> the first was occasionally used for the explanation of homosexuality.
> Plato's myth in the *Banquet* and the hermaphroditic statues of antiq-
> uity show how acute minds, working ahead of science, exercised
> themselves with these problems.[14]

For modern writers like Lawrence and Hardy, however, androgyny, as
Plato has Aristophanes conceive it, was a politically oppressive myth, to
be greeted with scepticism. In *Women in Love*, Birkin meditates on 'the
old age, before sex was, [when] we were mixed, each one a mixture'[15]

before repudiating this thesis: 'Why should we consider ourselves, men and women, as broken fragments of one whole? It is not true. We are not broken fragments of one whole. Rather we are the singling away into purity and clear being, of things that are mixed.'[16] Hardy rejected Aristophanes' myth in *Tess of the d'Urbervilles* by de-romanticising its sentimental assumptions:

> completeness is not to be prophesied, or even conceived as possible. Enough that in the present case, as in millions, it was not the two halves of a perfect whole that confronted each other at the perfect moment; a missing counterpart wandered independently about the earth waiting in crass obtuseness till the late time came. Out of which maladroit delay sprang anxieties, disappointments, shocks, catastrophes, and passing-strange destinies. (p. 83)[17]

In Angela Carter's *The Passion of New Eve*, Tristessa, the male-to-female transgendered subject, and Eve, the male-to-female transsexual subject, consummate their relationship, forming, momentarily, Plato's perfect hermaphrodite (as it is described in the text); but as that narrative demonstrates, the Platonic androgyne can only exist transitorily as a mythical construction that is damaged through contact with the real. The perfect couple is brutally demythologised and sundered, not by Zeus but by the military Children's Crusade who kill Tristessa. For Gore Vidal's legendary Myra Breckinridge, psychiatrists are *passé* and the index of that is the outmoded belief in androgynous unity: 'Dr Montag still believes that each sex is intended to be half of a unit, like those monsters mentioned in Plato's *Symposium*,' she tells Rusty; but sexual relations are a wrangle for supremacy for her, and in *Myron*, the sequel to *Myra Breckinridge*, Myra rejects Plato altogether: 'Those gorgeous hemispheres, crying to be wrenched apart in order that one might create the opposite to Plato's beast by substituting that dumb Greek's trendy ideal of the unnatural whole to my truer vision of forcibly divided and forever separated parts. No monist Myra!' (p. 291).

John Cowper Powys, writing to Frances Gregg in 1919, found the *Symposium* to be on target for an account of heterosexual love: 'I've just been reading in the *Symposium* what that old comedian Aristophanes says about love and I'm damned if he doesn't hit the mark with his one person cut in half or how two half-people hunting about for each other and begging Hephaistos to hammer them together ...'[18] Powys echoes a sentiment nursed by the narrator in Baron Corvo's *The Desire and Pursuit of the Whole*: 'And, as far as I know ... I really do think that Plato has touched the spot' (p. 13). By the mid-twentieth century, Lacan still claimed sovereignty for Aristophanes' story as an account of the forma-tion of subjectivity; it was, he asserted, 'a defiance to the centuries for it traverses them without anyone trying to do better'.[19] For American fem-inist critics like Catharine Stimpson writing in the mid-1970s: 'To reas-sure them of their humanity, to remind themselves that they have a tradition, both the androgyne and the homosexual look back to Plato's *Symposium* for an endorsing myth.'[20] Aristophanes' androgyne turns out to be a trope with multifarious possibilities, an index not only of sexual orientation, but also of cultural and social relations.

At stake in the difference between the androgyne and the hermaph-rodite, critics have argued, is the visibility, the material fact of the body: 'What sets the androgyne apart,' says Francette Pacteau, 'dwells in one gesture: the uncovering of the body.'[21] It is that display 'that positions the hermaphrodite on the side of the visible'. The androgyne is, then, the 'impossible referent', a sign (despite what Aristophanes argues) indicating a fantasy that unfolds along the axis of the gaze. 'I do not encounter an androgyne in the street,' Pacteau suggests, 'rather I encounter a figure whom I "see as" androgynous.'[22] Pacteau's reading of the androgyne shifts the focus from an embodied androgynous object to a subject whose narcissistic or fetishistic gaze fantasises a given figure as androgynous and who must, at the same time, function as the index of disavowal: I know this is really a man *or* a woman, *but* ...[23] If the hermaphrodite body (as we're supposed to picture it in *Middlesex*) doesn't leave all that much to the imagination, the apparent body of the androgyne annuls it: disembodied, the androgyne leaves everything to the imagination. In Hari Kunzru's *The Impressionist,* the androgyne represents a figure denoting secrecy and invisibility: 'Pran wonders if ... the power to remove oneself from sight is merely a deeper form of androgyny.' But the hermaphrodite is tangible: Pran, now reinvented as Bobby, 'shows them the hermaphrodite figure of the God, man on one side, woman on the other. He stands back as the women titter and the men make ribald jokes. Then discreetly, when they are not looking, he reaches forward and touches the stone for luck.'[24] The hermaphrodite marks a limit of sexual knowledge in Roth's *The Human Stain*: 'one of the boys was so innocent he didn't know what a hermaphrodite was.'[25] But then, the androgyne has been every-thing to the imagination, from the *fin de siècle*, in modernist and contemporary literature and film, androgyny has been consistently re-imagined and re-embodied, 'at once a real, empirical subject and an idealized abstraction, a figure of universal Man'.[26]

The double-sexed figure shifted in terms of its representation from classical mythology to discourses of medicine and psychiatry in nineteenth-century sexology. Although some practitioners within the field saw the unified double-sexed figure as emblematic of an atavistic and primitive civilisation, others like Richard von Krafft-Ebing, Professor of Psychiatry at the University of Vienna, constructed the androgyne as the womanly man, a pathologised identity that he placed as a sub-section in the category of 'Cerebral Neuroses' in his *Psychopathia Sexualis*. Freud adapted the 'popular view of the sexual instinct' taken from the 'poetic fable' as the basis for understanding 'sexual aberrations' in the first of his 'Three Essays on Sexuality' (1905), but was famously selective in his reading of Aristophanes' story, making the androgynous couple central to an understanding of hetero-normative desire so that, as Kari Weil suggests, 'Plato's theory will not conflict with Freud's presentation of homosexuality and lesbianism as "deviations"'.[27] His use of androgyny was modified, however, to fit a different theory in his psychoanalytic biography of Leonardo da Vinci in 1910. Freud's representation of androgyny found expression in the pre-Oedipal boy's fantasy of the imaginary embodiment of the androgynous/hermaphrodite mother (Freud doesn't distinguish between the two terms) and in an idealised sublimation of the androgyne, which was bound up in Leonardo's painterly aesthetic.

With classical models as their source, writers could look to antiquity to give authority to the hypotheses they were making in connecting sexual desire with creativity and genius. In his *Autobiography of an Androgyne*, Earl Lind suggested that he was giving the 'inner history' of ancient Greek hermaphrodite sculptures, and obligingly posed in his book as the statue of the Sleeping Hermaphrodite in the Louvre. The English writer Edward Carpenter claimed distinguished and heroic figures from Greek and Renaissance histories (Michaelangelo, Alexander the Great, Sappho) to secure lofty precedents for the modern 'intermediate type', artists and educators who combined positive elements of traditional male and female characteristics. His cultural regenerators were similar to those envisaged by socialist-feminist writers like Edward and Eleanor Marx-Aveling and Olive Schreiner. In *The Woman Question*, the Marx-Avelings had endorsed Kant's belief that 'man and woman constitute, when united, the whole and entire being; one sex completes the other':

But when each sex is incomplete, and the one incomplete to the most lamentable extent, and when as a rule, neither of them comes into real, thorough, habitual, free contact, mind to mind, with the other, the being is neither whole nor entire.[28]

But if such androgynous union was deployed as contributing towards the social good, rather than the pursuit or realisation of love, it was also part of a sub-cultural erotic, European imagination. In France, decadent writers like Rachilde scandalously incorporated the androgynous figure into stories that rummaged in the margins of erotic desire, teasing conventional heterosexual relations: in *Monsieur Vénus*, aristocratic women 'pass' as men; peasant men dress and behave as women in order to satisfy and disrupt social and sexual desire. Wilde gestured towards French decadence in his portrait of the bisexual sybarite Dorian Gray, described by Camille Paglia as the charismatic, Apollonian androgyne,[29] but such decadence appeared degraded and moribund by the time Radclyffe Hall came to represent a noble 'intermediate type' in the often pious spaces of *The Well of Loneliness* in 1928. The association of androgynous or intermediate identity with creative genius was part of the discursive representation of androgyny in the early twentieth century, rebutting sexological categorisations that saw androgyny as degenerative and injurious. Famously, Virginia Woolf thought that the writer should have an androgynous mind, and her sixth novel, *Orlando*, engaged with androgyny as both an oscillatory identity (Orlando is first a man, then a woman, and, cross-dressing, is able to re-inhabit masculinity) and as the product of complementary union. When Orlando marries, she recognises that her husband is also a woman, just as he recognises that Orlando is also a man. From pathology, to ideal, to fantasy, to sensibility, androgyny resurfaced in the late 1960s and 1970s as an achievable ontology before it was rejected as limiting and conservative: a trope, category, identity and fantasy that reinforced the characterisations that it challenged.

This book presents a chronology of representations of androgyny, beginning with the translation and subsequent proliferation and metamorphoses of Plato's *Symposium* from the mid- to the late nineteenth century onward. Two speeches from the *Symposium* – those of Aristophanes and of Pausanias – proved to be instrumental in constructing narratives of same-sex desire, from Xavier Mayne's *The Intersexes: A History of Similisexualism* to Edward Carpenter's popular writings on the 'intermediate sex'.

Through readings of Freud's psychoanalytic biography of Leonardo da Vinci, Earl Lind's *Autobiography of an Androgyne* and Rachilde's *Monsieur Vénus*, chapter 1 explores constructions of androgyny that posit it, variously, as the sublimated expression of repressed sexual desire, the pre-Oedipal male child's fantasy of a specific maternal embodiment, the story of the androgynous, homosexual 'womanly-man'. Each of these versions of androgyny foreground the androgyne's power to disrupt and disturb hetero-normative relationships, a power that seems at once desirable and to be feared. The figure of the androgyne, the fantasy of the androgyne, as it is constructed in literary (and psychoanalytic) imagination always presents us with an impasse. This is partly because the figure is shown to test the limits of the respectable and permissible in social and sexual life, and is therefore often seen in powerless retreat or isolation, and partly because the androgyne (or more generally, androgyny) is always bounded by the binary categories it also seeks to challenge. If there are similarities in the construction of the figure (as a category or as a subject, androgyny or the androgyne tends to be secretive, liminal, wavering, private) there are also intriguing differences: as a category and an identity, it has been pejorative, degenerative, embodied, projected, artistic, spiritual, regenerative.

The degenerative and regenerative potential of the androgyne is explored further in chapter 2 through readings of Rose Allatini's pacifist novel, *Despised and Rejected*, first published in 1918 and immediately banned under the terms of the Defence of the Realm Act. The novel seeks to revise internalised homophobia by drawing on Edward Carpenter's construction of the noble 'intermediate type', homosexual and artistic, who *could* be the regenerators of a boorish and moribund national culture, but who are never given the chance. The imprisonment of Dennis at the end of the narrative and the banning of the book speak eloquently to the limits of democracy and toleration at the end of the First World War. Radclyffe Hall's *The Well of Loneliness* also retrieves the 'invert' from its pathologised incarnation and re-presents Stephen Gordon as another noble intermediate, a writer apparently blessed with an 'androgynous writing mind' (Puddle, her governess, tells her that she can 'write with a curious double insight – write both men and women from a personal knowledge'). Whilst Hall explicitly rewrote sexological constructions of inversion, contemporary writers like Woolf and Lawrence appeared to turn away from them: Carpenter, important for Allatini and for Hall, was rejected by Lawrence as being 'not in my line', and he dismissed the idea of a third or intermediate sex as perversion in *Fantasia of the Unconscious*. His distaste for the intermediate type was expressed in *The Rainbow* in his construction of Ursula's uncle, Tom Brangwen, and her teacher, Winifred Inger: the effeminate industrialist and the mannish, educated woman lose themselves entirely in the world of the mind, at great cost to the redemptive sexual experience offered by the body. Lawrence, formulating a philosophy of writing from 1913 in 'The Study of Thomas Hardy', had been looking for an androgynous aesthetic that addressed a pure and transcendent sexual union devoid of social consciousness, and his exploration of a symbolic androgyny in *Women in Love* was partly expressed through Rupert Birkin's bisexuality. In these texts, same-sex orientation tended to be marked upon the body by masculinity or boyishness for women, femininity for men: when such individuals are located in the social, their fates are marked by trauma – imprisonment, exile, alienation.

Chapter 3 pays particular attention to Virginia Woolf, and considers her much-maligned representation of the 'androgynous writing mind' in *A Room of One's Own*. Hall, Woolf and Lawrence intersect in *A Room of One's Own*: Woolf, as Jane Marcus has pointed out, draws attention to the trial of *The Well of Loneliness* which took place at the same time that she was giving the speeches at Cambridge that she revised as *A Room*, and Woolf later wrote to Desmond MacCarthy that Lawrence was probably the writer she had in mind when she criticised Mr A the novelist. The chapter situates Woolf's call for the androgynous writing mind in different contexts: first as the culmination of the arguments she has been making in *A Room*, then among other images that she uses to try to net a symbol for the creative process, and finally more generally in the context of literary modernism. Woolf explores dual sexual identity as the location of sexual difference as it is marked on the body, in culture, through marriage and, crucially, in writing.

Chapter 4 explores the resurgence of interest in androgyny during feminism's second wave, and examines the renewed faith in androgynous ontology displayed in the work of writers of this period. If anything, androgyny became even more protean during the late 1960s and 1970s, serving as the expression of a range of sexual identities, social possibilities and imaginative freedoms. Androgyny thus came to figure asexuality, bisexuality, a credible force within culture or a purely imaginary concept; we might aspire to be androgynous by embracing masculine or feminine qualities, or we needn't bother since, according to the Jungian analyst June Singer, we already are androgynous: the archetypes of the anima and animus that lurk inside us ensure that. Literary representations of androgyny moved between sincerity (Ursula Le Guin's *The Left Hand of Darkness*, Marge Piercy's *Woman on the Edge of Time*) and parody. Gore Vidal's *Myron*, the 1974 sequel to *Myra Breckinridge*, made an oscillatory androgyny the site of civil war as Myron and Myra struggle to take control of a body both think of as their own. Their endless, fruitless struggle points to the futility of a desire to unite 'femininity' and 'masculinity': in *Myron*, femininity and masculinity are hopelessly mismatched. There are really two Myrons: the first is the film aficionado and 'fag nephew' of Uncle Buck Loner, who transforms himself into Myra, a fantasised assemblage of Hollywood's female movie icons. When Myron returns to re-inhabit the body that once was his, he turns into the epitome of middle-class conservatism, extending a trajectory that took him from gay man to bisexual woman to heterosexual man. The flamboyant Myra, the antithesis of the second Myron, cuts a strangely residuary figure. Myra and Myron not only embody a fundamental incompatibility between a specific kind of masculinity and femininity (thereby signalling the ludicrousness or impracticability of the androgynous ideal), they also suggest the male's abhorrence of being subsumed by woman (the fate of Hermaphroditus), a fear that affords Vidal an opportunity to mock a particular kind of straight maleness rather than simply theatricalising misogyny. Androgynous ontology promised an idealised alternative to the institutionalised effects of sexual division in Marge Piercy's *Woman on the Edge of Time*, offering a serene existence in the imaginary community of Mattapoisett. Its antithesis is the nightmarish offspring of technology, the inert cyborg, half-woman, half-machine, as Piercy imagined it, subject to the control of men who were themselves in thrall to multinational corporations. Towards the end of the decade, androgyny was a category more repudiated than welcomed: it threatened to obliterate sexual difference and reified the gendered categories it sought to dismantle. Jan Morris identified as androgynous whilst she was making the transition from man to woman, but the different appropriations of androgyny in Morris's autobiography *Conundrum* (1974) seem to crystallise its possibilities and difficulties. As ontology, it was temporary, a suspension between, rather than a union of, male and female identities. It was also an essentially private identity (Morris was understandably self-conscious about displaying a body that appeared to be simultaneously male and female) and mythological; she felt like a figure in a fable, either 'monstrous or divine', when she went swimming in a Welsh mountain lake. But androgyny was never more than a temporary identity or identification and, following her sex change, Morris readily identified with culturally approved constructions of femininity, a process that seems to figure androgyny as a wavering and insecure identity.

Chapter 5 explores representations of androgyny in Gore Vidal's *Myra Breckinridge* and Angela Carter's *The Passion of New Eve*, both texts that situate the androgyne as an image or reflection created in myth or fantasy, but unable to survive in reality. *Myra Breckinridge* speaks to the apparent possibility of a return to the ideal of androgyny as she looks forward to a time when 'man' 'has become free to blend with others, to exchange personalities with both women and men, to play out the most elaborate dreams in a world where there will be no limits to the human spirit's play'. The novel ends, however, by establishing those limits in the marriage of an ultra-conservative Myron and his equally conservative wife, Mary-Ann. Myra's life is always twinned with Myron's, and throughout her narrative, Myron's is an identity that she alternately requires and disowns. She needs to complete Myron's book of film criticism on *Parker Tyler and the Films of the Forties*, but her larger project involves 'realigning' the sexes in order to prevent a population explosion, and so she sets to work on radically re-educating two of her students, Rusty and Mary-Ann, who exemplify the boy and girl next door. Both *Myra Breckinridge* and Angela Carter's *The Passion of New Eve* explore identity as it is mediated through the cinematic gaze, and the most positive representations of femininity in these texts are those sanctioned by the male gaze. Writing about Greta Garbo, Carter claims that there was always a story going round that Garbo was really a man because she was too much like a woman; Tristessa, a little like Vidal's Myra, was 'somebody who's been completely constructed by the rules of the cinema'.[30]

Carter and Lindsay Clarke (whose novel *The Chymical Wedding* is the subject of chapter 6) both explore the possibility of androgynous unity through the symbolism of alchemy. Maleness and femaleness exist notionally in *The Passion of New Eve*: Carter negotiates what they might mean and be through myth, alchemy, the simulacra and the performative. Androgynous unity is momentarily possible but impossible to sustain, as the transsexual Eve comes to understand: when Eve and Tristessa embrace on the American flag, they make, as Eve says, the Platonic hermaphrodite, but the coupling is doomed when reality intrudes and Tristessa is shot by the boys of the Children's Crusade. Clarke's *The Chymical Wedding* engages with androgyny through the idea of the chymical wedding – in alchemy, the moment that signifies the symbolic unification of opposites. Moving between two narrative moments – the early 1980s and the mid-nineteenth century – Clarke unites disparate strands of history by making the present redeem the terrible events of the past, a process that also offers possible solutions to the fractures and atomisation of the modern period. In both the nineteenth- and twentieth-century parts of the book, the transformation brought about through the processes of alchemy (in which base metals are supposedly turned into gold) is replayed as a series of androgynous possibilities: Louisa Agnew is possessed by the androgynous spirit of Mercurius and longs to be united through the 'chymical wedding' – in which opposites are united and purified in androgynous unity – with Edwin Frere. That unity is shown to be an impossibility, bound as they all are by the social contracts that determined nineteenth-century social and sexual behaviour. Alchemy is rendered both obscure and legible through its intricate series of symbols, and *The Chymical Wedding* is a text that advocates the importance of poetry and of symbolism, a text that asks for a more nuanced understanding of how to re-read, how to excavate surface reality.

Susan Sontag claimed the androgyne as 'one of the great images of Camp sensibility' and cinema 'probably the greatest popularizer of Camp taste today'. For Sontag, androgyny implied an aesthetic of emptiness (she described Garbo's beauty as a 'haunting androgynous vacancy'). That emptiness often lies at the heart of androgynous representation. The androgyne wavers in Huysmans' *À Rebours*, as I discuss in chapter 1; it's an image caught in transition, a figure engendering instability for Des Esseintes, and again for the assembled wedding guests in Rachilde's *Monsieur Vénus*. When Raoule and Jacques dance at their wedding the guests are divided between attraction and repulsion, between desire and its repudiation. Androgyny is a trope expressive of a sensibility that cannot be heard, as we see in Allatini's *Depised and Rejected*, a sensibility that is articulated in private retreat, in Woolf's *A Room*. Even as androgyny was resurrected as an aspirational material identity in the 1960s and 1970s, feminist writers still felt that it should only be a temporary term and anticipated a time when it would no longer be needed or make sense, a longer transition than that momentary wavering depicted by Huysmans and Rachilde, but a transition none the less. Aristophanes' myth of the androgyne depicted it as a figure in mourning, grieving the loss of its other half, longing for reconciliation. As a figure, trope, characteristic, sensibility and embodiment, androgyny and the androgyne might be associated with melancholia, in Freud's sense, as well as with mourning. In 'Mourning and Melancholia', Freud suggests that melancholia works unconsciously, that it is 'in some way related to an unconscious loss of a love-object, in contradistinction to mourning, in which there is nothing unconscious about the loss'. The ubiquity of androgynous representation in literary imagination suggests that the androgyne functions as a kind of melancholic figure in which the lost 'lost' other becomes incorporated, but often with traumatic effect, invoking a bleak neutrality or impasse. This figure is invoked repeatedly, only to be annulled or repudiated, as though we both do and do not want and require it. It's that curious history of representation that this book explores.

1
Classical to Medical

First then, human beings were formerly not divided into two sexes, male and female; there was also a third, common to both others, the name of which remains, though the sex itself has disappeared. The androgynous sex, both in appearance and in name, was common to both male and female; its name alone labours under a reproach.

androgyny as a third sex.

Plato, *Symposium*

You must remember in our Universities, Plato is held to be little better than a misleader of youth.

Dr Folliott, *Crotchet Castle*

This chapter takes as its starting point the translation into English in 1871 of Plato's *Symposium*, a series of dialogues devoted to the praise and nature of love. Benjamin Jowett, the distinguished classics scholar, introduced Plato to the University of Oxford in his reform of the Greats Curriculum, enshrining Plato, as Linda Dowling has argued, 'at the institutional heart of elite Victorian values'.[1] Around the same time, the *Symposium* was reaching a wider audience: in 1839, Mary Shelley was in the process of arranging the posthumous publication of a complete edition of Shelley's works, including the translation of the *Symposium* that she had transcribed for him in the late summer of 1818. She was necessarily guarded about Plato's unequivocal validation of homosexuality, though, encountering objections to its publication in full (it would not be published in unexpurgated form until 1931). Within the university, Greek studies operated as a 'homosexual code'.[2] 'You've read the *Symposium*?' Clive Durham asks Maurice, in E.M. Forster's posthumously published novel of same-sex love. Maurice, responding to their embryonic desire, had not known that 'it' could be mentioned, 'and when Durham did so in the middle of the sunlit court a breath of liberty touched him'.[3] That sense of liberation, Dowling suggests, was to be both intellectual and emotional for late Victorian writers like John Addington Symonds, Walter Pater and Oscar Wilde. In the *Phaedrus* and the *Symposium*, Symonds 'discovered the true *liber amoris* ... It was just as though the voice of my own soul spoke to me through Plato.'[4] Wilde's invocation of Plato under Charles Gill's cross-examination during the Marquis of Queensberry's 1895 libel trial clearly emphasised the intellectual and emotional qualities of 'the Love that dare not speak its name', but by then, Plato's association with homosexuality was recognised beyond Oxford, and Wilde was imprisoned for being himself 'little better than a misleader of youth'.[5] The late Victorian and Edwardian writer Edward Carpenter thought that Wilde's court case and subsequent imprisonment produced 'a sheer panic ... over *all* questions of sex, and especially of course questions of the Intermediate Sex'.[6] Though Carpenter did not elaborate on what those questions were, one immediate consequence for him was Fisher Unwin's cancellation of *Love's Coming of Age*, which contained his pamphlet on 'Homogenic Love and its Place in a Free Society'.[7] A relationship between homosexual sexuality and the androgynous 'intermediate' sex or type was clearly established by the *fin de siècle*, although the function and the identity of the androgyne turned out to be remarkably protean, as this chapter explores. In psychoanalytic biography such as Freud's *Leonardo da Vinci*, autobiographical texts like Earl Lind's *Autobiography of an Androgyne*, and *fin-de-siècle* literature like Huysmans' *À Rebours* and Rachilde's *Monsieur Vénus*, the androgyne emerges variously as the manifestation of sublimation, narcissistic homosexuality, passive homosexuality and trans-sex identification: a figure insistently inside *and* outside of representation.

The speeches in sexology

Of the five speeches that comprise the *Symposium*'s encomium to Eros, Mary Shelley dismissed the speeches of two, Pausanias and Aristophanes, as being of 'minor importance', although these turned out to be foundational in the re-inscription and re-configuration of androgyny in sexological, medical and literary imaginations.[8] Aristophanes' speech tells the story of humanity's origins as twinned or dual beings. Originally, the sexes were conjoined, with two heads, four arms and four legs. These rotund figures were uniformly male and male, female and female or androgynously male and female, derived cosmologically from the sun (male), the earth (female) and the moon (the androgyne). As punishment for their extravagant pride and ambition, Zeus split the spherical creatures in two. During a period of mourning for their loss, the divided and unsexed creatures appeared to pine away, so Zeus rearranged their genitals, moving them to the front of the body, so ensuring that the androgynous couples would, at any rate, be able to procreate. The androgynous, or third sex,[9] says Aristophanes, once embodied, now survives only in name since the condition itself is now extinct. Humanity's fate is forever to attempt, however fleetingly, to make good that painful separation, and so we continue to embrace each other in an attempt to redeem the loss. For Jowett, 'the loves of this world are an indistinct anticipation of an ideal union which is not yet realized'.[10] Arguably, Aristophanes' conclusions endure within our own culture's romantic vernacular as we continue to look for our perfect 'other half' and long for the time when two, as the Spice Girls once put it, become one.

Pausanias' speech described two kinds of love: one vulgar and lustful, deriving from the goddess Venus Pandemos, practised by men and women, the other dignified and noble, deriving from the goddess Venus Uranus, practised between men, love that came to be known as 'Uranian'. These models of sensuous love and degraded love and a purer, unadulterated and noble same-sex love evolved into an intermediate, homosexual third sex, exemplified in Xavier Mayne's *The Intersexes: A History of Similisexualism As a Problem in Social Life*. Mayne's book, written several years before it was privately published in Rome in 1908, offered English readers 'popular information of the problem of homosexualism, similisexualism, urninigism, inverted sexuality, uranianism, as it is variously termed'.[11] He dedicated the book to the memory of Richard von Krafft-Ebing, Professor of Psychiatry at the University of Vienna, whose elaborate taxonomies pathologised same- or trans-sex identification as the degenerate inheritance of familial illnesses that ranged from nervous illness to epilepsy. Unlike Krafft-Ebing, Mayne defended 'the similisexual instinct' as one that 'defines a series of originally intermediary sexes – the so-called intersexual theory – rather than mere aberrations, degeneracies, psychic tangents, from the male and female'.[12] Borrowing from Pausanias' speech, Mayne understood the male intermediate to be an 'Urning' and of the 'Uranian' sex, though his thinking clearly owed a debt to two of the earliest and most prominent sexologists, Karl Ulrichs and Magnus Hirschfeld.

Hirschfeld constructed four categories of 'sexual intermediacy': Hermaphroditism, Androgyny, Metatropism and Transvestism.[13] Whilst

Hermaphroditism was distinguished by 'an intersexual formation of sex organs', Androgyny was 'an intersexually mixed form of other bodily qualities'.[14] The British sexologist Havelock Ellis claimed that Ulrichs had been the first within the field of sexology to use the term 'Uranian' 'based on the well-known myth in Plato's *Banquet*. Later'. Ellis wrote, 'he Germanized this term into "Urning" for the male and "Urningin" for the female, and referred to the condition itself as "Urningtum"'.[15] The Anglicised term, adopted and popularly and widely disseminated by the English liberal thinker and writer Edward Carpenter, was Uranian, the noble male homosexual, identified by Carpenter as an 'intermediate type'.

Mayne evidently drew on an admixture of Pausanias' and Aristophanes' speeches, and connected the inter-sexed, or third sexed, androgynous figure with the male Uranian and the female Uraniad: 'There are two Intersexes named here as the Uranian and the Uraniad, the one partaking most of the outwardly and inwardly masculine yet not fully a man, the other leaning toward the typic feminine yet not fully a woman, are each indisputably a blend of the two extreme sexes.'[16] Mayne then re-imagined Aristophanes' double-sexed figures by suggesting that they shared not only an anatomy, but also culturally produced traits: 'These Intersexes partake of the natures and temperaments and physique of both the male and the female, now to one extent, now to another.'[17] Acknowledging Ulrichs' sympathetic defence of the Uranian, Mayne alluded to Aristophanes' speech to further endorse his theory of the homosexual subject and of homosexual desire as androgynous, describing Aristophanes's androgynes as:

> a protosex, a bisexual human type which has been divided. Each of the moieties is ever seeking thro the world his missing fellow; each when met is immediately drawn to the other, no matter what outward, organic sex. In 'The Banquet,' Plato speaks also with definiteness enough of the theory of a composite sex, a third sex, an intersex, as having existed, but no longer in the scheme of creation and reproduction.[18]

Tracing the appearance of the homosexual as a species, Foucault summarised the repeated conflation of homosexuality, androgyny and the hermaphrodite: 'Homosexuality appeared as one of the forms of a sexuality when it was transposed from the practice of sodomy onto a kind of interior androgyny, a hermaphroditism of the soul.'[19]

That myth is, as Kari Weil has suggested, 'central ... to narratives of psychoanalytic theory'.[20] Freud drew explicitly on Aristophanes' speech in 'The Sexual Aberrations', the first of his *Three Essays on Sexuality*. Under the sub-heading 'Deviations in Respect of the Sexual Object', Freud recalled how '[t]he popular view of the sexual instinct is beautifully reflected in the poetic fable which tells how the original human beings were cut up into two halves – man and woman – and how these are always striving to unite again in love'.[21] He goes on to suggest, in what is evidently a selective reading of the 'poetic fable', that it 'comes as a great surprise therefore to learn that there are men whose sex object is a man and not a woman, and women whose sexual object is a woman and not a man'. Now, as Weil observes, 'Plato's theory will not conflict with Freud's presentation of homosexuality and lesbianism as "deviations"'.[22]

The androgyne in creation myths/the proliferation of androgyny

In the psychoanalytic scenario, the figure of the androgyne represents a fantasy of plenitude, offering recuperation from the loss entailed by the necessary adoption of a subject position as the child separates from the mother and enters language. The androgyne signals a nostalgic return to an original dyadic and symbiotic state that does not, for the pre-Oedipal infant, involve division or separation, as Freud argued in his psychoanalytic interpretation of Leonardo da Vinci's formative years. Aristophanes' story in the *Symposium* is a version of a story familiar to creation myths: the Fall from grace is the Fall from unity, and Faith offers redemption from division back to unified One-ness with the androgynous God-like source. M.H. Abrams points out, 'In its Western form this myth has roots in Plato's *Symposium* ... in Gnosticism, and in the Orphic and other mysteries; it has been the major pictorial medium for embodying and sustaining the doctrine that perfection is identical with simple unity ...'[23] Mircea Eliade cites the Midrash *Bereshit Rabba*, according to which Adam and Eve 'were made back to back, joined at the shoulders; then God divided them with an axe stroke'.[24] Aristophanes' story also echoes the book of Genesis, as Weil points out, 'Both in Genesis and in Aristophanes' account, sexual division is regarded as punishment for the Fall. For Aristophanes it is also its remedy–the union of the two sexes through divinely inspired love is the route towards regaining salvation.'[25] Barbara Charlesworth Gelpi, drawing on the work of Carolyn Heilbrun, notes out that whilst Christian interpretations 'make little or nothing of Adam's possible androgyny', the hermetic tradition expands on that possibility

> in the philosophy of such thinkers as Paracelsus and Jacob Boehme – in short, in the whole hermetic tradition – posits the first world, the real Paradise, as that in which Adam dwelt alone and believes that when Paradise returns the new, the renewed man, will, like Adam, be androgynous.[26]

From the Jewish Kabbala, the Vedic mysteries, Gnosticism, the Orphic mysteries[27] and Christian Hermetic lore, the androgyne is repeatedly cast as central to creation myths, demonstrating the expression of a totality and divine perfection, which we have lost and strive to re-attain. For Aristophanes, love is the redemptive force that will reunite the sundered pair; whilst for John Scotus Erigena, as Abrams describes it, '[t]he myth is that of primordial man as a cosmic androgyne, who has disintegrated into the material and bisexual world of alien and conflicting parts, yet retains the capacity for recovering his lost integrity'.[28] After the Fall,[29] as it were, we became consumed with the need to restore what had been lost.

In a book devoted to the 'mystery of the androgyne', written in 1938, Theodor Faithfull coined the term 'Androgynology' as a 'more appropriate word to describe the branch of psychological science [dealing] with the analysis and synthesis of the human psyche'.[30] Faithfull suggested that in psychoanalysis, Freud's clinical practice had produced yet another narrative form for understanding psychic duality: 'The same truth,' he points out, 'is expressed by the Hindus in dual sexual figures of a Buddha, and by other races by dual forms of expression of some tribal diety [*sic*].'[31] Freud compared the sexual instinct to 'the instinct of nutrition' in 'The Sexual Aberrations': suggesting that hunger and libido are correlative.[32] Following Freud and Lacan, the psychoanalytic critic Francette Pacteau has observed:

> The psychic development of the child fits perfectly the temporal sequence of Aristophanes' myth, from a being who extends beyond the boundaries of its own body, incorporating its environment as full and replete as Plato's little spherical things, to an ever 'starving' subject: somewhere in between when the smooth rolling motion is broken, the split and consequent loss.[33]

Theories made across different but related fields about our development as a species, as well as our development as individuals, have all borrowed from and developed the model that Aristophanes produced. Nineteenth-century scientific epistemologies posited humanity's original somatic state as hermaphrodite or androgynous (the terms were often used interchangeably), helping to legitimise arguments that protected and maintained the division of sexual roles, even if, as Foucault argues of some medical men, they were 'producing truth'[34] and knowledge rather than revealing it. In *The Descent of Man*, Darwin had argued that vertebrates appeared to have been originally 'hermaphrodite or androgynous'.[35] Havelock Ellis went on to suggest that Darwin was one of several who helped to revive the Platonic 'ancient medicophilosophic conception of organic bisexuality'.[36] It was a useful model for Ellis, who argued that 'Hermaphroditism ... far from being a phenomenon altogether abnormal amongst the higher vertebrates, should be viewed rather as a reversion to the primitive ancestral phase in which bisexualism was the normal disposition'.[37] Whilst Ellis sought to naturalise the aetiology of homosexuality, Darwin's thesis still implied that the androgynous or hermaphrodite was a primitive condition from which humans had evolved: where once there were two sexes in the primitive body, now there was one in an advanced culture. Freud both supported and elaborated on this thesis in 'The Sexual Aberrations', where he argued that 'a certain degree of anatomical hermaphroditism occurs normally' because, originally, we were bi-sexed.[38] But its occurrence, even if 'normal', can only be read as atavistic in this context.

Freud, in his psychoanalytic biography of Leonardo da Vinci, and Earl Lind in his *Autobiography of an Androgyne*, both made androgyny interchangeable with the figure of the hermaphrodite. For Freud, the androgyne/hermaphrodite was evidence of the obdurate trace of pre-Oedipal phantasy emanating from the male child's assumption that women's bodies are the same as men's, that everyone has a penis. In Freud's essay on Leonardo da Vinci, the androgyne figure functions as the sublimation of Leonardo's repressed homosexual desire, cementing, in the process, a connection between creativity and sexuality. That connection is evident in Lind's *Autobiography*, although it is manifested differently. He casts himself as the living embodiment of the Greek hermaphrodite statues, but it is his self-identification as androgynous that is of interest: a passive homosexual, he considers his true (or preferred) self to be female, and his purchase on his sense of self is bought from the material evidence of Krafft-Ebing's case studies where the androgyne is figured specifically as the womanly-man, in distinction to the gynandrous manly-woman.

The notion that the sexes might somehow change through a *redeploy-*ment of alliance[39] held a potent appeal for advocates of sexual and social change even as it posed a threat to cultural and national health for opponents attentive to the signs of degeneration. Medical assumptions about inversion were mapped on to both revolutionary and reactionary agendas by those rallying for or against changes along the axes of political, cultural, social and sexual conventions and identities. Whilst the emergence of the so-called intermediate type was condemned as anachronistic and symptomatic of cultural degeneration, intermediate identities, constructed from medical and mythical models, were acclaimed as the herald of social renewal for writers like Olive Schreiner, Edward Carpenter, Bryher, HD, Vita Sackville-West and Virginia Woolf.

In *The Sexual Life of Our Times* Iwan Bloch suggested that vestigial traces of hermaphroditism (he thought androgyny was both spiritual and fetishistic[40]) remained dormant but might potentially be 'transformed into kinetic energy'.[41] Whilst this sounds promisingly dynamic, Bloch had also argued that '[t]he contrast between the sexes becomes with advancing civilization continually sharper and more individualized'.[42] This argument, that the mark of the civilised race and the modern nation was inscribed by clear sexual division, was to become a familiar one, rehearsed by Lombroso and Ferrero in *The Female Offender*, and by Weininger in *Sex and Character*. To some extent, these narratives respond to the clamour for and emergence of social change, but also speak to the increasing visibility and legibility of an 'intermediate' type, who could be emblematic of the 'mythic mannish' New Woman or the 'newly discovered', commonly 'inverted' homosexual subject like Earl Lind. As Siobhan Somerville has pointed out,

> [o]ne of the most important ways in which the discourses of race and sexuality intertwined during this period was through the concept of degeneracy, understood as a kind of reverse evolutionary process, in which the usual progression towards more 'civilized' mental and physical development was replaced with regression instead, resulting in a weakened nervous system and the emergence of 'primitive' physical and mental traits.[43]

'Leonardo da Vinci'

Freud published his study of Leonardo da Vinci in 1910 (its first translations into English followed in New York in 1916 and in England in 1922), potentially widening the appeal and the function of psychoanalysis as an approach that might inform biographical methodology whilst inventing 'psychobiography', as Wayne Andersen has suggested, 'with his analysis of Leonardo's sexual disposition'.[44] (Jutta Birmele has suggested that Freud 'frequently returned to artists' biographies or literary topics to demonstrate the usefulness of psychoanalysis',[45] simultaneously redeeming psychoanalysis by 'latching onto an icon of high culture'.[46]) For if instincts and their transformations are at the limit of what is discernible in psychoanalysis (as Freud suggested in the conclusion to his study), then biographical interpretation might extend that limit. His study marked another distancing of psychoanalytic methodology from other medical constructions of the homosexual as a species. Rather than a theory of the homosexual as 'a distinct sexual species ... an intermediate sexual stage ... a "third" sex',[47] he presented a specific theory of homosexuality, its causality and the ways in which its effect might be traced through sublimation in art. The relationship between the androgyne and homosexuality was still a dependent one, but it was revealed through a psychoanalytic practice which investigated the psychic processes that other sexologists, Freud felt, had crudely neglected. His essay, in which he first developed his concept of narcissism, decoded the unconscious significance of a specific symbol of the hermaphrodite/androgyne, that of the Egyptian goddess Mut, depicted as a fecund, hermaphrodite figure complete with breasts and a penis.

Freud quotes two passages in his biography, which he thought illustrated Leonardo's 'confession of faith', and provided the key to his nature:

> One has no right to love or hate anything if one has not acquired a thorough knowledge of its nature. ('Leonardo', 163)[48]

> But such carping critics would do better to keep silent. For that line [of conduct] is the way to become acquainted with the Creator of so many wonderful things, and this is the way to love so great an Inventor. For in truth great love springs from great knowledge of the beloved object, and if you know it but little you will be able to love it only a little or not at all ... (p. 163)

Opposing Leonardo's deliberations, Freud argued that humans love or hate impulsively rather than reflectively, and read Leonardo as *really* saying 'one *should* love in such a way as to hold back the affect, subject it to the process of reflection and only let it take its course when it has stood up to the test of thought' (p. 163). In other words, Leonardo was able to control affect, or feeling, in the name of research and sublimate it in his art and his pursuit of knowledge As Freud wrote to Jung:

> At an early age he converted his sexuality into an urge for knowledge, and from then on the inability to finish anything he undertook became a pattern to which he had to conform in all his ventures: he was either sexually inactive or homosexual.[49]

Freud then tested this hypothesis by reading a passage that he thought was central to Leonardo's notebooks, the *Codex Atlanticus*: the fantasy of the vulture.[50] This is Leonardo's memory:

> It seems that I was always destined to be so deeply concerned with vultures; for I recall as one of my very earliest memories that while I was in my cradle a vulture came down to me, and opened my mouth with its tail, and struck me many times with its tail against my lips. ('Leonardo', 172)

Freud's reading of the memory, or phantasy, gestures towards its erotic content: a tail is a *'coda'*, 'one of the most familiar symbols and substitutive expressions for the male organ' (p. 176). And so the vulture's tail in the mouth of the infant may suggest a memory, or phantasy, of fellatio. Anxious not to alienate his readers on this controversial point, Freud directed them to Krafft-Ebing's *Psychopathia Sexualis*, whose patients (women, passive homosexuals who liked to adopt the role of women) indicated that it was a common phantasy, the roots of which lay in being suckled. The child's later familiarity with the cow's udder, he argued, merged the memory of suckling with an object that resembles a penis. But if the phantasy of the vulture is a phantasy of the phallus, or of fellatio, what has this to do with the mother?

In ancient Egypt, the mother is represented by the sign of the vulture, and the Egyptians worshipped a mother goddess who had the head of a vulture and was usually represented with a phallus: she was depicted with breasts and an erect penis. For Freud, this emblem of fertility signified an androgynous or hermaphrodite:

> Mythology may then offer the explanation that the addition of a phallus to the female body is intended to denote the primal creative force of nature, and that all these hermaphrodite divinities are expressions of the idea that only a combination of male and female elements can give a worthy representation of divine perfection. (p. 185)

For writers of antiquity, the vulture was regarded as a symbol of mother-hood, 'because only female vultures were believed to exist'.[51] The Egyptian Magus Horapollo Niliacus tells us that since there were no male vultures, the vulture reproduced by being impregnated by the wind.[52] Freud assumed that Leonardo would have had some familiarity with the story (a 'rather fantastic, if elegant, revelation', suggests Birmele),[53] and consolidates this belief by suggesting ('irreverently', Scherr argues)[54] that the story had some credibility with the Church 'so that they could have at their disposal a proof drawn from natural history to confront those who doubted sacred history' (p. 180). Wayne Andersen underlines the point:

> A manuscript by Horapollo was known in Florence by 1419. Pointing to passages that Horapollo devoted to the self-impregnating vulture, the editor of its republication in 1835 wrote in the preface, 'This story about the vulture was easily taken up by the Church Fathers in order to refute, by means of proof offered by the natural order, those who denied the Virgin Birth.'[55]

Assuming that Leonardo was familiar with the story, Freud suggested that an associative phantasy had been activated. For Leonardo was a 'vulture child': the child of a mother and apparently no father. (Leonardo had spent the first years of his life with his birth mother, Caterina, and was not adopted into his father's household until the age of five.) With the association of this memory came another: the pleasure he had experienced at his mother's breast. The cultural, or spiritual, value of the phantasy came with the association made by the Fathers of the Church in arguing for the truth of the virgin birth of Christ.

Freud's reading transformed the story of divine androgynes and her-maphrodites, symbols of plenitude, into a drama of desire contained by threat. The male child at the fulcrum of this drama assumes that women possess the same genital structure as his own:

> The child's assumption that his mother has a penis is thus the common source from which are derived androgynously-formed mother-goddesses such as the Egyptian Mut and the vulture's *'coda'* in Leonardo' childhood phantasy. It is in fact only due to a misun-derstanding that we describe these representations of gods as her-maphrodite in the medical sense of the word. In none of them is there a combination of the true genitals of both sexes – a combina-tion which, to the abhorrence of all beholders, is found in some

cases of malformation; all that has happened is that the male organ has been added to the breasts which are the mark of a mother, just as it was present in the child's first idea of his mother's body. (p. 189)

And so the meaning of the phantasy of the vulture with the tail lies in Leonardo's earliest imagining of his mother: the breast and penis, suckling and fellatio, are imbricated in phantasy and belong to a point in Leonardo's imagination when his mother's genitalia, he believed, were no different from his own. Furthermore, Leonardo was being passively suckled, rather than actively sucking, from which Freud concluded that Leonardo was making an unconscious connection between his earliest relationship with his mother and his sublimated homosexuality. This passive (or dependent) relation with his mother laid the foundation for narcissism: repressing his love for his mother, the narcissist puts himself in her place and chooses someone who resembles him to love.

The hermaphrodite/androgynous phantasy involving the vulture/ Mut/Mutter is a defence against castration anxiety. Leonardo's mother Freud argues, is abstracted and replicated in Leonardo's paintings, and the memory of the vulture becomes a resource through which Freud interprets the aesthetic whilst returning the artist's sensibility to phantasy and unconscious memory. The smile of the *Mona Lisa* is, Freud suggested, the recreated smile of his mother, 'the smile of bliss and rapture' (p. 209). What he paints is androgynous,[56] but not in the sense, says Freud, of the vulture phantasy:

> The figures are still androgynous, but no longer in the sense of the vulture phantasy. They are beautiful youths of feminine delicacy and with effeminate forms; they do not cast their eyes down, but gaze in mysterious triumph, as if they knew of a great achievement of happiness, about which silence must be kept. The familiar smile of fascination leads one to guess that it is a secret of love. It is possible that in these figures Leonardo has denied the unhappiness of his erotic life and has triumphed over it in his art, by representing the wishes of the boy, infatuated with his mother, as fulfilled in the blissful union of male and female natures. (pp. 210–11)

Freud's trajectory in this essay takes him from the mythological emblems of androgyny which symbolise the pre-Oedipal boy's unconscious phantasy and assumptions regarding the phallic mother, to the development of a narcissistic homosexuality, to the sublimated representation of that homosexuality in an art that returns the artist to depicting an androgynous figure that had also (though in a different embodied shape) constituted his earlier phantasy. Leonardo's imagining of the androgynous/hermaphrodite mother leads Freud to see it enacted in his paintings of Leda, St John the Baptist and Bacchus, his art a projection of an androgynous and repressed psychic disposition. The androgyne is thus an emblem of sublimated phantasy (Pater suggests that Leonardo's pictorial subjects were 'a cryptic language for fancies all his own'),[57] symptomatic, as Pacteau has argued, of repressed desire.

Autobiography of an Androgyne

Earl Lind's *Autobiography of an Androgyne*, published by the *Medico-Legal Journal* in 1918, offered a very different kind of analysis, shifting the figure of the androgyne from a trope to an embodied gendered identity and set of sexual practices.[58] The autobiography's limited print-run of 1,000 copies was available, by mail order only, to physicians, lawyers, legislators, psychologists and sociologists. Lind's story was *apparently* available, then, to those with a professional interest in regulating the body through the law and for the state; but his was also a body – and a story – that exceeded the boundaries set by juridical constraints since the androgyne, or fairy, as Lind understands himself, and the female impersonator were all visible presences in New York's Bowery region in the late nineteenth and early twentieth centuries.[59] Alternately adopting the pseudonyms 'Ralph Werther' and 'Jennie June', Lind (also a pseudonym) dedicated his book to 'NATURE'S Step-Children – the sexually abnormal by birth – in the hope that their lives may be rendered more tolerable through the publication of this Autobiography'. Offered under the aegis of 'the *scientia sexualis*', the often transgressive content of Lind's story meant that it potentially functioned, too, as an *ars erotica*.[60] Lind's belief in the androgyne as a category and as an identity appeared to reinforce the legitimacy of medical typologies, although his autobiography also contested the sexological assessment of the homosexual's body as degenerative and naturally criminal. Alfred Herzog's reluctant introduction to the *Autobiography* was written primarily to support the decriminalising of certain forms of homosexuality, 'in an endeavour to obtain justice and humane treatment for the Androgynes, that class of homosexualists in whom homosexuality is not an acquired vice but in whom it is congenital'.[61] His unwillingness to endorse the text arose because Lind appeared to take such apparent pleasure in an identity that he ought

(Herzog felt) to feel shamed by: 'he is at present extremely proud of the, to him, undisputable fact, that he is all of a woman's soul in a body which he believes to be one-third female and thus only two-thirds male.'[62]

Herzog contemplated the possibility that there existed a connection between homosexuality (what he called the 'aberration of sexual desires'), and a primitive 'hermaphrodism', since the homosexual is 'born with the body of a male, with perhaps some female characteristics, but with the soul of a female'.[63] The androgyne, recognisable through manner and mannerisms, was 'a male person with female ways'.[64] The homosexual, famously a category 'constituted from the moment it was characterized',[65] appeared, Foucault says, 'as one of the forms of sexuality, when it was transposed from the practice of sodomy onto a kind of interior androgyny, a hermaphrodism of the soul'.[66] As Jonathon Katz has pointed out, within sexological theory (specifically in the work of Ulrichs) there existed an 'unquestioning assumption that sexual love for a man must be feminine'. It is as though sexual desire could never be conceived outside the heterosexual matrix, and is always straitjacketed within the constraints of the male-female binary.[67] This is how Dennis Blackwood understands or takes account of his homosexuality in his prescriptive explanation of sexual orientation to Antoinette de Courcy in Rose Allatini's pacifist novel of 1918, *Despised and Rejected*: 'because there's a certain amount of the masculine element in you, and of the feminine element in me, we both have to suffer in the same way' (p. 220).

Lind wrote the autobiography in order to extend Krafft-Ebing's own work: he both did and did not see himself in the case studies, and although he felt that Krafft-Ebing had offered fresh insights into the androgyne in *Psychopathia Sexualis*, '[v]ery little of androgynism came under his observation'.[68] If the Professor of Psychiatry's taxonomies gave some legibility and scientific legitimacy to Lind's self-understanding, his act of self-telling reclaimed and resituated a different representation of the androgyne as 'a sexual type situated somewhere between the effeminate man and the transsexual, and the fairy as a sociological type who regularly inhabits the military barracks and the Bowery'.[69] In Krafft-Ebing's intricate categorisations, androgyny was just one sub-species of what he termed 'Cerebral Neuroses'. His precision is oddly belied by the eventual approximation of his findings. 'Cerebral Neuroses' fell into several headings: 'Paradoxia', 'Anaesthesia', 'Hyperaesthesia' and 'Paraesthesia'.[70] 'Paraesthesia' subdivided into Sadism, Masochism, Fetishism and Antipathic Sexuality, or the total absence of feeling towards the opposite sex (what Freud called 'absolute inverts' in 'The Sexual Aberrations'). Krafft-Ebing then further subdivided antipathic sexuality into different manifestations and characteristics. Androgyny-gynandry was his appellation for the individual who possesses the secondary sexual characteristics of the sex with which he identifies, as was the case with Lind (in the book's photographic illustrations, a plumpish man with the appearance of breasts), but the binomial term indicates that androgyny is the provenance of the womanly man (as Lind understands it), gynandry the provenance of the manly woman. (In *Idols of Perversity*, Bram Dijkstra writes disparagingly of *The Gynander*, the ninth volume of Josephin Peladan's *The Latin Decadence*. Dijkstra cites Tammuz, Peladan's 'spokesman', who defines the androgyne as 'the virginial adolescent male, still somewhat feminine' against the gynander, 'the woman who strives for male characteristics, the sexual usurper: the feminine aping the masculine!'[71])

Krafft-Ebing's Case Study 152, Mr v. H., was an example of androgyny, characterised by his cultural and aesthetic tastes, sexual orientation and feminised somatic features: 'Body fat was rich, skin was soft and feminine, facial hair was only thin, gait was mincing, manner shy and effeminate'.[72] Consonant with the findings of Krafft-Ebing's (and Havelock Ellis's) other studies of homosexuality, Mr v. H revealed a 'disinclination for masculine pursuits and his preference for feminine amusements were early remarked'.[73] He was described as a dreamy individual, weak, infantile, unable to lead a useful social existence, and characterising himself as an 'aesthete'. 'He learned very poorly,' Krafft-Ebing noted, 'spending his time in *couture* and artistic nothings, particularly in painting, for which he evinced a certain capability ...'[74]

Foucault suggests that 'sex would derive its meaning and its necessity from medical interventions', and whilst Lind partly recognised himself in Krafft-Ebing's case studies, he also shaped an identity from the community of fairies, androgynes and female impersonators that congregated around the Bowery. Mr v. H's 'androgyny' (or, indeed, his femininity) is pejoratively inscribed by Krafft-Ebing, whose Lamarckian constructions read any non-normative sexuality as emblematic of a progressively regressive degeneration, but Lind wrested androgyny from the domain of the clinic[75] by claiming, presumptively, that his own narrative represented the 'inner history' of hermaphrodite sculptures. (In declaring his home to be an art gallery, he clearly enjoyed the aesthete status.) He believed that the modern androgyne was distinct from, but also ultimately derived from, the ancient hermaphrodite, but whereas that figure had been a woman with male genitals, the modern (implicitly male) androgyne was 'an individual with male genitals, but whose physical structure otherwise, whose psychical constitution, and *vita sexualis* approach the female type'.[76] With no 'sharp dividing line between the sexes', he suggested that '[t]he two sexes gradually merge into each other'[77] with transitional stages in between. Lind's distinction between the classical hermaphrodite and modern androgyne, and his assumption that the hermaphrodite statues are primarily female (a woman with male genitals, rather than, in his schema, an androgyne man with breasts) is a telling one, related to pre-Oedipal fantasy. Pacteau has argued that:

> The common representation of the hermaphrodite is that of a figure endowed with breasts and a penis; the female genitalia do not figure. The male infant does not acknowledge a sex other than his own. Seen in this light, the hermaphrodite appears less as a woman with a penis and more as a man with breasts – the reiteration in the post-Oedipal of a primitive condition of early childhood which passed into the unconscious through repression ...[78]

Within the Freudian paradigm, the child acquires language and recognises sexual difference. The little boy has to give up his fantasy of the phallic mother, one that also helps to ward off the threat of castration (the phallic mother is, after all, a figure of powerful plenitude, possessor of both breasts and penis, as we saw in Freud's reading of Leonardo). The fantasy of the hermaphrodite, Pacteau continues, 'accommodates both belief in the phallic mother and processes of defence. In its function it is a protection against castration'. Both the androgyne and the hermaphrodite are, she argues, 'manifestations of a similar repressed desire',[79] and that desire clearly functions as a peculiarly male fantasy in which the boy child assimilates the body of his mother, narcissistically, to himself. Lind displaces one fantasy of the hermaphrodite as phallic mother and reasserts himself as the reluctant possessor of a male body (he had, he said, undergone partial castration), complete with breasts and 'female desires' towards men.

In elaborating his own taxonomy, Lind's autobiography repudiates the pathological representation of the androgyne by evoking classical statuary, a form anterior to sexology's historically specific interpretive frames. The implications of Lind's account suggest that since the (mythical) existence of the androgyne precedes its sexological/pathological incarnation, it might also be recuperated from sexology's pathology of it, dignified by both cultural form (the statue) and location (the museum). In posing as the classical 'Sleeping Hermaphrodite', Lind re-embodied the androgyne, 'coming into being', as Anne Herrmann has observed, 'as simulacrum', a copy of a copy without an original.[80] But what else can the self-styled androgyne be?

The autobiography of this androgyne is (initially at least) presented as the interior, mobile life of the inanimate sculpture, its cool perfection re-scripted as unspiritual and carnal. Lind adapts current epistemologies: sexology and evolutionary theory are mapped onto classical mythology and sculpture, and he reanimates them within a narrative of his own life that, to Herzog's contempt (and Lind's credit), he refuses to feel shamed by. Lind is selective with medical theories that give his narrative some scientific credibility before elaborating on his sexual adventures as a passive homosexual, a male-to-female transvestite, and a partial transsexual (his chapters have a new sub-heading on every page, 'I am Held up on Broadway', 'Glimpse into Hell's Kitchen at Night', 'An Evening in a Squad Room', 'Ethics of My Conduct', 'I Am Court-martialled'). Lind both does and does not celebrate the androgyne status, and experiences the same unease with his male body as Stephen Gordon does for her female one in *The Well of Loneliness*, when he confesses, 'I had been doomed to be a girl who must pass her earthly existence in a male body.'[81] Lind oscillated between different identifications that seem to observe orthodox binary assumptions: scholarly and reserved during the day, he transformed himself into 'Jennie June' by night, a metamorphosis that gave him sexual licence.

Lind's narrative is different from other narratives of an imaginary androgyny in so far as he understands the androgyne to have an embodied status and a sexual identity. That the androgyne might be a projection or fantasy, or that it might be paradigmatic of the kinds of transgression permitted by carnival, is evident in one of the most celebrated texts of European decadence, Husymans' *À Rebours* (1884; translated into English as *Against Nature*). For the jaded aristocrat Des Esseintes, the figure of the androgyne appears fleetingly, embodied in the powerful form of Miss Urania, 'an American girl with a supple figure, sinewy legs, muscles of steel, and arms of iron' (p. 110). Des Esseintes' attraction for Miss Urania is triggered by her apparent change in sex, engineering a fantasy of cross-sex identification, or, indeed, a fantasy of a homosexual practice and identity. In the *mal du siècle*, Miss Urania appears to be the antithesis of, for example, Balzac's luminous androgyne Séraphita/Séraphitus, described by Camille Paglia as the 'Apollonian angel'.[82] As Des Esseintes looks at the theatrical spectacle of Miss Urania, she is transformed into a man:

> Little by little, as he watched her, curious fancies took shape in his mind. The more he admired her suppleness and strength, the more he thought he saw an artificial change of sex operating in her; her mincing movements and feminine affectations became ever less obtrusive, and in their place there developed the agile, vigorous charms of a male. In short, after being a woman to begin with, then hesitating in a condition verging on the androgynous, she seemed to have made up her mind and become an integral, unmistakable man. (p. 111)

The condition of androgyny is, in this instance, one of bare possibility, noumenal, intuited; the androgyne is a fleeting figure without content, a spectre caught in a passing glance. The narrator names the androgyne only as the barely glimpsed liminal condition in which the masculine and the feminine momentarily coexist. What the nature of that transitional embodiment might be is, tantalisingly, never disclosed, as though it must operate outside, rather than constitute, the transgressive sexual space that Des Esseintes both controls and is controlled by. Huysmans opens up the possibility of a sadomasochistic masculinity and femininity, considering gender as a pose to be both voluntarily and involuntarily resumed or declined. But Des Esseintes' delight in the artificial cannot be sustained, and typically, and necessarily, it soon bores him. Miss Urania offers him a respite from the apparent burden of his masculinity, appearing to embody a fetishised version of it for him, offering him a transformative sexual experience in which he can assume the fantasy of a passive feminine role. But it is not passivity that he assumes, but impotence, and the usefulness of the feminine to him is quickly exhausted.

In his 1930s discussion of nineteenth-century erotic sensibilities, Mario Praz argues that in Gustave Moreau's paintings, it becomes impossible to distinguish the difference between men and women, or Good from Evil. It is perhaps not surprising, then, that Moreau is the aesthetic point of return for Des Esseintes. The erasure of sexual difference is aligned, in Praz's reading, with the breakdown of Christian morality and the consequent dissolution of sexual difference. For Des Esseintes, the androgyne offers only a momentary release from the ennui that, on occasion, his masculinity and sexuality entail. Whether it might offer redemption from that burden is difficult to know in a fantasy of sexual oscillation that appears to re-inscribe what he would like to transcend (the passive woman, the active man). But the naming of this envoy from the New World as Miss Urania is, of course, a telling gesture on Huysmans' part, for what lies on either side of liminal androgyny in the late nineteenth century is homosexuality, the index of which is trans-gender and trans-sex identification.

Monsieur Vénus

In Rachilde's *Monsieur Vénus* (1884), described by Maurice Barrès in his introduction of 1889 as 'one of the most excessive monographs of the *mal du siècle*',[83] the location of depravity and displacement is embodied and grotesquely *dis*embodied in the trans-gender identifications of the aristocratic Raoule de Vénerande, 'the child born of death' (p. 21), as her own father describes her. Order and disorder are explored through the text's five principal figures, all of whom have clear functions in the text. The chaste Aunt Elisabeth is a figure of spiritual and pious contemplation; Marie Silvert as the 'seething demon of debasement' is her antithesis, a grasping celebrant of social and material wealth. Raittolbe, the ex-hussar, is the avatar of normative heterosexual masculinity whose function is to realign manliness with masculinity and restore morality. Central to the text, though, is the relationship between the aristocratic Raoule de Vénérande and Jacques Silvert, an effeminate artisan who makes artificial flowers for a living until he meets Raoule. Raoule is instantly captivated by him and establishes him in a new studio. One evening, as Raoule is on her way to a rendezvous with Raittolbe, she is seized with a compulsion to visit Jacques as 'the body that was no longer hers had felt revulsion' (p. 42). When she visits the studio, Raoule is aroused by the sight of Jacques dressed in feminine nightwear (he claims that he's so poor, he doesn't know the difference). She invites him to 'the land of the mad' (p. 45) and gives him hashish. From then on, their clandestine relationship functions through Jacques' willing embrace of an inert femininity and Raoule's increasing sadistic and masculine persona.

Balzac explored the idealised androgyne in his philosophical novel *Séraphita*, 'the last great work of European literature,' Mircea Eliade suggests, 'that has the myth of the androgyne as its central theme'.[84] The luminous Séraphita/Séraphitus is beloved by all who look at him/her. His/her parents were followers of the Swedish philosopher Emmanuel Swedenborg, and s/he is born as though through a mysterious osmosis of Swedenborg's teachings rather than by any more carnal method.

And yet, embodied in the world, s/he is too good for it. At his/her death, Séraphita's devoted disciples, Wilfrid and Minna, will preach the doctrines of this spiritual creature to the newly emerging and material-istic culture of the nineteenth century. Séraphita/Séraphitus fleshes out Swedenborg's philosophies in a narrative that oscillates between his/her supernatural appearances and Pastor Becker's rendering of Swedenborg's teaching. The death of Séraphita/Séraphitus, the spiri-tual, Christ-like figure, suggests that it is the theory (or the faith) that is pervasive and lasting, not the embodiment or personification of the theory, so that the wraithlike Séraphita becomes a figure through which to symbolise and transmit an oscillatory androgyny as ideal. Though Mario Praz has said that Rachilde proclaimed the 'ideal of the androgyne' in *Monsieur Vénus*,[85] it might be argued that she refash-ioned the androgyne in the name of decadence without necessarily being too sure of what costume it might wear.

Monsieur Vénus explores the possibility of rupturing sexual and social norms by literally marrying an aristocrat to an artisan and by disengaging the hetero-normative alliance of male/masculine, female/feminine sex and gender roles: a woman whose identification is masculine marries a man who is cast in the role of inert and masochistic woman (p. 66), and for Jacques at least, to periodically lament and repudiate. When Raoule confesses her cross-gender identifications to her suitor Raittolbe, he is confounded by her explanation: '"My dear," she said abruptly, *"I am a man in love!"'* (p. 50). In Raittolbe's limited imagination, he cannot understand how a woman could love another woman without being Sapphic (and therefore masculine), but Raoule puts him right: lesbianism is the 'crime of the boarding school girl or the prostitute's foibles' (p. 50) – both immature and *déclassé*. In any case, she tells him, 'I am a man in love with a man, not a woman!' (p. 53). But as Raoule's relationship with Jacques develops, the condition of their love entails, for Jacques, an amnesia about his masculinity: 'The more he ceased to remember his sex, the more she multiplied around him opportunities to be womanly' (p. 67). Raoule is a man in love with a man whose passivity and gratitude for affection render him female.

When he is in pursuit of Raoule, Raittolbe proclaims love as an ideal: 'the union of souls in the union of beings' (p. 36), but that ideal is soon corrupted as everyone, with the sole exception of the saintly Aunt Elisabeth, has to confront the 'abyss'. When Raoule finally introduces Jacques to aristocratic society, the androgynous union that they as a couple embody is one that profoundly disturbs the assembled wedding guests who are not at all sure of what they're looking at. When Jacques takes Raoule to the dance floor they appear to merge into each other:

> With dreamy eyes Raittolbe watched them waltz. The bumpkin waltzed well, and with his supple body with its feminine undulations seemed made for this graceful movement. He did not contrive to support his partner, but with her he was a single form, a single figure, a single being. Seeing them close, turning and melting into an embrace where flesh, clothes notwithstanding, joined flesh, one could imagine the single godhead of love within two entities, the complete individual spoken of in the fabulous tales of the Brahmins, two distinct sexes in a single monster. (p. 108)

And yet, Jacques' appearance at Elisabeth's *salon* is slightly scandalous: none of the guests there can assign him to an orthodox place as an aristocratic or as unequivocally male, and his evidently androgynous appearance perturbs them. Like (and unlike) Balzac's idealised Séraphita/Séraphitus, he appears as both male *and* female to those who observe him:

> Jacques's head was thrown back, still with its lovelorn maiden's smile; his parted lips displayed his pearly teeth, and his eyes, enlarged by a bluish ring, still kept their moist shine. Beneath his thick head of hair could be seen his small ears, that bloomed like purple flowers. The same inexplicable shiver went through them all. (p. 109)

Since it is inexplicable, the 'shiver' seems to rest obscurely between repulsion and attraction, between the injunction of a prohibitive social law and the muted possibility of their uninhibited desires. (When Raittolbe kills Jacques in a duel, he too seems divided between wanting to 'rid society of an unspeakable being' (p. 141), and his barely acknowledged desires for Jacques.) Elisabeth's pious perspective is the one that throws into relief the apparently diabolical and inverted dynamic of Jacques' and Raoule's relationship: her response is to damn them and retreat to her convent, giving a clear moral verdict on the pair.

Jacques is not, Raoule stresses, hermaphrodite or impotent, but rather 'a handsome male of twenty-one years, whose soul, with its feminine instincts, is in the wrong container' (p. 54). Rachilde's narrative considers an erotic sensibility existing outside of hetero-normative practice, though it can still be seen to corroborate the confessional narratives of the 'invert' as these are filtered through sexological interpretation. If, as Julia Epstein has observed, 'cultural ideas saturate medical language',[86] the obverse is true, too. Medical typologies identified androgyny as a form of bisexuality, as hermaphroditism, and with cross-gender identification and homosexuality. Texts like the *Autobiography of an Androgyne* both legitimised *and* subverted the authority of those categorisations by inhabiting and then relocating them. In doing so, they made the androgyne synonymous with specific sexual practices within a specific sexual milieu: for Lind, with the passive transvestite fairy on the Bowery.

Monsieur Vénus is a narrative that continuously gestures to a series of sexual, gender and erotic transformations, but does so indecisively, since transgression is, in the end, rewarded by alienation. Describing the fate of the androgyne in the nineteenth century, Mircea Eliade linked its degradation to spiritual crisis: 'When the mind is no longer capable of perceiving the metaphysical significance of a symbol, it is understood at levels which become increasingly coarse.'[87] The one spiritual figure in the text, Aunt Elisabeth, refuses to countenance Raoule's marriage to Jacques or the nature of their relationship, but her retreat says more about the tolerance and the ability of the Church to function as a moral authority than it does about Raoule's sexual preferences. Raoule follows an undeveloped trajectory that takes her from an apparently heterosexual and feminine woman, poised to begin an affair with de Raittolbe, to a woman attracted to a feminine man, to a woman who inhabits a sadistic masculinity defined by her ability to keep the docile Jacques submissive and grateful (in what is possibly a satiric comment on the fate of femininity as it might be defined in hetero-normative relations). What *Monsieur Vénus* offers is a reverse discourse of masochistic female femininity and sadistic male masculinity, casting the male body as weak and receptive and the female body as strong and active. Rather than engaging in a radical or far-reaching revision of sexual role, the novel reconfirms masculinity – assumed by a character we know to be anatomically female, and femininity assumed by a character we know to be male – in the familiar active-passive binary. In the end, Jacques comes to understand that the nature of his depravity lies in his femininity: 'So much had he been *feminised* in the deepest recesses of his being that depravity had him in its grip like lockjaw!' (p. 140).

The power relations between Raoule and Jacques are further inverted not only by the roles they choose to adopt (and Rachilde keeps them explicitly gendered, the passive inert woman, the dominant sadistic male), but also by the fact that she is wealthy and he is not: economics lie at the heart of all sexual relations in this text, and sexuality, idealised by Raittolbe as 'the union of souls in the union of beings' (p. 36), transmogrifies into a commodity. (It is financed, ironically, by Aunt Elisabeth, who gives money to Marie Silvert, which enables her to open her brothel.) All relationships – social as well as sexual – seem in danger of corruption when rich merge with poor, masculinity with femininity. But the dissolution of boundaries has only private rather than public repercussions, and only the vulgar, like Marie Silvert, appear to thrive when they exploit such a breakdown rather than eschew or disavow it. The end, when it comes, is ghastly: Raoule, in her grief at Jacques' death, skins his body, and covers a mannequin with it. Raoule enters his tomb dressed sometimes as a man, sometimes as a woman. 'By replacing the living man with a mechanized dummy,' Diana Holmes has argued, 'Raoule ensures that Jacques remains the docile "fine instrument of pleasure" desired by both her masculine and her feminine selves.'[88] If Raoule preserves Jacques' perfection, she commits herself to a 'strange passion, sexless and lustful', as Praz describes it in *The Romantic Agony*.[89] Commenting on Plato's 'repulsive and ridiculous' theory of the androgyne, Swinburne found the literal or symbolic idea of the androgyne 'merely beautiful', a response to what he saw as the stagnating effect of the perfection embodied in the statue of Hermaphroditus: 'once attained on all sides [perfection] is a thing thenceforward barren of use or fruit; whereas the divided beauty of separate man and woman – a thing inferior and perfect – can serve all turns of life.'[90] When Raoule and Jacques' wedding guests leave the Vénérande mansion, they declare that they are leaving a tomb, effectively enunciating a moratorium on the womanly man and the manly woman.

The androgyne exists spectrally, as though it is always brought into being by the gaze,[91] lacking a secure ontology. Incarnated, the androgyne's deconstructive potential is always defeated by the circularity of argument it brings into being: the androgyne (and the idea of androgyny) concretises and simultaneously undoes gender binaries. Put crudely, women can perform a certain kind of masculinity and men can perform a certain kind of femininity, but these do not transform a difference that works through opposition and still reasserts what masculine and feminine behaviours are supposed to be. Without a single or concretising interpretive frame, and across diverse critical practices, consensus is impossible for androgyny as a trope and as a material figure because it becomes such an over determined signifier, from the dissemination and proliferation of the *Symposium* to European decadence, from Freud's psychoanalytic excavations in the unconscious to positive reclamation of an androgyne identity cast pejoratively by sexology as evidence of degeneration. Narrative and embodied representations of androgyny evolved during the late nineteenth and early twentieth centuries through conflation. Aristophanes' trope of the androgynous couple became a useful one in representations of same-sex sexuality because sex, gendered identity and sexual orientation were part of a legible and familiar narrative that reified a connection between male or female anatomy with masculine or feminine gender and with heterosexual sexuality. Same sex desires or cross-gender identification might be read as variations of, or deviations from, that normality as they are configured by it, but whilst they challenged and threatened its authority, they could never displace its centrality or power. The originally heterosexual androgyne was co-opted into discourses that explained, even as they constructed, same-sex desire and, in the case of Earl Lind, inter-sexed bodies. Although androgyny is evidently a ubiquitous trope, it is also just as evidently not a transcendent one. But if androgyny functioned as a trope that had a useful explanatory purpose in understanding psychic and sexual motivation, it was also, as I show in chapter 2, one that had its limitations too.

2
Despised and Rejected

Earl Lind's robust sexual history and absorption in sensuous pleasure in *Autobiography of an Androgyne* constituted precisely the kind of sexual adventuring that Edward Carpenter censured in *The Intermediate Sex*: 'to confuse Uranians (as is so often done) with libertines having no law but curiosity in self-indulgence is to do them a great wrong.'[1] It was a denunciation that the character Barnaby echoes (*pace* Carpenter) in Rose Allatini's pacifist novel of 1918, *Despised and Rejected*: 'Of course there are those who enjoy it – who wallow in the perverted sensations of their own abnormality, as normal sensualists wallow in their own "permissible" lusts' (p. 348). Barnaby, needless to say, isn't one of them. For Carpenter, as for Allatini, to emphasise a connection between being 'intermediate' and being artistic was also to legitimise same-sex desire by making it useful: the intermediate type was the potential saviour of enervated post-war modernity, come to revivify English culture both socially and artistically, filling the gap, as Carpenter put it, created by 'the alienation of the sexes from each other, of which much complaint is so often made today'.[2]

Whilst narrative representations of androgyny in the late nineteenth and early twentieth centuries served as explanations for same-sex (though mainly homosexual) sensibilities and desires, there was a recognisable shift in how androgyny came to be reconfigured as the 'intermediate type' or 'intermediate sex' by writers like Carpenter and Allatini. Whereas Krafft-Ebing's case studies theorised, even as they constructed, degenerate subjectivities, Carpenter took his intermediate types out of the consulting room and away from the asylum, arguing that they had a great part to play in 'general society'. The antithesis of Krafft-Ebing's pitiable patients, Carpenter's 'Uranians', promised to be the upholders and regenerators of civilisation, not least because (like

Radclyffe Hall's Stephen Gordon)[3] they had the 'double point of view': 'with their extraordinary gift for, and experience in affairs of the heart – from the double point of view, both of the man and the woman – it is not difficult to see that these people have a special work to do as reconcilers and interpreters of the two sexes to each other.'[4]

Carpenter's self-appointed task was to legitimise or authorise what degrees of intermediacy were and were not appropriate, but in the 'extreme specimens' (as he clinically describes them) their corruption is marked by the ways femininity and masculinity apparently invade and infect the male and female body, marking the *en travestie* as travesty. At a stroke, he naturalises and reifies the orthodox relationship between gender identity and the sexed body, even as he indicates some of the ways in which they can also be re-ordered. His sketch of the 'extreme' type of intermediate suggests a surprisingly illiberal repudiation of queer identities, marking the androgynous intermediate type as distinct from Lind's representation of the androgyne as fairy. The extreme male intermediate is 'effeminate … sentimental, lackadaisical, mincing in gait and manners, something of a chatterbox, skilful at the needle and in woman's work'.[5] The extreme intermediate woman is egregious, like her male counterpart: 'markedly aggressive, sensuous rather than sentimental in love, often untidy, and *outré* in attire, her voice rather low in pitch; her dwelling room decorated with sporting scenes, pistols, etc., and not without a suspicion of the fragrant weed in the atmosphere.'[6] Carpenter never discloses whether his models of the 'extreme specimens' are based on his reading of case studies, or whether they are drawn from observation or prejudice, but their 'extreme' is strategic in helping him to present the 'normal' intermediate not just as the ideal, but also as one who might permissibly 'pass' in hetero-normative culture without attracting a second glance.

Despised and Rejected

Rose Allatini's anti-war novel *Despised and Rejected* (1918), which she published under the pseudonym A.T. Fitzroy, was clearly influenced by Carpenter in its attempts to refashion and dignify the cultural implications of homosexual desire, the sublimation of which was presented as both intermediate and intrinsic to a noble and civilised modern culture. The original advertisement for the book described it as being partly concerned with 'the so-called Uranians, whose domestic attachments are more in the way of friendship than of ordinary marriage',[7] although the novel remains circumspect about those 'domestic attachments'. The normal Uranian that Carpenter presents as the idealised standard has an androgynous quality that simultaneously reifies as it revises and displaces masculinity and femininity. The Uranian, 'while possessing thoroughly masculine powers of mind and body, combines them with the tenderer and more emotional soul-nature of the woman'.[8] The ideal Uranian, as Carpenter imagined him, 'is often a dreamer, of brooding, reserved habits, often a musician, or a man of culture'.[9] Dennis Blackwood is constructed according to this model, although he cannot see a redemptive alternative to his internalised homophobia:

> Abnormal, perverted – against nature – he could hear the epithets that would be hurled against him, and that he would deserve. Yes, but what had nature been about, in giving him the soul of a woman in the body of a man? (*Despised and Rejected*, 107)

This novel's task, then, is to explain what nature had 'been about' in making Dennis Blackwood homosexual. The novel was banned under the Defence of the Realm Act in October 1918 for its eloquent defence of pacifism and conscientious objection, but *not*, surprisingly, for its representation of homosexuality and bisexuality, explored in the triangular relationship of Dennis Blackwood, Antoinette de Courcy and Alan Rutherford. Dennis, the central figure in the novel, has a quasi-sexual relationship with the bisexual and boyish Antoinette: he proposes marriage, she accepts and eventually he retracts his proposal, by which time she has realised that, though she loves women, she loves him too. It leads an uncharacteristically insensitive Dennis to proclaim: 'We're both right over the border-line of the normal – I more than you, because no woman could ever attract me in the least' (p. 250). For Laura Doan, 'Antoinette is an intermediate in the fullest sense of the word since, unlike Dennis, she has the capacity to love an intermediate of the opposite sex and thus contribute to the biological reproduction of a new race'.[10] But Dennis's heart had once throbbed to 'a new and strange music' on meeting the handsome and cultured Alan, and when they meet again by chance in London during the war, any possibility that he might have a sexual relationship with Antoinette evaporates. Antoinette unwittingly echoes Dennis's impasse (he can't write music when men like Alan are being sacrificed in the war) when she is unable to articulate what she feels for Hester Cawthorn: 'Impossible to express and impossible to set free' (p. 56). For Dennis, this dilemma – the impossibility of expression – becomes a musical and sexual block. Antoinette, on the other hand, finds it thrilling as it necessitates the secret and therefore sublime expression of a sexuality that is socially unacceptable. Two competing readings of homosexuality are juggled in the text: the internalised homophobia that constitutes Dennis's self-loathing legitimised by the medicalisation of sexuality; and the benign reading of the so-called intermediate 'Uranian' type, which rewrites the pathology of the homosexual.

Dennis is unable to articulate his feelings for Alan, and so music functions as the aesthetic encryption of his repressed homosexuality, as the literally unspeakable aesthetic index of the intermediate, an art form that specifically requires people to listen. It was also an art form that for Carpenter 'lies nearest to the Urning nature',[11] and for Bloch was the vocation of the Urning.[12] And so the promise of a new aesthetic and the nascent intermediate type are intimately implicated each in the other, although this blossoming art is muted by the punitive regime of Britain's dominant and nationalistic order in 1918. Dennis endures hard labour and solitary confinement as punishment for his pacifist beliefs, and defeated, he is unable to compose or play. Allatini's story offers an alternative to a militaristic or phallic culture, but also shows that that alternative, in the Britain of 1918, could be imagined but not realised.

Allatini's novel (like Hall's *The Well of Loneliness*) works strategically with rudimentary character types, from the young German girl, Ottilie, a guest of the Blackwood family, to the vapid suburbanites of Eastwold where people are paradigmatically old and married or young and about to be married. Functional characterisation serves Allatini's didactic purpose, though, as she stages a cynical look at nationalism, simpering or passive femininity, and herd-like and aggressive masculinity. *Despised and Rejected* is also an eloquent paean to pacifism and conscientious objection. This latter position is allied to the independence and integrity of the socialists and artists who are committed to a pacific and tolerant humanity, and holds the promise of a redemptive rather than degenerate new order.

Historical narratives of the First World War could reflect, construct and privilege the experience of men in such a way that war would be concretised, to borrow Daniel Pick's phrase, as a 'phallic index of culture'.[13] Field Marshal Haig's reservations about war reports sent home by government-appointed journalists were based on an anxiety that the fighting would be made palatable as 'little stories of heroism … to make good reading for Mary Ann in the kitchen and the man in the street'.[14] His use of the name Mary Ann, popular slang for homosexual, was presumably deliberate, and it was certainly contemptuous as he grouped without distinction effeminate homosexuality, women and non-combatants.[15] War writing, one might infer, had to produce the heterosexual boy's own story. Samuel Hynes has argued that, in spite of the homosocial aspects of war,[16] heterosexuality was paramount by the end of the conflict ('masculinity in 1918 was manifested in two ways, in heterosexuality and in war')[17] and he recognises that Dennis Blackwood is punished for flouting those conventions. Such a sentiment is underlined by Dennis Blackwood's father in *Despised and Rejected*: 'if a man's got no fight in him, he's unnatural, that's what I say, unnatural' (p. 289). Dennis *does* have a fight in him, and so too does Alan, but not the one that Mr Blackwood imagines. Alan contrasts the current war with an ancient heroism: 'I think we fought side by side before now. In ancient Greece, perhaps, or Rome. Sometimes I have dreams ... and in those dreams you are always my comrade in battle, my comrade in love' (p. 289). In ancient Greece, a comedy called *The Astrateutoi* was also known as *The Androgynoi*, a term signifying men who have not done their military service.[18] But Allatini redeems the pejorative coupling of pacifism and femininity as she recuperates the 'androgynoi' for the budding intermediate type. Her homosexuals, that is to say, are less 'Mary Ann in the kitchen' and more cast in the mould of Carpenter's heroic Uranians. In raising the difference between an heroic age in which homosexuality was privileged, and her contemporary age of mechanical reproduction, in which the homosexual was pathologised, Allatini explores 'the so-called intersexual theory'[19] by making Dennis central to a sense of cultural regeneration. She does this through his musical compositions.

In order to escape his oppressive suburban community, Dennis escapes to London to stay with Neil Barnaby, the librettist for an opera they are both working on: *Karen and the Red Shoes*. Dennis, like Karen, becomes enslaved to his art, but Allatini has him break free from the morality of Hans Christian Andersen's story.[20] Karen's desire for the red shoes is punished by the demands of an unforgiving Christian authority, but Dennis evacuates the power of Andersen's story by developing a new interpretation of his musical aesthetic, which will unite and redeem the warring world.

And yet there is another strand to this, too. His desire to set *Karen and the Red Shoes* to music seems to belong to the transitional period of the pre-war and wartime years. The pre-war world is represented as one determined by leisure, a world of parties, dressing up, community, amateur theatricals. The dominant artistic form seems to be the fairy story, from Dennis's opera to the last theatrical fancy dress held before the outbreak of war where the characters dress as figures from fairy tales and children's stories – Red Riding Hood, the Snow Queen, Little Boy Blue – although no one seems able to read the sinister signs and subtexts of these stories. Mrs Blackwood claims that she can read her husband and elder son like an open book; but the kind of book Dennis's 'type' might feature in would not be part of her reading matter: those privately printed monographs, essays and medical case histories constituted a secret sub-cultural discourse, invisible to the dominant world at large and available mainly to those with a professional interest, evident from the frontispiece of Lind's *Autobiography of an Androgyne*. Even Dennis and Antoinette do not appear to have a basis for understanding 'what' they are in the taxonomies of sexual desire. If he is a closed book to his mother, then he's a closed book to himself, too, and his sexuality remains a riddle to him.

Dennis's journey to the metropolis is partly an escape from social censure (family and community all expect Dennis to volunteer to go to war); but it also functions as a rejection of bad art and a celebration of the necessity of 'high' art for the continuation of civilised values. In common with much literature of this period, the rhetoric of war peppers the text: 'Why, music's half the battle!' (p. 13) urges the dandified and theatrical Mr Griggs. But his attempt to jolly people along serves only to caricature Dennis's serious artistic and moral concerns. Dennis is thus established outside of a mainstream establishment which is artistically banal, amateur and motivated by a herd dynamic: although the theatricals provide the community with an *esprit de corps*, they move as one, afraid to stand outside the groundswell of opinion. (Dennis's elder brother Clive takes part in the theatricals 'because he did not want to make himself conspicuous by refusing', p. 21). When war was declared in 1914, Sir Charles Stanford, then Professor of Music at Cambridge University and Professor of Composition and Orchestral Playing at London's Royal College of Music, was among those who thought that it would produce great art.[21] Allatini considers this notion, though presumably what she explores is not what Sir Charles had in mind. Her contribution to the debate is to think about the representation of homosexuality (specifically, the Uranian and the Intermediate Sex) in terms of a musical aesthetic and as an imperative for social and cultural change with regard to sexual desires and subjectivities. 'Music' thus begins as a code for homosexuality. In one particularly long epistolary outpouring, Dennis tells Antoinette about a school friend, Eric Rubinstein, who was also an outsider,[22] for not only was he Jewish, he also played the violin 'like an artist' (p. 80). The alliance between Jewishness and homosexuality or effeminacy was commonplace in sexological texts of this period, as we see in Mayne's suggestion of synonymous exchange – 'Show me a Jew and you show me an Uranian.' A like statement might run: 'Show me a musician and you show me a homosexual.'[23] Eric senses that Dennis is 'musical' too, a fact that he conceals from his friends for fear of being ostracised. And so he

> tried to forget that there was something inside my brain that turned everything I felt and experienced into music, which clamoured to be released, and which I refused to release, because I knew that if I did so, it would widen still more the gulf between me and the others. (p. 79)

Indeed, he goes to great lengths to conceal his 'musical' tendencies, refusing to take lessons because the music master 'might have spotted me' (p. 79). Music functions (or seems to) as both metaphor and sublime: it cannot be explained, but it can be experienced. Picking out chords on the piano one day releases his pent-up repression: 'I knew then that I'd got to be a musician, even if it did mean being different and lonely. I knew I'd got to suffer, and by suffering – create' (p. 83). It is while he is waiting for his trial that Dennis comes to realise that the suppression of what is natural to him is the real perversion, the 'continuous struggle between brain and body, the continuous struggle to suppress his instincts and force them into ways not natural to them' (p. 304). *Karen and the Red Shoes*, his incomplete pre-war work, belongs to a condition that he calls his 'imagined aestheticism' (p. 304), opposed to his newly realised aestheticism, which comes with the new conviction of his political morality and his sexuality.

Dennis begins work on his symphonic poem, *War*, which comes to represent all the cross-currents in his own life. *War* honours and gives shape to chaos, making sense of it, as though to defy the notion that art might, after all, represent it. Alan, now imprisoned for his conscientious objection to the war, remains the motivation for his new musical composition; his work, then, is founded from a newly imagined and realised aestheticism, and his pacifism, socialism and sexuality are crucial to his art.

Just before the outbreak of war, he meets Antoinette at a masquerade party (he does not need a costume, his identity is itself a masquerade: as Xavier Mayne puts it: 'The Mask, ever the Mask! It becomes the natural face of the wearer.')[24] The very point at which he is about to disclose his 'real' identity to her is the moment at which the German Ottilie, dressed as Britannia, intrudes upon their intimacy. Allatini's syncretic symbol is clear: the emblem of nationalism may well be a costume or disguise (worn, ironically, by the national enemy), but both nationalism and war prohibit the discussion and the expression of homosexuality. Music and war may be irreconcilable to Dennis's sensibilities, but the very spectre of nationalism inhibits the confession of privately held homosexual desire. And so he undertakes a journey round England, where icons of family and emblems of nation are what he must discard. It is on this journey that he meets Alan in a forge, symbolically recalling the figure of Hephaestus, who might forge together the sundered androgynes in Aristophanes' speech about our somatic and sexual origins.

Barnaby 'reads' Dennis for Antoinette at the end, and in doing so, rewrites one of the familiar emblems of the war, 'sacrifice': women like her, he tells her, have to be 'sacrificed' for the love between men. He had guessed Dennis's sexuality after all: 'It's a woman's passion as well as a man's that he feels for Alan; virile yet tender' (p. 347). The physically crippled Barnaby is the voice of a hopeful tolerance, but he also speaks the ideas of Carpenter, articulating a version of the caveats and defences made in *The Intermediate Sex*. Barnaby condemns sensuous homosexuality as a kind of pornography: 'Of course there are those who enjoy it – who wallow in the perverted sensations of their own abnormality' (p. 348). But there are others, like Dennis and Alan, who belong to the Intermediate Sex:

> But perhaps these men who stand mid-way between the extremes of the two sexes are the advance-guard of a more enlightened civilisa-tion. They're despised and rejected of their fellow-men today. What they suffer in a world not yet ready to admit their right to existence, their right to love, no normal person can realise; but I believe that the time is not so far distant when we shall recognise in the best of our intermediate types the leaders and masters of the race. (p. 348)

And yet, although the representation of the intermediate type is pre-sented as redemptive and scriptural ('For out of their suffering, out of pain and confusion and darkness, will arise something great'), it's still located within eugenic thought, so that the resurrection of the androg-ynous type speaks also to a kind of proto-fascism. The intermediate type, as Barnaby perceives him, doesn't mingle in the multi-cultural fabric: he will be the master of the race; the intermediate who rebels against social regulation stands to initiate a new form of it. But really, what form would that take; in what context might it happen? The narrative voice makes an earnest statement at the end, in what amounts to a desire for a transcendent sex that exists outside the prescriptions of power in restoring original unity:

> For out of their suffering, out of pain and confusion and darkness, will arise something great – God-given: the human soul complete in itself, perfectly balanced, not limited by the psychological bounds of one sex, but combining the power and the intellect of the one with the subtlety and intuition of the other; a dual nature, possessing the extended range, the attributes of both sides, and therefore loving and beloved of both alike. (p. 349)

After the war, Susan Kingsley Kent has argued, the hope that sexual equality could be possible was shattered: 'Dichotomization, polarization and conflict became the models through which political, social, literary, artistic, sexual and psychological experience was lived.'[25] Barnaby's plea fell on deaf ears, and not least because Allatini's novel was banned a month before the end of the war. Her narrative offers an alternative to sexual dichotomies, not as an atavistic return to an extinct primitive state of androgynous unity, but as an aspiration for a civilisation that must be radically rewritten as tolerant, balanced and intermediate. In the end, this is a thwarted ambition: Dennis is stuck in solitary confinement, unable to write and unable to play the piano, since his hands have been destroyed through hard labour. There is no one, literally, to hear what he might have to say, and rather than standing at the advance of a new social order, the intermediate type signals a retreat into a closed aesthetic space, excluded from an increasingly alienated and inharmonious world. The invisibility that shrouded Dennis also befell her own novel: banned under the Defence of the Realm Act, it didn't see the light of day until it was reprinted in 1975 by the Arno Press in New York, and by the Gay Men's Press in London in 1988.

The Well of Loneliness

Retreat of a different order marks the infamous climax of *The Well of Loneliness* when Stephen, having renounced her lover, pleads to God in her solitude for 'the right to our existence'. Though *The Well of Loneliness* was famously banned for obscenity in 1928, Beverley

Nichols declared it to be 'about as vicious as *Pride and Prejudice* ... its powers of corruption ... hardly equal to those of a grocer's catalogue'.[26] Stephen Gordon tends not to be read explicitly within narratives or representations of androgyny, although her 'type' had been so read by John Addington Symonds in *A Problem in Greek Ethics*: 'The woman who seduces the girl she loves, is, in the girls' phrase, "over-masculine", "androgynous".'[27] Within Krafft-Ebing's categorisation of androgyny-gynandry, Stephen, the gynandrous manly woman, might have been the counterpart of Jonathon Brockett, the more androgynous womanly man. Yet, although Hall mined sexological case studies when she was writing *The Well of Loneliness* (Una Troubridge read them aloud to her),[28] those typologies do not work as models that adequately speak to the complexities of Stephen's vexed sense of her own embodiment or her gifts as a writer. Stephen Gordon troubles categorisation, an effect of the narratorial mode that Hall uses. Stephen is compassionately represented by an omniscient narrative voice that moves from intimately relaying her anguish and uncertainties, to reporting how others, representative of broader cultural opinion, see her. Against Stephen's self-fashioned identity, the narrator pitches the views of others, creating a diverse sense of how Stephen sees herself in the world and how she is perceived and re-perceived by those around her. Stephen is thus created from a series of competing interpretive models of subjectivity and sexuality prevalent over the 30 years or so of the novel's historical location.

Recent readings of the text have thoroughly mined *The Well of Loneliness*, exploring the semiotics of masculine sartorial style,[29] and considering Stephen as a subject of 'transsexual aspiration or transgender subjectivity'.[30] Laura Doan and Jay Prosser's vibrant collection of essays in *Palatable Poison* interprets *The Well* in a wide array of different arguments, including its ecological and biblical significances, its engagement with the First World War, and its place within the category of lesbian modernism. As recent readings of *The Well of Loneliness* attest, Stephen emerges from a welter of critical reappraisals as a kind of multilateral figure – lesbian, invert, aspirational transsexual, transgender subject – and as a compound dramatisation of sexological theories.

Susan Kingsley Kent has read Stephen Gordon as 'a quintessential model of the blurring of gender and sexual lines',[31] which gestures to perceptions of androgyny as a coalescence of the gender binary, but Laura Doan has pointed to the more specific influence of Carpenter's writings in this text, not just as a model for Stephen but also for Mary, Stephen's lover, and Martin, Stephen's closest friend. In a persuasive reading, Doan argues that just as Stephen looks as though she is internalising Krafft-Ebing's theories of inversion, the timely intervention of Puddle, Stephen's loyal governess, dislodges those master narratives in favour of Carpenter's theories of intermediacy, and together they form 'an incipient interpretive community, with the older instructing the younger in the ways of sexological systems of knowledge'.[32]

The sub-title of Carpenter's *The Intermediate Sex – A Study of Some Transitional Types of Men and Women* – reinforces precisely that sense of evolutionary change that Stephen might be said to embody and that characterises the historical location of *The Well of Loneliness*, which moves from late Victorian England to post-war Europe. Stephen Gordon is frequently singled out as exemplifying a 'type', but what 'type' she represents largely depends on the perspective of who is looking, and so she appears to be inverted, a gifted intermediate, masculine and, on two occasions, deemed to possess a 'feminine' beauty. Stephen is also 'an unsexed creature of pose', and 'it': as Judith Butler observes, 'Those bodily figures who do not fit into either gender fall outside the human, indeed, constitute the domain of the dehumanized and the abject against which the human itself is constituted.'[33]

Stephen is a necessary figure of abjection for the English county set who represent an exclusive and dominant hetero-normal desire. A liminal figure, she is both 'grotesque and splendid' as we see in a description of her miserable outing (so to speak) to her neighbours, the Antrims:

> She stood there an enraged and ridiculous figure in her Liberty smock, with her hard, boyish forearms. Her long hair had partly escaped from its ribbon, and the bow sagged down limply, crooked and foolish. All that was heavy in her face sprang into view, the strong line of the jaw, the square, massive brow, the eyebrows too thick and too wide for beauty. And yet there was a kind of large splendour about her – absurd though she was, she was splendid at that moment – grotesque and splendid, like some primitive thing conceived in an age of transition.[34]

If the narrative depicts that 'age of transition' as archaic or primeval, the age of transition is evidently bound up in the contemporary moment too, characterised by succession and exchange: the horse is replaced by the motor car, the country is abandoned for the city, class-bound England is dropped for a (marginally) more egalitarian Europe, and the First World War itself marks the shift from the 'old' to the 'new' so that 'types' like Dickie West, the aviator, represent a visibly new and self-confident generation of unapologetic but over-compensatory 'inverts'.[35] Stephen, always refracted through the eyes of others, is at times represented as an idealised 'type' with the potential to redeem the widening spheres of a rather soppy contemporary English femininity (symbolised by Violet Antrim) and a type of masculinity that, if it's not bullish (Roger Antrim), is going to seed (Colonel Antrim, Ralph Crossby). That chance is wasted, though, and since she figures abjection (from their point of view), she must always remain liminally outside the boundaries that define the English county set, although her nostalgic attachment to the class that repudiates her also means that she remains outside the Parisian enclave of inverts living on the Left Bank.

Carpenter's construction of the intermediate type suggests a desire for reconciliation and balance between masculinity and femininity. It is difficult to construct Stephen as intermediate within such a frame since what she constantly repudiates is her femininity or femaleness, and so she troubles the categories that comfortably accommodated Allatini's rendering of intermediate identity. As Kingsley Kent points out: 'Lacking "oneness" within herself and with others implies that Stephen does not understand herself to be an integrated whole; rather she feels *dis*integrated.'[36] It's true that before Stephen discovers the works of Krafft-Ebing and Ulrichs in her father's library, she often feels at odds with herself; she doesn't understand herself, feels herself to be 'queer'. But she also, repeatedly, experiences moments of unification with places, language and people, and her desire to achieve 'completion' recalls the Platonic/Aristophanic myth of complementary union and desire. Under Puddle's tutelage, for example, she learns 'a great feeling for balance in sentences and words' (p. 67). Jonathon Brockett praises this gift whilst berating her terrible second book: 'you've a perfect ear for balance' (p. 232). Her father encourages her to develop an equity of body and mind (p. 58). She has strong identification with place ('Morton and I are one', p. 142). But she also has a strong identification with people, specifically with her two lovers, Angela Crossby and Mary Llewellyn. With Angela, she feels 'we're perfect, a perfect thing, you and I – not two separate people but one' (p. 144) and when they kiss, Angela experiences a kind of transcendence and fusion with Stephen in a moment of unrestrained expression: 'All that she was, and all that she had been and would be again...was fused at that moment into one mighty impulse, one imperative need' (p. 144). In London, Stephen explains her writer's block (implicitly symptomatic of sexual repression and frustration) to Puddle by confiding that, like her first novel *The Furrow*, she's 'not complete' (p. 217). Bringing relief to both her writer's block and her sense of incompletion comes Mary Llewelyn. At Orotova 'all things would seem to be welded together, to be one, even as they two were now one' (p. 320). The book's most infamous line, 'and that night they were not divided' (p. 316), also recalls Aristophanes' myth of the restorative fusion of genders and the unity of the couple.

The trope of the couple recurs throughout the text, but Hall repeatedly dismantles it when it reinforces hetero-normative binary structures. Stephen's parents, Sir Philip and Lady Anna, suggest a perfect, harmonious unity that staunchly affirms binary traditions: male/female, mind/body, erudite/unlearned, sophisticated/innocent, even English coloniser/Irish colonised. As it turns out, it's an ideal coupling (from a patriarchal point of view) that is doomed: Sir Philip is killed and Lady Anna seems to shrivel. In middle age *she* (rather than her 'invert' daughter) displays 'a certain tendency towards regression' (p. 63) and endures a kind of living death, with Morton little more than a sepulchre. English masculinity, too, seems set in a kind of decline, embodied as it is in the henpecked and 'anaemic' (p. 108) Colonel Antrim, or the cranky nouveau-riche Ralph Crossby ('a nagging, mean-minded cur of a man', p. 148).

Stephen's childhood contemporaries, Violet ('No woman's complete till she's married', p. 173) and Roger Antrim, are characterised by a hyperbolic femininity and masculinity, qualities revealed as peevish and boorish when they appear under threat from Stephen (she's much better at being a boy than Roger is). But though Stephen is the product and heir to her parents' perfect binary legacy, she is also a destructive third term, who will dislodge these pervasive binaries by combining and reconfiguring them. At first, she's an awkward third term, dolefully confiding: 'Oh, Puddle, it's my fault; I've come in between them' (p. 111) as her parents' relationship starts to fissure. At formal dinners, 'the solemn and very ridiculous' procession of men and women walking arm in arm, two by two, is disordered by Stephen: 'Intolerable thought, she had stopped the procession!' (p. 75). Such cessation seems both literal and figurative. Inadvertently, she drives a wedge between her parents, emblem of the perfect couple, as though 'thrust in between them' (p. 80). And yet, although Stephen repudiates a femininity that is both awkward and alien to her, she is also perceived as an intermediate type. Stephen is bewildering and bewitching for the bored, sensuous, decadent Angela Crossby, and like Virginia Woolf's androgynous Orlando and Carpenter's intermediate types, Stephen 'seemed to combine the strength of a man with the gentler and more subtle strength of a woman' (p. 178). (Roger Antrim is a 'crude young animal' by comparison.) Martin Hallam sees her as both male and female, though never at the same time: 'He had offered this girl the cold husks of his friendship, insulting her youth, her womanhood, her beauty – for he saw her now with the eyes of a lover' (p. 96). Mary, too, apprising Stephen, notes 'the strong, thin line of her thighs ... the curve of her breasts – slight and compact, of a certain beauty. She had taken off her jacket and looked very tall in her soft silk shirt and her skirt of dark serge' (p. 323).

The balance that Angela Crossby notes is one that Jonathon Brockett sees too, but is emblematic of her atrophying talent: 'You're so strong in some ways yet so timid – such a mixture' (p. 233). Brockett is an epicene figure, a character based, according to Diana Souhami, on Noel Coward, 'even to the bags under his eyes' and 'feminine white hands'.[37] Terry Castle's work on the relationship between Hall and Coward affirms Brockett as a portrait of Coward. In her study of the friendship between them, she draws attention to a series of photographic 'binary portraits' that Coward appeared in during the 1920s and 1930s, in which he posed with different women, back to back, facing or in matching profile. The effect, Castle notes, is to undo sexual difference so that '[m]en and women meet on the same plane, as affectionate comrades or androgynous reflections'.[38] Unique to those androgynous representations were the sexual dynamics that informed them: 'one has the sense,' Castle suggests, 'of a new sort of male-female connection being celebrated: a creative marriage of male and female homosexual sensibilities'.[39] But if androgynous representation is refashioned according to the modish sartorial look of the 1920s, it's still, after all, a self-reflective gaze: each is mirrored back to other, the epicene man, the boyish woman, androgynous figures who constitute and are constituted by a stylish but contentless look.

The artist's relation to, and interest in, androgyny has been well rehearsed in several critical studies of the modernist period.[40] Reviewers of Virginia Woolf's *A Room of One's Own*, which contains one of the twentieth century's most famous explications of androgyny, signalled agreement with Woolf's conclusions rather than expressing surprise or criticism, an index of how commonplace androgyny was in discussions about creativity. (Marjorie Carling, for example, thinks of the artist Walter Bidlake, in Huxley's *Point Counter Point*, as combining 'the best points of both sexes'.)[41] Puddle tells Stephen that she will be a good writer because, like Virginia Woolf's androgynously minded writer, she can 'write with a curious double insight – write both men and women from a personal knowledge' (p. 208). Valerie Seymour returns to this towards the end of the text: 'But supposing you could bring the two sides of your nature into some sort of friendly amalgamation and compel them to serve you and through you your work – well then I really don't see what's to stop you. The question is can you ever bring them together?' (p. 414). The answer is never given, or if it is, is oblique: Stephen engineers the relationship between Mary and Martin, the two lesser types of intermediates, and in doing so, helps to pair the potentially procreative 'normal female and male intermediate types'.[42] Where does that leave Stephen Gordon? Rhetorically, her climactic *cri de coeur* appears to label her an inter-textual relic of nineteenth-century sexological case studies, echoing as she does Krafft-Ebing's gynandrous Count Sandor/Sarolta:

'O God, Thou All-pitying, Almighty One! Thou seest my distress; Thou knowest how I suffer. Incline Thyself to me; extend Thy helping hand to me, deserted by all the world. Only God is just.'[43]

'God,' she gasped, 'we believe; we have told You we believe ... We have not denied You, then rise up and defend us. Acknowledge us, oh God, before the whole world. Give us also the right to our existence!' (p. 447)

In Bryher's *roman à clef, Two Selves* (1923), the boyish-girl Nancy longs to read the Futurist Manifesto, discuss *vers libre* and embrace a sense of masculinity that she had repressed according to the conventions of her Victorian childhood. Coterminous with the acknowledgement of sexual difference in *Two Selves* is the entry into a modernity that she is itching for. One might argue that Bryher's asexual androgyny, the elision of sexual difference because there is no difference, marks both an embodied state that she will grow out of and a psychological one: but the fact that her coming of age is congruent with the century itself suggests that the non-difference of androgyny is a trope that – HD's interest in dual or bi-sexuality notwithstanding – belongs to the *fin de siècle*.[44] In *Two Selves* Bryher repudiates what we might read as the Platonic topos of androgyny; rather than offering the self-contained, serene unity of the couple, it tropes, instead, an unhappy division and disintegration within the self:

Two selves. Jammed against each other, disjointed and ill-fitting. An obedient Nancy with heavy plaits tied over two ears that answered 'yes, no, yes, no,' according as the wind blew. A boy, a brain, that planned adventures and sought wisdom. Two personalities uneasy by their juxtaposition. (*Two Selves*, 5)

That sense of uneasiness is produced by Nancy's frustration about what being a girl entails, as she describes it:

Oh to be a boy and have the world. What was the use of existence to a woman, what compensation could there be for loss of freedom? ... A man has liberty, the disposal of his life so largely in his hands, but a girl – she had no wish to write books woven of pretty pictures ... To possess the intellect, the hopes, the ambitions of a man, unsoftened by any attribute ... (*Development*, 136–7)

It's not the balance of androgyny that Nancy longs for but the cultural privilege of masculinity: Bryher's identification with and desire for masculinity went deeper than that though: she should have been a boy, she told HD, she was just a girl 'by accident'.[45] Whilst she was undergoing psychoanalysis with Freud in 1933, HD wrote to Bryher about some photographs of her that she had shown him. 'Papa', as HD called Freud, had 'made a most brilliant remark. He looked at the pictures through a second pair of double lenses that he puts on, and said, 'but surely I have seen that face in a *quattrocento* picture ... she is ONLY boy.'[46] 'How 'tail-up-curling-with-excitement,' replied Bryher.[47] It's an interesting exchange: if Bryher is a boy, Freud has to look and look again, 'through a second pair of double lenses'. Bryher's response is no less interesting: though her letters to HD are, in any case, full of animals and animal imagery[48] the erection of the excited tail hardly needs the intervention of Freud to elucidate.

'[B]eing a little boy' was an incongruity that Daphne du Maurier felt she had to grow out of. In a letter to Ellen Doubleday, she invited her to:

[imagine] D. du M as a little girl like Flave [Flavia, du Maurier's daughter], only very shy, always biting her nails. But never being a little girl. Always being a little boy. And growing up with a boy's mind and a boy's heart ... so that at eighteen this half-breed fell in love, as a boy would, with someone quite twelve years older than himself who was French and had all the understanding in the world, and he loved her in every conceivable way ...[49]

It wasn't quite true: the popular novelist Ethel Mannin recalled two photographs given to her by du Maurier: one was a studio photo, but

> the other [was] a snapshot of her aboard her yacht [which] shows her with slacks tucked into wellingtons, her short hair blowing across her face, and is inscribed on the back, in the red ink she always affected, 'Daphne as a boy' – though in point of fact she looks more boyish in the studio portrait.[50]

Being a boy was, for du Maurier, a way of rationalising same-sex desires by reframing them as heterosexual, and permitting herself to rebut lesbianism: 'by God and by Christ if anyone should call that sort of love by that unattractive word that begins with 'L', I'd tear their guts out.'[51] Whereas Bryher longed to (and did) embrace masculinity and lesbianism, du Maurier evidently felt the need to disavow hers: adult women couldn't remain boyish, and so 'the boy was locked in a box forever'.[52] If boyishness was a way of articulating same-sex desire by masking it as essentially heterosexual, it was also, for du Maurier, the figure of a specific, idiosyncratic vitality. When she went to live at 'Menabilly' (the model for 'Manderley' in *Rebecca*) she disinterred the boy who (unsurprisingly after years in a box) 'was neither girl nor boy but disembodied spirit' and together they 'dance[d] in the evening when there was no one there to see'.[53] Like Bryher, du Maurier felt that she, too, had two personalities, which she came to label No. 1 and No. 2. The second, the boy, was the figure that enabled her to write – as she told Flavia, 'he certainly has a lot to do with my writing'.[54] Du Maurier's understanding of what the 'boy' constituted is interesting in terms of how she negotiated her sexuality (if she loves as a boy, she must be heterosexual, not the 'L' word, at any rate); but the 'boy' is also sublimated in her writing where the repressed, once thought dead, return to haunt the living.

D.H. Lawrence bemoaned the revival of the 'hermaphrodite fallacy' in his 1923 essay *Fantasia of the Unconscious*, a text that John Worthen suggests was 'almost entirely oriented to the male reader'.[55] But in 1914, in his unfinished essay 'The Study of Thomas Hardy', Lawrence had been searching for a 'metaphysic' or philosophy of writing which suggested both the desirability and the impossibility of attaining an androgynous aesthetic:

> There shall be the art which knows the struggle between the two conflicting laws, and knows the final reconciliation, where both are

equal, two in one, complete. This is the supreme art, which yet remains to be done. Some men have attempted it, and left us the results of their efforts. But it remains to be fully done.[56]

The intellectual difficulty that Lawrence wrestled with was, for Carpenter, intrinsic to a set of specific concerns about the toleration of homosexuality. Carpenter based his theory of the intermediate sex on Karl Ulrichs' postulation that 'there were men, for instance, who might be described as of feminine soul enclosed in a male body (*anima muliebris in corpore virili inclusa*), or in other cases, women whose definition would be just the reverse'.[57] Ulrichs' work was important, he claimed, 'because it was one of the first attempts, in modern times, to recognize the existence of what might be called an Intermediate sex'.[58] In developing a specific history and profile of the 'intermediate type' or the 'intermediate sex', located in socialism and feminism, Carpenter reconstructed intermediates not as individuals who should be defined *exclusively* by sexual orientation and gender, but as 'diviners or prophets', the exemplars of whom had been 'some of the world's greatest leaders and artists ... dowered either wholly or in part with the Uranian temperament – as in the cases of Michael Angelo, Shakespeare, Marlowe, Alexander the Great, Julius Caesar, or among women, Christine of Sweden, Sappho the poetess, and others'.[59] (In 'The Sexual Aberrations', in *Three Essays on Sexuality*, for example, Freud noted the 'specially high intellectual development and ethical culture' of the invert, noting that 'It must be allowed that the spokesmen of "Uranism" are justified in asserting that some of the most prominent men in all recorded history were inverts ...'[60]) The trope of androgyny had functioned as an 'idealizing rhetoric', as Richard Dellamora suggests in *Hellenism and Homosexuality*, enabling Victorian writers to revise constructions of masculinity by feminising it (whilst avoiding effeminacy) in order to explore the homoerotic dynamics of male-male relationships. In citing Tennyson's *In Memoriam* as an exemplar of this 'idealizing rhetoric', Dellamora echoes Carpenter, who singled out Tennyson's *In Memoriam* as his 'finest work' in 'The Homogenic Attachment'.[61] Clearly, this is a model that privileges a trope of masculinity made whole by the assimilation of tropes of femininity: Carpenter, so locked into binary models, suggested that the male intermediate was identifiable by his affinity with the arts, the female intermediate by her affinity with the sciences, but the limitations and the possibilities of that binary model were also explored by modernist writers with different investments in the trope of androgyny.[62] The marriage of Will and Anna Brangwen in *The Rainbow* is one defined by patterns of conflict and resolution: after Will destroys his carving of Adam and Eve (Anna scorns the impudence of men for suggesting that woman was born from man) they walk home from Marsh Farm 'along opposite horizons' (*The Rainbow*, 166). Prompted by his feelings of isolation from Anna, who has just discovered that she is pregnant, he wants reunion with her, the implication being that femininity, assimilated into masculinity, will complete him:

> He wanted her to come to him, to complete him, to stand before him so that his eyes did not, should not meet the naked darkness. Nothing mattered to him but that she should come and complete him. For he was ridden by the awful sense of his own limitation. It was as if he ended uncompleted, as yet uncreated on the darkness, and he wanted her to come and liberate him into the whole. (p. 166)

On the face of it, that paragraph suggests that androgyny is a masculine fantasy that subsumes and requires femininity in order to complete itself: what women gain from the union seems hardly to matter. Lawrence's response to androgynous unity was more complex than that, however. He had shown an interest, albeit brief, in Edward Carpenter, reading *Love's Coming-of-Age* with Jessie Chambers, before telling William and Sallie Hopkin in September 1915 that Carpenter was 'not in my line'.[63] By the time he came to write *Fantasia of the Unconscious* in 1922 he had staged a *volte face* from his earlier and extensive meditations about the necessary reconciliation of the male and female marriage of 'two-in-one' in 'The Study of Thomas Hardy', flatly declaring that 'every single cell in every male child is male and every single cell in every female child is female. The talk about a third sex, or about the intermediate sex, is just to pervert the issue.'[64] In *The Rainbow* Lawrence thought of androgynous unity less as a trope that permitted writing about bisexual or same-sex desire than as one that affirmed the necessity of sexual difference, a difference that would also be unified and would transcend and redeem the deadening effects of culture through sex itself.[65] He used androgyny as a figurative trope at the beginning of *Women in Love* to affirm sexual difference, but also to establish the necessity of bisexuality; as Birkin tells Gerald: 'You've got to get rid of the *exclusiveness* of married love. And you've got to admit the unadmitted love of man for man. It makes for a greater freedom for everybody, a greater power of individuality both in men and women' (p. 352).

When Birkin walks into Ursula's elementary botany lesson, he dismisses her instruction to have the children simply sketch the catkins and tells her to give them crayons

> so that they can make the gynaecious flowers red, and the androgynous yellow. I'd chalk them in plain, chalk in nothing else, merely the red and the yellow. Outline scarcely matters in this case. There is just one fact to emphasise. (p. 36)

But it's not clear what that one fact is since the male-female 'androgynous' is not the opposite of the female 'gynaecious': what Birkin appears to implicitly ask the children to figure is his own ideal condition of bisexuality, though that is masked by his insistence that the children recognise the essential difference between the 'red little spiky stigmas of the female flower, dangling yellow male catkin, yellow pollen flying from one to the other. Make a pictorial record of the fact, as a child does when drawing a face – two eyes, one nose, mouth with teeth – so –' (p. 36). The yellow of the androgynous flowers is a symbolic motif that is repeated throughout the novel, and it tends to signify a refiguring of sexuality. Travelling to London together, Gerald points out an essay to Birkin which says that 'there must arise a man who will give new values to things, give us new truths, a new attitude to life, or else we shall be a crumbling nothingness in a few years, a country in ruin' (p. 54). As they discuss the possibility of abandoning the old order, they come to talk about love and Birkin is illuminated with light, the colour of the androgynous yellow catkins: 'The evening light, flooding yellow along the fields, lit up Birkin's face with a tense, abstract steadfastness' (p. 58). It is Birkin's hope, then, that there will be a new embodiment: 'Humanity is a dead letter. There will be a new embodiment, in a new way. Let humanity disappear as quick as possible' (p. 59). After Birkin annihilates Hermione intellectually during dinner, Ursula appears in 'yellow with dull silver veiling' as though to complement Birkin's colours. When the two discuss love, there's 'a beam of understanding between them' (p. 130) and 'A strange, wicked yellow light shone at him in her eyes' (p. 130). When Birkin asks Ursula to tell him about herself, 'a flash of wild gaiety went over her face, a strange flash of yellow light, coming from her eyes' (p. 153). 'What I want is a strange conjunction with you,' he tells Ursula, ' – not meeting and mingling; – you are quite right: – but an equilibrium, a pure balance of two single beings: – as the stars balance each other'

(p. 148). That equilibrium is possible, though, only outside of a culture or consciousness, as Birkin explains to Ursula:

> 'There is,' he said, in a voice of pure abstraction, 'a final me which is stark and impersonal and beyond responsibility. So there is a final you. And it is there I would want to meet you – not in the emotional, loving plane – but there beyond, where there is no speech and no terms of agreement. There we are two stark, unknown beings, two utterly strange creatures, I would want to approach you, and you me. – And there could be no obligation, because there is no standard for action there, because no understanding has been reaped from that plane.' (p. 146)

The conditions of the social are seen to deform or corrupt masculinity and femininity, and the corruption of masculinity and femininity is clearly demonstrated in Lawrence's depiction of the manly-woman and the womanly-man in *The Rainbow*.

Intermediacy for Lawrence, though, was sterile rather than regenerative, and he explored it as a deadening cause and effect of the modern condition in the figures of Ursula's uncle, Tom Brangwen, and her teacher, Winifred Inger. Tom is an affectless figure, lacking agency: 'He scarcely existed except through other people. When he was alone he was unresolved' (*The Rainbow*, 223).[66] He is also the womanly man: 'He had a subtle, quick, critical intelligence, a mind that was like a scale or balance. There was something of a woman in all this' (p. 223). He watches over his brother Fred 'with a woman's poignant attention and self-less care' (p. 224). When he accompanies Ursula to the station to wave Skrebensky off to South Africa, he's the 'almost effeminately dressed-man' (p. 308). As Lawrence went on to demonstrate again with the figure of Halliday with his 'soft, rather degenerate face' in *Women in Love* (p. 68), the appearance of femininity in men is the sign of degradation, making him a 'half-man' (p. 81).

He is, though, clearly a figure of corruption who 'belonged to nowhere, to no society' (p. 226). At the funeral of the elder Tom Brangwen, Ursula catches sight of the otherwise controlled Uncle Tom, and the narrative gives a first insight into a kind of bestial corruption that this slick and womanly man carries about him. Though he withholds his grief in public, Ursula catches him baring his teeth, fists upraised, 'like an animal which grimaces with torment' (p. 234). Afterwards, his grief seems an affectation, a politeness and she sees him differently, 'in all his elegant demeanour, bestial, almost corrupt'

(p. 234). Skrebensky's 'real' masculinity is measured against Tom's womanliness, but the necessary first failure of his relationship with Ursula means that her nascent sexuality now 'flamed into a kind of disease within her' (p. 309). That disease is worked out through her relationship with Winifred Inger in the chapter titled 'Shame'.

At this stage in her life, whilst she is still a student, the nascent Ursula is not unlike Tom: 'She gave something to other people, but she was never herself, since she *had* no self' (p. 311). It's the 'man's world' that she wants to venture into and make a conquest of, 'the world of daily work and duty and existence as a working member of the community' (p. 310). And it's whilst her 'real' self is in abeyance that Ursula suddenly finds 'a queer awareness' existing between herself and Winifred Inger, her class-mistress. Winifred *is* the New Woman: independent, educated (her BA is from Newnham), she is, like Ursula's friend Maggie, interested in 'the Women's Movement'. When their sexual relationship begins, 'Their lives suddenly seemed to fuse into one, inseparable' (p. 316). At the height of their passion, seen through Ursula's eyes, Winifred sounds like one of Carpenter's best intermediate types: 'proud and free as a man, yet exquisite as a woman' (p. 312). Yet she is also the embodiment of a wider social malaise that infects the proper relationship (as it's constructed and strived for in the narrative) between men and women, marking the failure of modern masculinity and femininity. Implicitly, women like Winifred come into being because, as she says, '[t]he men will do no more – they have lost their capacity for doing ... They don't come to one and love one, they come to an idea' (p. 318). And yet the same-sex relationship is also deadening for Ursula, and as her passion dwindles, Winifred, once idealised as noble, reverts, as Anne Fernihough points out, to being regressively big, earthy, thick, whilst Tom 'had something marshy about him ... the same brackish nauseating effect of a marsh, where life and decaying are one' (p. 325).[67] If Ursula's matchmaking between Tom and Winifred seems contrived (the educated and independent woman suddenly loses her will), it is also, presumably, a measure of the moribund state of sexual relations between the modern types of men and women. Passively, Winifred understands that Ursula intends that she should marry Tom, and out of their respective feelings of ennui, Tom and Winifred settle for each other: mechanical, educated, passive, centre-less modern individuals. In Wiggiston, Tom's spiritual home (like Tevershall in *Lady Chatterley's Lover*), people are massed and lifeless, their individuality gone, they service and are defined by the industry that has them in its thrall. In Wiggiston, 'There was no meeting place, no centre, no artery, no organic formation. There it lay, like the new foundations of a red-brick confusion rapidly spreading, like a skin-disease' (p. 320). The rootless Tom is at home in this living entombment. Winifred, rather like Ursula, is both attracted and repelled by him (p. 321). In her he detects 'a kinship with his own dark corruption. Immediately, he knew they were akin' (p. 322). As Michael Squires says: 'Moving forward is also moving backward; growth harbours atrophy; dependence breeds bondage.'[68] Tom and Winifred represent a vicious impasse: 'her uncle Tom and her mistress remained there among the horde, cynically reviling the monstrous state and yet adhering to it, like a man who reviles his mistress yet who is in love with her' (p. 324). What the two have in common is their love of the machine, the location of Winifred's 'perfect unison' – 'in the monstrous mechanism that held all matter, living or dead, in its service, did she achieve her consummation and her perfect unison, her immortality' (p. 325).

The moribund relationship between Tom and Winifred is akin to a dead skin that Ursula needs to slough off:

> It was in these weeks that Ursula grew up. She stayed two weeks at Wiggiston, and she hated it. All was grey, dry ash, cold and dead and ugly. But she stayed. She stayed also to get rid of Winifred. The girl's hatred and her sense of repulsiveness in her mistress and in her uncle seemed to throw the other two together. They drew together as if against her. (p. 325)

Winifred Inger's fate is an odd one, not least because she's seen through at least three different narrative perspectives. Whilst Ursula is jaded and then besotted, Winifred cuts an impressive figure: noble, educated, independent, firm and strong. When Ursula arrives at a point of self-awareness, Winifred has a 'clayey, inert, unquickened flesh' (p. 325), reminding Ursula of 'great prehistoric lizards' (p. 325). But both Winifred and Tom are repudiated by the narrative voice that ends the chapter: passionless, affectless, they represent the 'other' in terms of a negative complementarity, a negative two-in-oneness: the apathetic industrialist and the educated woman are perfect mates. The ideal is restored with the return of Skrebensky: 'they were one stream, one dark fecundity, and she clung at the core of him, with her lips holding open the very bottommost source of him' (p. 414). Skrebensky represents her 'dark, vital self' (p. 416). In him, she has 'her mate, her complement, her sharer in fruition' (p. 416). There are two kinds of self, as Lawrence explores them in *The Rainbow*: the private and sexual self which offers both union and transcendence, and the deadened social self.

Ursula and Skrebensky discuss marriage, but 'To make public their connection would be to put it in range with all the things which nullified him, and from which he was for the moment entirely dissociated. If he married he would have to assume his social self. And the thought of assuming his social self made him at once diffident and abstract' (p. 419). Social life is 'dead reality' (p. 419) and 'dead reality' perverts and corrupts regenerative and necessary maleness and femaleness. 'One's social wife was almost a material symbol. Whereas now she was something more vivid to him than anything in conventional life could be, she gave the complete lie to all conventional life, he and she stood together, dark, fluid, infinitely potent, giving the lie to the dead whole which contained them' (p. 419).

Diana Collecott suggests that Lawrence's writings on art and psychoanalysis influenced HD in *Bid Me To Live*, evident in Julia Ashton's discussion of female and male artists as being 'woman-man' and 'man-woman' respectively.[69] The other influence, she suggests, was Virginia Woolf, specifically her theory of the androgynous writing mind in *A Room of One's Own*, in which she describes the cerebral unification of the two sexes. Lawrence, Hall and Woolf make for a strange *ménage*, but the point of connection for the three is their very different explorations of a relationship between sexuality, social identity, writing and the pursuit of a sensibility that might be the aesthetic index of all those dimensions.

Both Lawrence and Radclyffe Hall feature, if obliquely, in the final chapter of *A Room of One's Own*, both situated in relation to the narrator's theory of the androgynous writing mind. All three writers published famous and infamous books in 1928: the celebrated *Orlando* was published just over a week before Woolf gave the speeches at Cambridge that she later revised as *A Room of One's Own*. At the same time, *The Well of Loneliness* was in the process of being successfully tried for obscenity. Lawrence's *Lady Chatterley's Lover* ('the most evil outpouring that has ever besmirched the literature of our country'),[70] privately printed in Italy, was also banned for obscenity in 1928 (Woolf makes the briefest of allusions to it in *Orlando* when the biographer suggests that having a dalliance with the gamekeeper is safer than writing). Of the three, *Orlando* was a bestseller (although Vita Sackville-West's mother, who glued a photograph of Woolf into her copy and scrawled 'The awful face of a madwoman' against it, might well have ranked it alongside the other two).[71]

As Jane Marcus has pointed out, Woolf made a joking and seductive allusion to *The Well of Loneliness* in the original speeches that she had given at Cambridge in 1928.[72] When Woolf tested her theory of what it might mean to be 'man-womanly' and 'woman-manly', though, she drew a blank when she came to the modern writer, singling out Mr A the novelist and Mr B the critic as exemplars of a modernity characterised by leaden criticism and masculine egotism. Though we never learn the identity of Mr B, Woolf did reveal the identity of the meretricious Mr A to be D.H. Lawrence: 'He was not in my upper mind; but no doubt was in the lower,' she told Desmond McCarthy. [73] She admitted in a letter to Ethel Smyth that she was blinkered when it came to assessing the literary worth of her contemporaries and singled Lawrence out: 'Think how little I appreciate [him]'.[74] Mr A is certainly a disappointment to the woman critic/reader of *A Room* whose narrative climax fails, in the end, to satisfy:

And then Alan, I thought, has passions; and here I turned page after page very fast, feeling that the crisis was approaching, and so it was. It took place on the beach under the sun. It was done very openly. It was done very vigorously. Nothing could have been more indecent. (*A Room*, 90)

Well, she had been looking for incandescence, not the sun shining on the beach. At any rate, Woolf touched a nerve when she imagined that male writers were threatened by women's emerging political consciousness, symbolised by 'a few women in black bonnets':

[Man] becomes more feminine than woman ever was, and worships his own femininity, calling it the highest. In short, he begins to exhibit all the signs of sexual complexity. He begins to imagine that he is really half female. And certainly woman seems very male. So the hermaphrodite fallacy revives again.

But it is all a fallacy. Man in the midst of all his effeminacy, is still male and nothing but male. And woman, though she harangue in Parliament or patrol the streets with a helmet on her head, is still completely female. They are only playing each other's roles, because the poles have swung into reversion.[75]

On this evidence at least, that reversion was an inversion of, and affront to, the proper and natural order of sexual relations for Lawrence, an inversion he represented in the mediocre marriage of Tom Brangwen and Winifred Inger. Far from aspiring to transcendence in art and eschewing the consequences of sexual difference, Woolf's Mary Beton, *A Room*'s narrator, may well exemplify Lawrence's 'cocksure' woman, laying votes or empty ink bottles rather than eggs, although she is, unsurprisingly, much more sympathetically cast from the perspective offered by Woolf.[76] As Linda Ruth Williams describes her, the cocksure woman was 'the woman who wears the trousers, who has sex in her head, and whose modern mind is fixated upon the primacy of looking and knowing'.[77] Williams' description appears to fit Mary Beton well (from a Lawrentian perspective), though, not least because of her transformation of bodily sexual experience into the cerebral activity of the creative androgynous writing mind. But it also calls to mind Rupert Birkin's distaste for Hermione: 'It all takes place in your head, under that skull of yours' (*Women in Love*, 41). As Fiona Becket has pointed out:

> The phrase 'in the head' was a pejorative verbal formula that Lawrence often employed: in *Fantasia* he repeatedly uses the phrase 'sex in the head' to describe a deliberate, if not prurient, concentration among his contemporaries on sex where regrettably 'sensual passion' has been displaced by a 'mental-conscious' fixation on genital pleasure.[78]

He had criticised Whitman in *Studies in Classic American Literature*: 'You have mentalised your deep sensual body, and that's the death of it.'[79]

In the context of *A Room of One's Own*, Hall and Lawrence have little in common, aside from the dubious distinction of having had their most recent work banned for obscenity, but within the broader context of wartime and post-war writing, they did share, along with Woolf, an interest in rethinking writing strategies and embodied subjectivity. Lawrence explored an androgynous 'metaphysic' in essays like 'The Study of Thomas Hardy', 'The Crown' and in his fiction, notably *The Rainbow* and *Women in Love*. Writing to Arthur McLeod in 1914, he suggested that 'the source of all living is in the interchange and the meeting and mingling of these two: man-life and woman-life, man knowledge and woman-knowledge, man-being and woman-being'.[80] 'The Study of Thomas Hardy' was (as Woolf's imagined trope of the androgynous mind is for her) 'a celebration of marriage – the marriage of opposites':[81]

> In marriage, in utter interlocked marriage, man and woman cease to be two beings and become one, one and one only, not two in one as

with us, but absolute One, a geometric absolute, timeless, the
Absolute, the Divine. ('Study of Thomas Hardy', 75)

Woolf explicitly named the desire for unity between men and women
'androgyny', which she cast as the location of a new and transcendent
literary sensibility in *A Room of One's Own* and *Orlando*, although even
within those texts, the trope of androgyny allows her to explore very
different things: the foundation for an aesthetic in *A Room*, a narrative
space to trace a relation between writing, the body and sexual desire in
Orlando.

Despised and Rejected and *The Well of Loneliness* both inhabit and
revise medical constructions of inversion and intermediacy. Both texts
offer a reverse discourse, but both were stalled by the censorship of the
law, which read those texts as counterproductive rather than reproduc-
tive for the state of the nation. They are, of course, very different, and
if they have a common aim (both make a plea, implicitly and explicitly, for the toleration of same-sex relationships calibrated through discourses of intermediacy and inversion), the approach and the politics
of Allatini and Hall could not have been more different, certainly with
regard to their view of what the war meant in terms of opportunity (for
Stephen and Mary) or annihilation (for Dennis and Alan). Allatini's
text is easier to place within contemporary narratives or representations of an androgynous intermediacy because she adheres to
Carpenter's construction of the intermediate type. Read alongside
Despised and Rejected, *The Well of Loneliness* inhabits a wider range of
medically constructed identities. If Stephen's masculine embodiment
speaks to an uncertain 'age of transition', it also recalls the body of the
boy-girl Zeldo, Nicholas Crabbe's androgynous and recuperative 'other
half' in Frederick Rolfe's *The Desire and Pursuit of the Whole*: 'Surely
Nature had been interrupted when She made this creature, a grand
broad-chested thin-flanked waistless boy by intention but a girl by
defect' (p. 9). Plato's description of androgyny was clearly a useful
interpretive frame for Rolfe to situate Nicholas and Zelda/Zeldo within:
as split parts of the androgynous couple, they complement each other
perfectly. Evidently, constructions of androgyny are not just ahistoric,
they are also developmental. However, even if there is always content
and context for androgynous representation in *The Well*, it's a representation that remains unstable because it is always located differently,
as a sensibility, a matter of insight, the result of a glance or the gaze as
Stephen is repeatedly refracted through the prismatic gaze of those
around her. I am mindful here of Judith Halberstam's critique of

androgyny as both unspecific and an act of erasure which homogenises the specificity and lived experience of female masculinity.[82] But female masculinity was also specifically readable through evolving tropes of the gynandrous-androgynous and intermediate subject, a subject category constructed in the late nineteenth century and still given currency (perhaps as short change) in the twentieth by Allatini and Hall. In making intermediate subjectivity central to sexuality and creativity, and by making Stephen and Dennis virtuous and gifted, they redeemed the 'intermediate' or 'invert' from their pathologised incarnations in the pantheon of sexological case studies, but they also left these figures in a kind of impasse, both in terms of the situations they find themselves in (they're both isolated at the end of each narrative) but also in terms of the kind of fiction that represents them. Written in the decade of high modernism, both texts evince a concern for cultural change and value in music and in literature, but in style and narrative structure, they sit as resolutely outside the modernist canon as Woolf and Lawrence sit within it.

Lawrence's engagement with modernity is, at the same time, the expression of a desire to disengage with it, a paradox evoked through, for him, idealised and corrupted forms of sexuality. Both forms comprise or require androgynous, intermediate identities, but his censorious voice suggests that one is right, one wrong. Androgynous sexuality in culture corrupts the possibility of a redemptive two-in-oneness. In order to cure a malaise fostered by culture's insistence on sexual division, androgyny can be achieved only outside the society that deforms the sexual ideal. But even writers who wished to legitimise intermediate identities could do so only by locating their 'types' in spaces beyond culture, rendering androgyny the subject of disapproval: we both must and must not see it, from the ostracised Dennis Blackwood to the exiled Stephen Gordon. If Du Maurier's impalpable boy in the box, emblem of the literary impulse and, covertly, of her sexuality, ends up a wraith-like spirit as she dances with it in the private retreat of Menabilly, her masculine aspect, like a *pentimento*, stills vies with the appearance of her femininity in the studio portrait she gave to Ethel Mannin: Daphne as a woman is still haunted by 'Daphne as a boy', who somehow wriggles back into the picture. Appearance also seems crucial to constructions and representations of androgyny in modern literature. Freud must look and look again through his special double lens when he peers so intently at the picture of Bryher, who, even then, only reminds him of another representation in a quattrocento painting as image is exchanged for image. Noel

Coward's double portraits of the epicene man and boyish girl depict androgyny as a rather narcissistic, modish 'still' rather than an achievable or even complex ontology. Even so, androgyny seems defined and produced by a specific moment that simultaneously questions its possibility in the social and imagines it outside that which is culturally determined and recognisable. When Woolf's narrator looks through the window of her private room and considers the possibility of a disembodied androgynous mind, she does so only in a contemplative moment that exists in spite of the modern industrial world: to represent the mind as androgynous was, for Woolf, to float above the groundswell of cultural and feminist politics and to re-engage literature (represented by Tennyson and Christina Rossetti in *A Room*) in a productive dialogue with itself. Representations of androgyny circulate rather than settle: as image, in and out of culture, as sexuality, as embodiment and as sensibility for these writers and in the texts explored in this chapter. If historical change and rupture are also crucial to these writers' representations of intermediate, androgynous identity, it is mined most thoroughly, perhaps, in Woolf's *Orlando*, the subject of the next chapter.

3
Virginia Woolf

When Virginia Woolf gave the two talks at Cambridge that she later revised as *A Room of One's Own*, she had in her mind the other literary event *du jour:* the trial of Radclyffe Hall's *The Well of Loneliness*. The contiguity of these two events prompted Jane Marcus to construct a lesbian sub-text to the speeches, reading them as examples of 'sapphistry' – the seduction of the woman reader by the woman writer.[1] Woolf made an evident allusion to the obscenity trial then in progress when she teased her audience with the possibility of what two women, Chloe and Olivia, might have shared:

> The words covered the bottom of the page; the pages had stuck. While fumbling to open them there flashed into my mind the inevitable policeman ... the order to attend the Court ... the verdict; this book is obscene ...[2]

In the event, it is a laboratory they share, not a bed, but for some feminist critics, the radical nature of her joke seemed diluted when she introduced the subject of the androgynous writing mind: 'every woman reader I know,' said Jane Marcus, 'sees this passage as Woolf's mnemonic device to force herself out of her feminist and lesbian fantasy world', back to a vision of 'heterosexuality makes the world go round'.[3] Later twentieth-century appraisals of Woolf's representation of the androgynous writing mind have uniformly considered it as the index of a failure of one kind or another. Elaine Showalter famously read Woolf's 'flight into androgyny' as a vitiation of feminist nerve (I discuss Showalter's critique in the context of 1970s feminism in chapter 4). Michèle Barrett thought that the transcendence promised by the androgynous mind signalled Woolf's ambivalence about the rival claims of art and politics.[4] The difficulty for Woolf, as Morag Shiach has observed, was 'of finding an androgynous image to express her creative and political aspirations'.[5] It was a point that Stephen Heath made in *The Sexual Fix*: Woolf's metaphorical presentation of marriage as a symbol for androgyny 'returned [her], even against the possibilities of her thesis, to what is a representation of woman, in relation to a certain domination and evaluation from men, the place of man'.[6] Heath's point is one that is made repeatedly about the limitations of androgyny, a model that is invoked to undo binaries but that inevitably reinforces them. Woolf located androgyny first as a form of balanced coexistence, redolent of Jung's anima and animus: 'in each of us two powers preside, one male, one female; and in the man's brain the man predominates over the woman, and in the woman's brain the woman predominates over the man' (*A Room*, 88). That develops into a model of cohabitation: 'The normal and comfortable state of being is that when the two live in harmony together, spiritually co-operating' (p. 88), and finally to a state of marriage:

> Some marriage of opposites has to be consummated. The whole of the mind must lie wide open if we are to get the sense that the writer is communicating his experience with perfect fullness. ... The writer, I thought, once his experience is over, must lie back and let his mind celebrate its nuptials in the darkness. He must not look or question what is being done. (p. 94)

Of course, the description is problematic: the female part of the mind appears to have been abandoned, leaving writing as an onanistic pleasure rather than a collaborative pursuit, precisely the kind of writing that the narrator has criticised ('one blushes at all these capital letters as if one had been caught eavesdropping at some purely masculine orgy', p. 92). It would be tempting to argue that this failure is strategic or deliberate: androgyny seems both a private practice and a nostalgic fantasy now rendered impossible in the wake of twentieth-century feminist consciousness. (Proust is the only contemporary writer cited in the selective list of (male) androgynous literati, and even that seems contradictory since earlier in the text Proust was 'a man terribly hampered and partial in his knowledge of women', p. 75.)[7] The shift to male consciousness and the impotence of a writing practice that fails to penetrate the surface of the mind only reinforces a sense that tropes of potent masculinity continue to be privileged rather than questioned or resolved. One of the difficulties facing Woolf/Mary Beton is that she has rejected feminism as a practice that fosters a political consciousness about sex roles, a consciousness that then squats unwanted in the private room of literary imagination. Feminism precisely *does* threaten social hegemonies: the myth of the androgyne or androgyny as a trope of the literary imagination does not. But it is not a theory of social transformation that Woolf/Mary Beton offers; it is an exploration of the condition of the writer's mind.

The contemporary reviews of *A Room of One's Own*, sharing as they do Woolf's historical and cultural moment, did not signal dissent with her use of androgyny, but they do affirm an understanding of androgyny as dissociated from feminism and as an acceptable sensibility for the artist figure. In fact, androgyny emerges as a mode or trope that confirms repressive stereotypes of gender rather than subverting them. The *Times Literary Supplement* reviewer suggested that Woolf 'persuasively develops' Coleridge's belief in the androgynous mind, but said that there was 'nothing very startling in the belief that, with artistic natures at least, the man's mind has a share of the feminine and the woman's of the masculine'. M.E. Kelsey, reviewing in the *Sewanee Review*, simply recorded Woolf's argument about the androgynous mind, declaring obscurely that Woolf herself was 'more man-womanly than woman-manly', primarily because she had 'as masculine a wit as any purely male writer of the day'.[8] Vita Sackville-West, reviewing for the *Listener*, also suggested that Woolf, though 'too sensible to be a thorough-going feminist', was herself androgynous since she enjoyed 'the feminine qualities of, let us say, fantasy and irresponsibility, allied to all the masculine qualities that go with a strong, authoritative brain'.[9]

Sackville-West's elaboration of the androgynous mind developed it in a direction that Woolf's narrator may not have anticipated or wanted, precisely because she refits it into prescriptive cultural models that associates femininity with fantasy and irresponsibility and masculinity with strength and authoritativeness. The androgynous writing mind is evidently metaphorical, as Woolf imagines it, but it also follows and precedes other metaphorical explorations in Woolf's work of how to figure or imagine the woman writing. Right at the beginning of *A Room of One's Own*, Woolf, in the persona of 'Mary Beton, Mary Seton, Mary Carmichael or … any name you please' (p. 4), asks her audience to picture her sitting on the banks of a river, lost in a reverie, contemplating the topic of women and fiction. The woman writer in search of an idea is figured as a woman fishing, an image that Woolf returned to in the draft of another speech she went on to make in

& also had £. *[handwritten marginal note]*

1931, 'Professions for Women', again in a diary entry made in 1937, where she asks herself whether 'another novel will ever swim up', and yet again in a letter written to Lady Robert Cecil, 'But it is only a sketch for a book – a fling of my line (like the old gents on the Tyne) over a bubbling and boiling stream, so full of fish one cant pick and choose'.[10] In 'Professions for Women', Woolf's woman writer experiences an insight and then a failure of vision, which places imagination as both phallic and feminine:

> She was not thinking; she was not reasoning; she was not construct-ing a plot; she was letting her imagination down into the depths of her consciousness while she sat above holding on by a thin <but quite necessary> thread of reason. She was letting her imagination feed unfettered upon every crumb of her experience; she was letting her imagination sweep unchecked round every rock and cranny of the world that lies submerged in our unconscious being.
>
> Then suddenly this fisherwoman gave a cry of dismay. What had happened? The line had suddenly slackened; her imagination had floated limply and dully and lifelessly upon the surface. The reason hauled the imagination on shore and said What on earth is the matter with you? And the imagination began pulling on its stock-ings and replied, rather more tartly and disagreeably; its all your fault. You should have given me more experience to go on. I cant do the whole work for myself.[11]

'Imagination' fails because it lacks experience, presumably of sex, but the sexual itself is also the location of fear, and this time 'Reason' steps in to check it:

> The imagination [*darts away*] has rushed away; it has taken to the depths; it has sunk – heaven knows where – into what dark pool of extraordinary experience. The reason has to cry 'Stop!' The novelist has to pull on the line and haul the imagination to the surface. The imagination comes to the top in a state of fury.[12]

– and not surprisingly, with such brutal retrenchment from erotic reverie. In both passages, women seem unable to have any relation to the sexual: either they know nothing because their knowledge has been repressed, or they know too much and culture demands prohi-bition. 'Reason' and 'imagination' fail to co-operate in the 1931 speech because writing, coming from a site which appears to be the unconscious, eddies at an intersection where social proscription and unrepressed sexuality collide. 'That dark pool of extraordinary experience' is exactly what 'reason' cannot let 'imagination' explore: 'I cannot make use of what you tell me – about women's bodies for instance – their passions.'[13]

This draft passage marks a return, then, to Woolf's original woman writer sitting on the banks of the river thinking about women and fiction in *A Room of One's Own*: letting down her line of thought, she catches an idea, hauls it in, dismisses it as small fry and throws it back. Even so, this is the germ of something, and as it darts about in her mind, she is so absorbed that she finds herself walking across a grass plot in one of the Oxbridge colleges. The Beadle who comes to right this wrong (as a woman and therefore an outsider, she is not privileged to walk on the grass) chases her away, but in doing so, her idea is also chased into hiding. The intervention of the Beadle and his insistence that there are rules determining where one should walk is at once real and emblematic for Woolf of how the woman writer is placed and how her thinking gets shaped – but she also raises an issue about the conditions necessary for the production of thought and writing. It is not order that she's looking for in writing; she makes that clear from the outset when she celebrates the 'wild flash of imagination, that lightning crack of genius' that leaves Lamb's essays 'starred with poetry' (p. 6). Woolf builds her argument slowly as she plots her account of the differences between men and women – the respective wealth of their colleges, what they eat, and so on. From the affluent comfort of the men's college where she first dines, she looks out of the window and sees a Manx cat, and the sight of that 'abrupt and truncated animal' makes her think about loss, which leads her to think about the First World War as a dividing point that separates one kind of social intercourse that was possible before the war, and a different kind of social intercourse that was possible after it: 'in those days,' she reflects, 'they were accompanied by a sort of humming noise, not articulate, but musical, exciting, which changed the value of the words themselves' (p. 11). She found that exciting transformation in a literary exchange where she, as reader, can put into dialogue Tennyson's *Maud* and Christina Rossetti's 'A Birthday' as examples of the parity between men and women writers' romantic desires. She implies that one of the consequences of the war was the destruction of romance between men and women: the contemporary writer at any rate, she felt, no longer sang 'so passionately about the coming of their loves' (p. 14), and the contemporary woman reader, as she goes on to conclude, is left as though eavesdropping at a masculine orgy, her sensibility in revolt from the indecency of Alan's exploits on the beach in the work of Mr A. the novelist. *Maud* and 'A Birthday' are expressions of a romantic desire accessible to *both* men and women writers and readers. As she went on to caricature Professor von X in the reading room of the British Museum, she realised that 'the black snake' of anger was clouding her plans for objective research because what that research revealed to her was the hatred that men apparently had for women. 'England,' she went on to declare, 'is under the rule of a patriarchy' (p. 30). As she considers the material conditions that have historically governed women's lives, she begins to question 'what is the state of mind that is most propitious to the act of creation?' (p. 46), which leads her to think that the chances of ideas coming 'from the writer's mind whole and entire' (p. 47) are slim. She considers this in relation to Shakespeare, 'because the mind of an artist, in order to achieve the prodigious effort of freeing whole and entire the work that is in him, must be incandescent ... There must be no obstacle in it, no foreign matter unconsumed' (p. 51). She then goes on to reiterate that 'If ever a human being got his work expressed completely, it was Shakespeare. If ever a mind was incandescent, unimpeded, I thought, turning again to the bookcase, it was Shakespeare's mind' (p. 52). She goes on to demonstrate in her thumbnail sketch of women writers throughout history that such unimpeded expression has never been possible for women, since material and ideological factors distort the woman writer's imaginary in advance. Furthermore, the scale of values that exists everywhere ('This is an important book, the critic assumes, because it deals with war. This is an insignificant book because it deals with the feelings of women', p. 67) meant that the woman writer was either apologetic ('she was 'only a woman') (or defensive she was 'as good as a man', p. 67).

In the modern period, though, she senses some change. The evidence for that lies in the novel that she's reading – Mary Carmichael's *Life's Adventure* – the novel in which we discover that 'Chloe likes Olivia', a significant step not necessarily for the implied lesbian relationship, but for the fact that women's relationships might be seen more generally in relation to other women and not in relation to men. What she would like to celebrate about Carmichael's novel is the fact that she had 'mastered the first great lesson; she wrote as a woman, but as a woman who has forgotten that she is a woman, so that her pages were full of that curious sexual quality which comes only when sex is unconscious of itself' (*A Room*, 84). She had also wondered whether the separate worlds of men and women – the professional and the domestic – might not animate and enliven each other so that for him, 'the sight of her creating in a different medium from his own would so quicken his creative power that insensibly his sterile mind would begin to plot again' (p. 78) (problematically, she does not say what the women in her domestic setting gains from this). Sexual difference is important, she concludes: 'It would be a thousand pities if women wrote like men, or lived like men, or looked like men, for if two sexes are quite inadequate, considering the vastness and variety of the world, how should we manage with one only?' (p. 79). What the narrator returns to throughout her ruminations are questions of difference and the conditions necessary for the production of writing; economic independence and privacy are the two famous requisites, but it is the condition of the writer's mind that she is interested in. The desirability of the androgynous writing mind begins to draw these arguments together.

Mary Beton's exploration of androgyny is bound up with modernist concerns about how to apprehend the androgynous mind in terms of a literary sensibility. When the narrator wonders whether it is, after all, '[an effort] to be thinking these two days, of one sex as distinct from the other' (p. 87), she is doing what HD later urges in *Trilogy*: 'Chasm, schism in consciousness/must be bridged over.' Mary Beton's amateurish sketch of the androgynous mind as a model of unity and integration concludes the trajectory of her arguments which take her from thinking about how the woman writer is shaped and conditioned, to what kinds of conditions are necessary for the production of art that is unfettered by the demands and conditions of history and politics. She delights throughout in the incandescent mind of Shakespeare and in the imaginative power of literature, a power that modern literature appears to have lost. Lamb's essays, then, are more exciting than Beerbohm's, just as she prefers Coleridge's literary criticism, which 'explodes and gives birth to all kinds of other ideas', to that of the contemporary critic Mr B who is careful, dutiful, full of learning but deadening to read.

Woolf had previously argued that an androgynous ontology is vital to creativity. Writing to her sister Vanessa Bell two years earlier, Woolf claimed that all great artists (she was thinking of her sister's lover, the bisexual Duncan Grant) were 'hermaphrodite, androgynous'.[14] Her statements about androgyny in *A Room of One's Own* are the culmination of a long-standing effort to develop a trope that calibrated bodily and cerebral functions. Her version of androgyny is one that recalls not only Lawrence's scorn for a too-cerebral 'sex in the head', but also HD's belief in the 'vision of the womb' as a source of artistic creativity.[15] In Woolf's sixth novel, *The Waves*, Bernard, the writer, imagines his future biographer describing his androgynous identity: '"joined to the sensibility of a woman" (I am here quoting my own biographer) "Bernard possessed the logical sobriety of a man"' (p. 48). And yet this too neat attribution isn't always so clearly circumscribed: 'nor do I always know if I am man or woman, Bernard or Neville, Louis, Susan, Jinny, or Rhoda – so strange is the contact of one with another' (p. 188). The question of sexual difference is anxiously raised by Louis, only to be rationalised by Rhoda: 'Are they men or are they women? They still wear the ambiguous draperies of the flowing tide in which they have been immersed' (p. 154). But Rhoda tells him, '[t]hey are only men, only women. Wonder and awe change as they put off the draperies of the flowing tide' (p. 154). The acquisition of individuality is both unwanted and inevitably painful for the six voices of *The Waves*: 'We saw for a moment laid out among us the body of the complete human being whom we have failed to be, but at the same time, cannot forget' (p. 185). Unity is a nostalgic reference point for them, and attainable only through writing: 'we melt into each other with phrases. We are edged with mist. We make an unsubstantial territory' (p. 7). In Woolf's fiction, androgynous sensibility figures a unity that tended to be an expression for writing, rather than ontology, though there are exceptions. In her first novel, *The Voyage Out* (1915), Mrs Dalloway (making her first appearance in Woolf's *oeuvre*) praises Richard Dalloway 'He's man and woman as well' (p. 57), whilst Evelyn Murgatroyd praises the writer Terence Hewett, 'There's something of a woman in him' (p. 262).[16] The character of Hewett has been the focus of critical attention that reads him as androgynous, but masculinity is, none the less, eschewed in these visions of androgyny as Evelyn and Mrs Dalloway, looking at Richard and Terence, see femininity narcissistically reflected back at them. The figure of the male is further elided in androgynous representation in Woolf's second novel, *Night and Day* (1919). Katharine Hilbery, seen in conjunction with her cousin Cassandra, affirms androgyny as a unifying bond between two women: 'they represented very well the manly and womanly sides of the feminine nature, and, for foundation, there was the profound unity of blood between them' (pp. 328–9).

Woolf's most famous and sustained exploration of androgyny found expression in *Orlando*, published on 11 October 1928, just nine days before she gave the two speeches at Cambridge University that would become *A Room of One's Own*. Leonard Woolf and her niece, Angelica

Bell, went to the first talk at Newnham, and Vita Sackville-West, the model for Orlando and the novel's dedicatee, accompanied her to the second talk, at Girton, prompting Kathleen Raine, then an undergraduate, to describe them as 'the two most beautiful women I had ever seen'.[17] The proximity of the novel to the lectures has contributed to biographical readings that secure Woolf's representations of androgyny to a modish bisexuality, and see *A Room* as being integral to a writerly aesthetic.[18]

Her tactical invocation of androgynous oscillation in *Orlando* allowed her to explore bisexual desire as well as to question who and what authorises and legitimates normative gender and sexuality. But her exploration of androgynous sensibility followed a particular kind of trajectory, and Woolf ended up fashioning a version of androgyny that was English in its provenance, and modernist in its aesthetic desires. In her recent study of what she calls 'the modern androgyne imagination', Lisa Rado has argued that Orlando, failing to find emotional contact or relations with his parents, turns in the end to androgyny. It's a thesis that suggests androgyny is, after all, a consciously acquired identity, a consolation, the result of a calculated if neurotic choice, since it requires the repudiation of the body and a retreat into an aesthetic, presumably non-sexual, space. In this scenario, androgyny emerges as a state that betokens irreconcilability rather than unity: if it offers a refuge from the failure of emotional contact, it is also, ultimately, the location of abjection, and Rado argues, intriguingly, that Orlando suffers catastrophic mental breakdown in the novel's final, surreal chapter. Rather than offering a celebration of androgyny, she suggests, Orlando's 'androgynous psyche falls apart'[19] as she is increasingly alienated from her own body, and the novel, far from being the joke or the writer's holiday that Woolf had envisaged, enacts a ghastly fantasy where the dead live once more and the logic that distinguishes fantasy from reality is 'permanently broken'. In this reading, androgyny is determined and motivated by different trajectories and choices that end in disintegration and a terrible rather than celebratory disembodiment at the novel's close.

Arguably, Orlando's androgyny comes into being with his dramatic sex change from man to woman, a metamorphosis that proffers a critique, even within the paradigms of the privileged social status that she enjoys, of the limited social, sexual and creative possibilities open to women. The power of the Law to determine sexed identity, and the limitations of that power, are explored and exposed as Orlando's fluid bisexual identity is disguised through Woolf's dramatic and spirited ploy in the eighteenth-century sections of the book. Orlando then 'returns' to androgyny as though of necessity, as the prevailing spirit of the nineteenth century (as she is affected by it) threatens to obliterate her sense of self (which is bound up with her ability to write) by confining her to the production of nothing better than saccharine verse. The book's satire, as is well documented, lies in mocking inflexible constructions of sexuality and gender, as well as offering a counterpart of sorts to the cultural-material history of women's writing that she offered in *A Room of One's Own*. Orlando's gendered and sexed subjectivity is evidently produced and guided by the spirit of the age, but is also just as evidently in revolt against it, and androgyny as the successive alternation of male and female identities finds a successful resolution in both sexual and literary enterprise: the marriage of Orlando and Shelmerdine, and the completion of *The Oak Tree*. And whilst Vita Sackville-West was reputedly disappointed by Orlando's marriage to Shelmerdine, arguing that it diluted her (Mary Campbell, Vita's then lover, maintained that Orlando was a much paler version of the more vital Vita), the marriage suggests that the androgynous sensibility conferred by it is crucial to writing.

Orlando's pluralistic androgynous status can engage with a series of concerns: sexual desire and orientation, sexual practices and – always, and crucially – writing. Woolf's engagement with the ideals (and imperatives) of androgyny also constitute a decisive shift in early twentieth-century representations, moving androgyny away from its pathologised, degenerate and decadent incarnations to consolidate instead a relationship with feminism, polymorphous sexuality, writing and a creative literary criticism.[20] Orlando also dramatises a specific mode of androgyny, constituting what Luc Brisson terms a 'successive' rather than simultaneous androgyne: Orlando 'lives alternation not resolution', as Makiko Minow-Pinkney puts it.[21]

Lesbianism, cross-dressing, transsexualism, writing, transcendence and the symbolic implications of the heterosexual couple do lie in the hinterland of Woolf's two major works on androgyny, but she mined from her circle of friends, rather than trawling the medical textbooks as Hall did for *The Well of Loneliness*. In her biography of Woolf, Hermione Lee traces a series of incidents that coalesced in the writing of *Orlando*: Vita's sexual fling with Mary Hutchinson (the former mistress of Woolf's brother-in-law, Clive Bell), Woolf's three-day visit to see the lesbian couple Ethel Sands and Nan Hudson in France, 'a sudden burst of amorous letters'[22] from Philip Morrell, reminding her of her half-brother George Duckworth, Vita's relationship with Mary Campbell. Woolf went to Long Barn, Vita's home, where Vita had dressed her young son Nigel as a Russian boy. 'Don't. It makes me look like a girl,' he'd said. She had gone to a fancy dress party at the Keynes's where photos of a 'pretty young woman who had become a man' were circulated.[23]

Letters and diary entries during the period of her thinking about *Orlando* and the *Room* talks also indicated an interest in different forms of transcendence. A diary entry written in February 1927 outlined an idea of unity, which was characterised by Sidney and Beatrice Webb and represented by the soul: 'Their secret is that they have by nature no divisions of soul to fritter them away: their impact is solid & entire.'[24] The childless couple, she thought, comparing herself and Leonard Woolf with the Webbs, was symbolic, 'standing for something, united'.[25] And then, from her boredom with trying to write *Phases of Fiction*, came the idea of writing *Orlando*, a text that clearly explores phases of fiction in relation to matters of sexual difference.

Sackville-West's confessional understanding of her own sexuality, published as *Portrait of a Marriage*, reveals not only a debt to the sexologists, but also anguish about a 'duality' that she saw as 'a curse'. She was frequently described in androgynous terms. Evelyn Irons, a journalist on the *Daily Mail* and one of Sackville-West's many lovers, referred to their 'hermaphrodite minds'.[26] Mary Campbell alluded to Vita as a being who transcended sexual division:

> I can never think of your sex, only of your humanity. I could love you in breeches, or in skirts, or in any other garments, or in none. I know you must be a woman – evidence your husband and sons. But I don't think of you as a woman, or as a man either. Perhaps as someone who is both, the complete human being who transcends both.[27]

Peter Quennell recalled seeing Vita at Sissinghurst: 'she resembled a puissant blend of both sexes – Lady Chatterley and her lover rolled into one'.[28] In her writing tower at Sissinghurst, Vita kept the six volumes of Havelock Ellis's *Studies in the Psychology of Sex*, Edward Carpenter's *The Intermediate Sex* and Otto Weininger's *Sex and Character*, annotating passages about male and female characteristics.[29] In the confessional *Portrait*, she initially struggles under a reluctant if wilful imperative: 'I hate writing this, but I must, I must' (p. 38). If her confession promised catharsis or a glimmer of redemption, it was also an offering to medical knowledge of

> the perfectly accepted theory that cases of dual personality do exist, in which the feminine and the masculine elements alternately preponderate. I advance this in an impersonal and scientific spirit,

and claim that I am qualified to speak with the intimacy a professional scientist could acquire only after years of study and indirect
information, because I have the object of study always to hand, in
my own heart, and can gauge the exact truthfulness of what my
own experience tells me. (p. 108)

Vita's oscillation, privately recorded here, found a public but very different expression in *Orlando*: 'Different though the sexes are, they
intermix. In every human being a vacillation between one sex to the
other takes place' (p. 121).[30] Whilst this is offered as a celebratory
unfettering, since the assumption of masculinity is always a release
from the evident constraints of femininity in this text, it is also an
example of what Lawrence regarded as a 'false conclusion':

> Our ideal has taught us to be gentle and wistful: rather girlish and
> yielding, and *very* yielding in our sympathies. In fact, many young
> men feel so very like what they imagine a girl must feel, that hence
> they draw the conclusion that they must have a large share of the
> female sex inside them. False conclusion.[31]

Whilst Sackville-West appeared to rely on a more Platonic myth of sexuality in her descriptions of her duality, Woolf, as Sarah Annes Brown
has argued, invoked an Ovidian intertext in *Orlando* (though there is at
least one important incidence of a Platonic intertext).[32] Sarah Annes
Brown locates two main Ovidian subtexts in *Orlando*: the stories of
Daphne and Apollo and of Salmacis and Hermaphroditus. She
identifies the tapestry we 'see' whilst Orlando is in the process of
slicing the head of the Moor in the opening scene as a depiction of
Daphne, and suggests that 'Daphne's story is being reinvented as an
emblem of complementary harmony between the sexes'.[33] Woolf's narrative, certainly in the first section (in its limited first issue, it was
called 'Childhood and Youth'), toys with modernity and intermediacy
and its opposite, the distinct contrasts of the Elizabethan era. Indeed,
the intermediate so characterises *Orlando* that androgyny seems just
another manifestation of a pervasive dialectical uncertainty.

Orlando itself is of uncertain provenance, positioned somewhere
between novel and biography. Woolf had wanted the text to be 'half-
laughing, half-serious',[34] although after it was finished, it seemed to
her neither one thing nor the other: 'It may fall between stools, be too
long for a joke, and too frivolous for a serious book.'[35] Orlando, too, is
a mongrel of sorts: if his forbears 'had been noble since they had been

at all' (p. 4), his arrival muddies the pedigree since there is evidence of peasant ancestry on his grandmother's side. These murky distinctions carry over into other areas, as well: at one point, the biographer suggests that 'the philosopher is right who says that nothing thicker than a knife's blade separates happiness from melancholy' (p. 24).

The carnival prompted by the Great Frost seems to preserve impossible contradictions, from the want felt in the countryside to the opulent pleasures of the Elizabethan court, to the figures frozen beneath the waters, caught in an eerie life-in-death stasis. If polarities are only precariously separated, or held in an irresolvable tension, they also clash brazenly, as when the Archduchess Harriet 'stared at Orlando with a stare in which timidity and audacity were most strangely combine' (p. 69). In Constantinople, Orlando is a mysterious but also a liminal figure: though he is 'English root and fibre' he exults 'to the depths of his heart in this wild panorama' (p. 75); though he is aristocratic, 'He wondered if, in the season of the Crusades, one of his ancestors had taken up with a Circassian peasant woman' (p. 75). Whilst these examples point to a play with distinctions usually held to be separate, they also help to contextualise Orlando's change of sex, which dramatically disturbs and reconfigures the male-female binary.

The Elizabethan Orlando (though he much resembles Sasha, the female object of his desire) belongs to an age of clear distinctions, and the biographer suggests that it is perhaps the condition of our present age (i.e., 1928) to be one of indeterminacy, as opposed to Elizabethan clarity.[36] The Elizabethan was an age where there could be no doubt of Orlando's sex, where day was divided from night, land from water and everything was altogether more brilliant: 'Sunsets were redder and more intense; dawns were whiter and more auroral. Of our crepuscular half-lights and lingering twilights they knew nothing' (p. 12). The description of 'our crepuscular half-lights' also calls to mind Jung's description of the anima and animus – '[t]hese two crepuscular figures from the dark hinterland of the psyche – truly the semi-grotesque guardians of the threshold'[37] – implying that inter-sexed identity is surely, if obscurely, within us.

Narcissism underlines Orlando's attraction to Sasha, as he falls in love with the image of himself. Elizabeth I's appraisal of Orlando precedes Orlando's own appraisal of Sasha:

> Eyes, mouth, nose, breast, hips, hands – she ran them over; her lips twitched visibly as she looked; but when she saw his legs she laughed out loud. He was the very image of a noble gentleman. But inwardly? (p. 10)

Legs, hands, carriage, were a boy's, but no boy ever had a mouth like that; no boy had those breasts; no boy had eyes which looked as if they had been fished from the bottom of the sea. (p. 19)

Sasha's eyes, which look as though they've been fished from the bottom of the sea, echo too Orlando's, which are like 'drenched violets' (p. 4). The Ovidian intertext (Narcissus dies gazing at his unattainable but lovely watery reflection; Echo, his 'female double' as Isobel Armstrong reminds us,[38] is the onlooker at Narcissus's death) quietly announces the theme of metamorphosis, but it is significant, too, that the story of Tiresias – changed from man to woman and then to man again – precedes that of Narcissus and Echo in the *Metamorphoses*. Both Lisa Rado and Maria di Battista have suggested that the apparently ambiguously sexed Sasha, Orlando's first serious love, is an 'androgynous muse' (Rado) and a 'poetic muse' (di Battista).[39] Sasha, is, though, the muse that fails since Orlando can only mimic the conventional tropes of Elizabethan love poetry in the frustrated pursuit of an aesthetic sensibility that he can call his own. His failure suggests that there may be, for Woolf, an inauthentic as well as an authentic androgynous sensibility (and Woolf mines the relationship between the authentic and inauthentic, the mimetic and the real intermittently through the novel). And although Sasha betrays Orlando, prompting the first of his trances, this does not necessarily indicate sexual withdrawal into an aesthetic androgyny (as Rado argues). The aesthetic and the body are intimately imbricated in Woolf's text: even after recovering from his first trance, when he appears to have repressed all memory of the Great Frost which ended with Sasha's betrayal and her unannounced departure, it is never a complete repression; pallid images of Sasha are overlaid, like *pentimenti*, with a remembered inspirational image of Shakespeare's writing. Shakespeare, it should be noted, was one of Mary Beton's androgynous writers, along with Keats, Sterne, Cowper, Lamb and Coleridge, in *A Room of One's Own*.

When Orlando flees from the lustful desires of the Archduchess Harriet (the Archduke Harry in disguise) the biographer distinguishes between two kinds of love, and the images of the vulgar Venus Pandemos and the noble Venus Uranus resonate with the twinned Platonic androgyne:

For Love, to which we may now return, has two faces; one white, the other black; two bodies; one smooth, the other hairy. It has two hands, two feet, two tails, two, indeed of every member and each one is the exact opposite of the other. Yet so strictly are they joined together that you cannot separate them. (p. 72)

Though the scene has been read as indicative of Orlando's repudiation of the body and its desires,[40] a rational love and non-rational lust exist in an interminable dialectical tension in which his lust for the Archduchess is explained through a series of metaphorical displacements. Lust is the vulture, scavenging over the bodies of the dead, Love is the exotic bird of paradise. And when Lust threatens to invade the opulent domestic space that he has nourished, it threatens Orlando's creative writing space too: 'Vainly, it seemed, had he furnished his house with silver and hung the walls with arras, when at any moment a dung bedraggled fowl could settle upon his writing table (p. 73). The repudiation of the black, hairy lust of the Archduchess will, of course, eventually be redeemed by the advent of smooth, white love in the form of Shelmerdine and Orlando's subsequent completion of the lauded poem *The Oak Tree*. The binaries of lust/love, black/white, hairy/smooth suggest an uncomfortably racialised dynamic – uncomfortable not least for the developmental trajectory that is implied: black, hairy lust to white, smooth love. But here, too, one might argue, is an inauthentic androgyny, mimicked by cross-dressing and a temporary assumption of femininity. The arousal of lust (rather than the body) has to be repudiated before Orlando can accede to an authentic androgynous redemptive love as she and Shelmerdine simultaneously recognise a complementary and innate femaleness and maleness within each other in England's green and pleasant land. Importantly, that recognition arises from the fact that, for Orlando at any rate, both gendered and sexed identities have been experienced rather than, in the case of the Archduke, assumed as a disguise to facilitate a desire.

In order to escape the threat posed by the Archduke/Archduchess, Orlando requests King Charles to send him as Ambassador Extraordinary to Constantinople, and it is here that he changes sex. The circumstances leading up to the change of sex are reported only through a deliberate and strategic elusiveness – 'we have least information to go on ... the fire which followed, [had] so damaged or destroyed all those papers from which any trustworthy record could be drawn, that what we can give is lamentably incomplete' (p. 74). The biographer's narrative picks its way through the remaining fragments of the diaries and letters of the English men and women in Constantinople to present a patchwork of deliberately obfuscatory comments that, because they cannot account for Orlando's apparently miraculous transformation, deliberately and strategically mystify it. Two major events coalesce: his elevation to a dukedom and his marriage to Rosina Pepita (biographically, Rosina Pepita was Vita Sackville-West's maternal grandmother), thus uniting and confirming those two aspects of Orlando's aristocratic and peasant lineage that had been anecdotal. If this offers one kind of resolution, it is short-lived, since his second trance follows shortly afterward. Orlando only wakes from this during a violent insurrection, as the seismic upheavals in the body politic are replicated in the soma itself, producing a new political – and strategically elliptical – body. This political body is, of course, always mediated through specific attention to different narrative forms and functions: fragments of letters and diaries tell this episode, and the appearance of three courtly masque figures dramatise it, as Purity, Chastity and Modesty elaborate the symbolic – and literary – status of this sex change.

To emphasise symbolic and literary status is to renounce medical typologies of the sexed subject. Orlando's change of sex from man to woman is a triumph of understatement and narratorial *hauteur*: Orlando 'looked himself up and down in a long looking-glass, without showing any signs of discomposure, and went, presumably, to his bath' (p. 87). (The biographer shows a similar insouciance when Orlando returns to England: 'Whether, then, Orlando was most man or woman, it is difficult to say and cannot now be decided', p. 122.) Woolf's narrative blurs, or evacuates, the disclosures, anxieties and neuroses which distinguish sexological case histories and studies, signalling a marked refusal to probe intimately as sexology's practitioners and subjects had done: 'Let biologists and psychologists determine,' the narrator announces, but it's clearly not of any interest to him – or her (p. 88). It is the antithesis of case studies like Krafft-Ebing's 'autobiography of a transsexual' in which a doctor wakes to find himself female:

> But who could describe my fright when, on the next morning, I awoke and found myself feeling as if completely changed into a woman; and when, on standing and walking, I felt a vulva and breasts! When I at last raised myself out of bed, I felt that a complete transformation had taken place in me.[41]

And yet arguably, there isn't any need for the biographer to penetrate or offer psychological depth, since depth is there encoded on the surface of the body as the interior and the unthinkable is presented for inspection. The narrative just declines to moralise or pathologise as Freud, for example, did in his case study of Dr (or Judge) Schreber, who, Freud deduced, fantasised about being a woman in order to ward off anxieties about his homosexuality: 'his delusion of being transformed into a woman was a pathological idea'.[42] The biographer dispenses with all the hand-wringing: the intermediate body and its coterminous intermediate sexuality are still presented as an index of culture, but cultural degeneration seems hardly at stake here, as the sex change, Woolf's fantastic sleight of hand, permits her to explore bisexuality without censure.

If allegorical figures like 'Chastity', 'Purity' and 'Modesty' are presented realistically, what is the status of the material body of the biographical subject? Both Rachel Bowlby and Karen Lawrence have drawn attention to the similarity of Orlando's change from man to woman to Freud's account of the Oedipal journey of the little girl, in which she assumes that she will one day turn into a man until she is forced to realise that, after all, she will not.[43] Orlando's sex change thus makes legible and visible what we might assume to be interior, unconscious drives, an inversion that makes otherwise invisible processes interpretable for the biographer. For Karen Lawrence, 'what is figured in the moment of unveiling is a more androgynous fantasy of the elimination of the "truth" of sexual difference'.[44] Whilst the fantasy itself is not necessarily androgynous, the scene does rather affirm the fact of sexual difference even if the biographer's introductory assertion ('there could be no doubt of his sex') now has to be restated with one important qualification:

> Orlando had become a woman – there is no denying it. But in every other respect, Orlando remained precisely as he had been. The change of sex, though it altered their future, did nothing whatever to alter their identity. (p. 87)

Bowlby's parallel is interesting, though, not least because it grounds Orlando in metaphor where the temporal and physical impossibilities of the text suggest a series of displacements or replacements. Orlando's sudden change of anatomical sex is, perhaps, one way of representing psychic states of masculinity and femininity which, on one level, were embodied in this narrative venture to give a playful shape to what were otherwise scandalous (homo)sexual realities, as well as literally unthinkable ones in the plotting out of the Oedipal drama. It is not just the little girl's Oedipal drama that is discernible in Orlando's change from man to woman, but also Freud's case study of 'The

Psychogenesis of a Case of Homosexuality in a Woman'. In this study, the woman's shift in desire from man (her father) to woman involves a transformation of feeling, necessitating what Freud describes as a change of sex: 'She changed into a man and took her mother in place of her father as the object of her love.'[45] As Mandy Merck has pointed out in her reading of Freud's essay, the homosexual clearly has to identify with the opposite sex in order to be one.

Orlando's change of sex does pose crucial questions about desire and identity, which the assumption of an androgynously sexed being clearly facilitates. When Orlando was anatomically male, his relationship with Sasha had begun as a moment of homosexual desire since he thought that Sasha was male too. Initially repressed, Orlando's realisation that Sasha was, after all, female sanctions the relationship, a heterosexually inflected one we had understood to be based on the anatomical difference between the two of them. When Orlando becomes an anatomical woman, her sexual orientation must always be a bisexual one: in a narrative that insists on the periodic recuperation of past events, masculinity and femininity, and the desire for men and women, are palimpsestically revealed and concealed. Like Tiresias (and Freud's Dr Schreber) Orlando has the pleasure of experiencing (or fantasising) life as both a man and a woman, although unlike Tiresias, sex change (or feminisation) is not meted out as punishment. Nor is transsexual identification the means by which to repress homosexual desire (as in Freud's reading of Schreber's case),[46] although the first two instances of sexual attraction depicted in the novel, Orlando's for Sasha and the Archduke's for Orlando, do turn on the repression of same-sex desire.

As a woman sailing back to England, she comes to a better understanding of the relationship between women and men, and this moment of insight arises because, somewhere between her departure from the East and her arrival in the West, she is suspended between being a man and being a woman: 'for the time being she seemed to vacillate; she was man, she was woman; she knew the secrets, shared the weaknesses of each' (p. 100). And not only is she afforded cultural insight into how men and women collude with and require their versions of each other, but she is possessed of a deeper sexual insight.

> And as all Orlando's loves had been women, now, through the culpable laggardry of the human frame to adapt itself to convention, though she herself was a woman, it was still a woman she loved; and if the consciousness of being the same sex had any effect at all,

it was to quicken and deepen those feelings which she had had as a man. For now a thousand hints and mysteries became plain to her that were then dark. (p. 103)

In one way, perhaps, lesbianism is about being a better kind of man (Suzanne Young conflates the androgyne with the 'mannish lesbian')[47] and being a better kind of man is really, in the end, about being a woman. At any rate, being a man (which Orlando always partially is) is not determined by the signs of biological or anatomical difference. If Orlando's Tiresian perspective affords her insight into the sexual pleasures of both men and women, it also unsettles the reified relationships that cement a particular anatomy to a particular gender and a particular sexuality:

Now, the obscurity, which divides the sexes and lets linger innumerable impurities in its gloom, was removed, and if there is anything in what the poet says about truth and beauty, this affection gained what it lost in falsity. At last, she cried, she knew Sasha as she was ... (p. 103)

And yet, it is the law courts that are to decide her gender, amongst other things, since she arrives in England to face a series of charges: that she was dead and therefore couldn't own any property, that she was a woman (which amounted to the same thing) and that she had had three sons by Rosina Pepita, all claiming her property. Farcically, the Law has to determine whether Orlando is a woman or not, but of course the point is to highlight the elusiveness of gender as Woolf reveals (and produces) the performative nature of the sexed and gendered subject. It's Orlando's private thoughts, her nightly reflections, that suggest the randomly accumulated shards that make us up: 'Hair, pastry, tobacco – of what odds and ends are we compounded' (p. 113).

Orlando's pleasure in sexual oscillation is interrupted by the oppressive social expectations that arise in the nineteenth century, and which threaten to overwhelm her by forcing her into a pure femininity that requires the expulsion or denial of her masculinity as 'the sexes drew further and further apart' (p. 147). During her period of enforced femininity in the nineteenth century, Orlando takes to writing her poem again, but writing is impossible, she comes to realise, because she isn't married, and the more she worries about this, and the fact that everyone else seems to be married, the more she is prevented from writing.

But conventional marriage offers the wrong kind of union: the men and women she sees plodding down the road together look as though they are mechanically conjoined automata, spiritless androgynes: 'Orlando could only suppose that some new discovery had been made about the race; that they were somehow stuck together, couple after couple, but who had made it, and when, she could not guess' (p. 157). The marriage that she imagines for Orlando is, in part, based on her knowledge of Vita Sackville-West's marriage to Harold Nicolson. But marriage is also intrinsic to Woolf's vision of the writer's relationship with the imagination, a relationship she was revising as she worked on the drafts of the speech that became *A Room of One's Own*.

When writing happens in *Orlando*, nothing happens, as though the transaction between pen and paper is a private contract between Orlando and her imagination, but of course, when nothing happens this too (to borrow from Althusser) is also an event. The biographer's boredom whilst Orlando is writing lends an unstable irony to the text, that there's nothing to write about because imagination and thought are of no importance, that since Orlando is a woman, she'll soon give up the pretence of writing, that it will be fine if she thinks of making an assignation with her gamekeeper (not at all fine, as Lawrence was in the process of discovering). But the biographer implies that Orlando, at least during the writing of her poem, did not love, never slipped off her petticoat, and so without love or death, the biographer laments, there is nothing more to write about, as though to echo (and parody) the youthful Orlando, who slid between the extremes of life and death since there was nothing in between. But this is disavowal on the part of the biographer, in whose text everything is, precisely, 'in-between'. Woolf re-imagined the solitary act of writing in the final chapter of the drafts of *A Room of One's Own* where she outlined her aspiration for androgyny:

> Let me now advance a little more amateur psychology, & suppose that this union of the two sexes in one brain can only take place at hush of midnight. Not a light must burn; not a wheel grate on the cobbles. In fact the writer must be profoundly steeped in oblivion that his faculties, are unaware of the least supervision & bring & go about their task like conspirators at dead of night.[48]

The 'marriage night' as Woolf went on to visualise it in her manuscript was not the encounter between a man and a woman but between the woman writer and the successful articulation of her creative vision:

> Draw the curtain, & let the marriage take place, & ever presume for
> a moment to say, now I am a woman, now I am a man; they have to
> be allowed to do that job for themselves. And the only way to attain
> this oblivion is to exercise every day, night after night, every faculty
> freely; so that when the marriage night comes you, the writer, can
> sink into oblivion ...[49]

That oblivion evokes sexual ecstasy, an ecstasy that Woolf associates
with writing throughout this text. Lisa Rado draws attention to
Orlando's sexual imagination when he first meets Sasha, arguing that
he has to aestheticise her in order to contain her. Woolf's images, she
suggests, invoke sexual ecstasy: 'Orlando ran wild in his transports and
swept her over the ice, faster, faster, vowing that he would chase the
flame, dive for the gem, and so on and so on, the words coming on
the pants of his breath ...' (p. 25) The mature Orlando has a steadier
relationship with words, and, metaphorically, a more measured and
controlled sexuality: she dips the pen into the ink, it's wet but not
dripping, and the words, though 'they were a little long in coming ...
come they did' (p. 173). But it isn't, after all, the passionate experience
of women's bodies that Orlando wants to write about: nor is it anything particularly modish: like Sackville-West she wants to write a pastoral, a paean to the land, to close the gap between the word and the
thing itself, to make signifier and signified organic rather than arbitrary. In one scene, the biographer conveys the sexual act through the
intrusion of a barrel organ – its gasps and groans fill the page 'until the
moment comes which it is impossible to deny is coming' (p. 191) – and
the narrative pans over London like a camera lens, landing us in Kew
Gardens, scrutinising 'bulbs, hairy and red, thrust into the earth in
October, flowering now' (pp. 191–2) so that the sexual body and the
sexual act are metaphorically displaced onto the (fertile) land, possibly
an implicit reference to Sackville-West's own critically acclaimed narrative poem *The Land,* as the biographer appears to return to a memory
of the conception of Orlando's child, and to her sexual pleasure.

Orlando is rescued from her moribund life by the lavishly named
Marmaduke Bonthrop Shelmerdine. Shelmerdine is a marginal but necessary figure, who comes to redeem masculinity as partially and necessarily female. In one letter Sackville-West had written to Nicolson, in 1928,
she had again suggested a notion of necessary unity between people, a
reciprocity that their own marriage, in this instance, seemed to lack:

> Men and women who marry ought to be positive and negative
> respectively – complementary elements. But when two people like

us marry, it resolves itself into a compromise which is truly satisfactory to neither. You love foreign politics; and I love literature and peace and a secluded life. Oh my dear, my infinitely dear Hadji, you ought never to have married me.[50]

Woolf re-scripted this impasse, transforming it into the perfect union of opposites in Orlando's marriage to her adventurer husband: he is an adventurer, set on foreign travel; she is a writer, craving solitude. The putative conflict of these desires in fact turns on a more fundamental mutuality as they recognise the 'masculine' and 'feminine' sides of each other and, in marriage, form another perfect union. When Woolf reworked the emblem of marriage in *A Room of One's Own* to represent the trope of androgyny, femaleness was eschewed in favour of masculine pronouns and writing turned into a phallic activity, but in *Orlando*, and in the drafts of *A Room*, androgyny was still a more integrated metaphor.

When Orlando and Shelmerdine realise that they are in love, they immediately suspect the truth: that he is also a woman, that she is also a man, and it is (simplistically) this androgynous union that releases Orlando from the stifling fate that the mores of the nineteenth century appeared to have bequeathed her. She can be a 'real woman' on her own terms which threaten (or gesture to) to undermine the powerful terms bequeathed by the judiciary and its juridical norms which determine finally (and inadequately) that Orlando is really a woman (p. 166). Theirs is also a specifically English, or Anglicised, union – what Karen Lawrence elsewhere has described as 'the repatriation of the imagination ... that figures the mating of the poetical genius with the *genus loci* of English nature'.[51]

Orlando does reach a form of personal freedom with Shelmerdine, as each sympathetically draws out the 'masculine' and 'feminine' qualities of the other, but it is where her new identity takes her that is so interesting, as she moves in and out of doors, through London to Kent and to her ancestral home, through her past and into a moment that seems to transcend the present itself, a trajectory always implicated with writing. Taking her manuscript to London, she meets Nick Greene, the old poet-critic now metamorphosed into the academic literary critic and still declaring that the age of literary genius is over, underlining the transitory nature of literary and critical value.

It's a crowded last chapter that sees Orlando reading literary criticism by the Serpentine, watching toy boats become real boats as though the mimetic is finally supplanted by the authentic; the imaginary realised materially. Images of city and country mingle randomly in Orlando's mind as the narrative trails through the defence of personal happiness against the institutionalised and professional life to a sphere of transcendence gained through sleep and dreams and the rising to the surface of unconscious, unformed, poeticised thoughts.

Her identity becomes increasingly fragmented as she motors out of London, her androgynous self further subdivided and displaced into a history of the different selves that she had once inhabited. Masculinity and femininity are, in the end, as much embedded in idiosyncratic experience, the illusion of Orlando's apparently random memories (retrieved as edited highlights of Woolf's text), as they are in any more ideologically produced and regulated ways. Amongst the selves that Orlando can call to mind are the boy in the act of slicing the moor's head, filling a bowl of rose water for Elizabeth I, falling in love with Sasha, becoming a courtier, an ambassador, a traveller, a gipsy, a fine lady, a patroness of letters or simply a girl in love with life. And all of these selves, the biographer argues, form a composite self which is the real one and which is also composed not just of actions but of characteristics – snobbish, facile, glib, romantic, and so on – an identity that we would come to understand as performative – constitutive of the acts that iterate and enact it.

Writing is crucial to this text, and once Orlando has completed *The Oak Tree*, the biographer's attention turns as much to its reception as it does to the sexual desires of the biographical subject. Sackville-West was dazzled by Woolf's tribute to her: 'I feel like one of those wax figures in a shop window, on which you have hung a robe stitched with jewels ... how could you have hung so splendid a garment on so poor a peg.'[52] Orlando becomes a figure through whom Woolf was able to range over different relationships to sex and gender, sex, gender and writing, literary production, the shifting nature of censorship and ideology. In the end, there is no key to unlocking the nature of the successful or transcendent text: we are never given access to the *Oak Tree*, never allowed to witness what happens when writing happens. Literary values, we are reminded, are determined by a powerful few, and what constitutes value is historically determined, specific and contingent.

Orlando is at odds with the modern world and though she is meant to be of her time when she begins writing the poem, she's clearly not of the modern industrialised world, an alienation Orlando shares with Mary Beton, the narrator of *A Room* who observes the London cityscape and laments its ignorance of culture ('Nobody, it seemed, was reading *Antony and Cleopatra*. London was wholly indifferent, it appeared to Shakespeare's plays', p. 86). Trains and cars are all strange to her and the metropolis itself is transformed from the eighteenth-century city that she recalls, as though it never existed in the nineteenth. London, after the intimate interaction between herself and her manuscript, represents alienation and a great cacophony of sound. The twentieth century, perhaps as a consequence, moves with such rapidity that the passing of time is barely discernible (though Woolf makes time for a quick private joke, when the biographer notes Edward VII leaving a house opposite Orlando's – Alice Keppel, the King's mistress, was the mother of Violet Trefusis, Sackville-West's lover, one of the key figures in *Portrait of a Marriage* and reputedly the model for the treacherous Sasha).

As Orlando leaves Greene, she walks through London, ponders on life and, in a moment of panic, telegraphs Shelmerdine. The telegraph, because of its cost and its urgency, compels the broken, fragmented phrase, a disruption of syntactical and semantic rules, where the truncated word may stand for the whole, a reminder of the fragmented narratives that survive the bloody insurrection shortly before Orlando's change of sex. It is perfect for Orlando and Shelmerdine who have formulated a private language where meaning now has the exactitude that the boyish Orlando had been looking for, but which cannot be measured by normative grammatical or syntactical rules, a positive rupture of language's symbolic order.

When Orlando wonders how the unremarkable signs of activity going on around her could be translated or transformed in the literary text, her creative mind transforms the anodyne toy boats floating on the lake on the Serpentine to become a scene of imaginable terror, with Shelmerdine's boat riding the devastating crest of a wave, and where a thousand lives appear to perish, and then, as suddenly, calm is restored and all is safe. Later, the camera roves over the city, taking in the urban industrial landscape, the clerks, the servant girls, as though to echo Eliot's Tiresias, glancing over the city 'at the violet hour', inviting a contrast between its mechanisation against the fertility of the natural land. (The 'human engine' of the 'taxi throbbing waiting' that Tiresias notes also recalls Woolf's the taxi that motors Woolf's androgynous modern couple away in *A Room*.)

As Orlando remembers the memory of 'a fire in a field against minarets near Constantinople' (p. 192), the image of the Orient is overlaid with the image of sterile modernity, bringing us back momentarily to the moment of Orlando's change of anatomical sex. And the surreal passage culminates in the birth of Orlando's son, the male child who, in Freud's reckoning, would see no distinction between his anatomical body and his mother's.

The beginning of the twentieth century seems to signal the end of a particularly phallic Victorian age: though the shrinkage is alarming, still 'there was not a trace of that vast erection which she had thought everlasting' (p. 194). Modernity exercises a particular fascination for Orlando, the electric lights and the diminution of the grand symbols of the last era: even the women appear narrow, the men's faces 'as bare as the palms of one's hand' (p. 194). This diminution is neither good nor bad but suggests an acceptable levelling: 'Vegetables were less fertile; families were much smaller. Curtains and covers had been frizzled up and walls were bare so that new brilliantly coloured pictures of real things, like streets, umbrellas, apples, were hung in frames, or painted upon the wood' (p. 194).

The demands of the present moment are both terrifying and mundane: the present shores us up against the past on one side and the unknowable future on the other. The banal exigencies of commodity culture jostle with an Orlando who remains resolutely phantasmagoric:

> Shade and scent enveloped her. The present fell from her like drops of scalding water. Light swayed up and down like thin stuffs puffed out by a summer breeze. She took a list from her bag and began reading in a curious stiff voice at first as if she were holding the words – boy's boots, bath salts, sardines ... (p. 196)

But the sign always threatens to disintegrate or to metamorphose into something else, as though the text delivers the meta-language of criticism creatively, enacting what it is, collapsing the distinctions between signifier and signified: this is alliteration, this is sibilance. Woolf nets language as meta-discourse and symbol, as always already something else: 'Bath and boots became blunt, obtuse; sardines serrated itself like a saw' (p. 196). Under the instability and the literariness of the sign, meaning, like the body, is always in the process of metamorphosis, of transition, as is Orlando's location in time and place, now at the mercy of arbitrary phonemic slippage. One moment, she stands ordering sheets in Marshall and Snelgrove's, the next, the shop becomes a ship from where she sees the masts of the Russian ship and the ambiguous figure of Sasha becomes, in a moment, the distinctly unambiguous 'fat, furred woman' as Orlando imagines (or sees?) Sasha.[53] This purveyor of words, we are reminded, is fundamentally and crucially *in* words, too.

Driving out of London, Orlando's self dissolves, but the return to her ancestral home represents the coming together of all the historical selves that she has been. The house now is consigned to history, and her awareness of the present moment consigns the memories of the past to an at least temporary oblivion, and a different Orlando re-emerges, one who seems to stare into the abyss of her consciousness. Past and present converge as the dead and living mingle and Shelmerdine arrives, miraculously, by aeroplane, so that the two lovers are reunited and the wild goose, symbol of the failure to net language, to match vision with sign, flies above the reunited pair as the text ends on the present moment, and the day of its publication.

In *Orlando,* the image of the literary critic and the retrieved image of the *salon* represent the hub of an imagined literary enterprise, but it is one that Orlando regards as stifling in part because of its exaggerated manliness and femininity: 'they're all so manly; and then, I do detest Duchesses; and I don't like cake' (p. 187). Woolf went on to explore this disrelish of the modern critic's torpid treatment of literature as part of her appraisal of the androgynous writing mind in *A Room of One's Own.* Modern sex consciousness (or feminism) fostered masculine egotism which 'blocked the fountain of creative energy and shored it within narrow limits' (*A Room*, 90) for Mr A the novelist. Mr B the critic, though full of learning, wrote with a deadening insularity, so that 'when one took a sentence of Mr B into the mind it falls plump to the ground – dead' (p. 91). Coleridge, on the other hand, invoked in *A Room* as an advocate of the androgynous mind, was a critic whose cre-ativity gave 'birth to all kinds of other ideas, and that is the only sort of writing of which one can say that it has the secret of perpetual life' (p. 91). Criticism should not contain and limit the infinite possibilities promised by the literary text, and nor should the writer respond defen-sively to the pressing concerns of the age, which makes him 'impeded and inhibited and self-conscious' (p. 91). Mary Beton doesn't want to be told what to think, and she wants literature to be available to women as well as to men, not to feel as though she's been 'caught eavesdropping at some purely masculine orgy' (p. 92). Woolf's imagin-ing of the androgynous mind is, of course, partly defined in resistance and response to a self-consciousness that she regarded as constraining for both writer and critic, and that she saw as endemic in modern culture.

When Orlando encounters Nick Greene she senses a growing disap-pointment with literature, rather like James Ramsay's disappointment on arriving at the Lighthouse: the material object itself is disappoint-ing, but the private imagination is the consoling refuge where litera-ture, like the lighthouse, can be the 'other thing' too, safe from the demands of the commercial market. Orlando comes to the realisation, then, that she had conceptualised literature through a series of jaded similes: wild as the wind, hot as fire, swift as lightning. But literature was the other thing too: embodied in Nick Greene, it's the voice of an elderly man talking about duchesses: the other 'meaning' of literature, presumably, is in the authoritative care of a paternalistic authority and the aristocratic patron: it is shaped by commerce and patronage, always a threat to the soaring free spirit of the writer. The modern literary critic now seems to have replaced the Angel in the House as the censorious figure who prohibits freedom of speech, but Nick Greene venerates her manuscript because it derives from a literary heritage that he supports and because it is un-modish, it cannot be pinned down to any particular age.

On completion of her manuscript, Orlando decides that it is, after all, a living thing, which needs reading. It is the reader, then, not the writer, who will instil meaning and, therefore, life to the literary text. Whilst the biographer seems deliberately to dispel any notion of charisma, emphasising instead the biographer's requirement for the subject's active life, none the less 'the charismatic image of artistic activity as pure, disinterested creation by an isolated artist'[54] is presented here, complete with the palpable distaste aroused by the commercial production of the literary text as commodity, an act of possible self-mockery on the part of Woolf, herself a publisher as well as a writer. The chapter culminates, then, with a quasi- (but only quasi-) Barthesian birth of text and reader (the author, after all, never really seems in danger of dying in this novel). In fact, that last section of the text offers a compact history of the birth of both reader and writer, and their construction through marriage, copulation, birth, history, nature, capitalism, consumerism. And all of it is narrated with conscious attention to language, to the act of narrating itself.

In *A Room*, Woolf's (or Mary Beton's) invocation of Coleridge's view of the great androgynous writing mind marks a return to an earlier version of androgyny that is aligned with the English Romantic imagination, but she is selective with her quotation since Coleridge clearly aligns the figure of the genius with that of male writers in other passages in *Table Talk*. That she is selective suggests that she recuperates male androgyny by re-imagining it as female, since it is the woman writer that concerns her throughout *A Room*. She is also clearly concerned with masculinised Fascist culture and its apparent exclusion of femininity: 'The Fascist poem, one may fear, will be a horrid little abortion such as one sees in a glass jar in the museum of some county town.

Such monsters never live long ... one has never seen a prodigy of that sort cropping grass in a field' (p. 93). Androgyny is, then, offered as a corrective to what she saw as an exaggerated, excessive masculinity. In *Orlando*, the re-assumption of Orlando's masculinity through her marriage to Shelmerdine helps to recuperate a writing impoverished by an excess of femininity unwillingly acquired during the nineteenth century. But what does it mean to write of a 're-assumption of masculinity' or the expulsion of femininity in the strutting machismo of Italian Fascist politics? In the end, it is difficult to ascertain whether Woolf is reinforcing stereotypes of masculinity and femininity rather than transcending them, and problematically, Woolf might well be seen to follow Herbert Spencer's perception of George Eliot as a great writer: as Nancy L Paxton notes, 'Spencer goes on in his *Autobiography* to depict Eliot retrospectively as a sort of hermaphrodite, calling her intellect "masculine," as if he could not imagine her large and powerful mind to be feminine like the rest of her.'[55]

But perhaps the success or failure of Woolf's enterprise is no longer the critical issue at stake: the surrounding narrative drafts of *A Room*, read alongside *Orlando*, and considered in relation to Woolf's relationship with Vita Sackville-West, opens a reading of androgyny that engages with bisexuality and a narrative exploration of the body that concerns itself with words as struggling substitutes for the real and as adequate vehicles for transporting the real into a rich, imaginative fantasy. That slippery oscillation between bisexed identities and sexuality is one attempt to elude these prescriptive and monolithic identities, which appear to crush Orlando. As a man whose sex could never be in question his imitative writing lacks authenticity; as a woman whose sex is settled by the law courts her writing falls into sentimentality. As a figure who finally engages, through the trope of marriage, with being a man and being a woman, Orlando is able to produce poetry which is both a literary and a critical triumph. But since we have never seen it, it seems in the end a gestural victory. If Woolf salvages a version of androgyny from its melancholic inscriptions, she none the less restores it as an emblem of mourning, marking it less as a retreat from the body, as some critics have claimed, and more as a device that might permit the modern writer to cease a sexual hostility engendered by twentieth-century sexual politics. *A Room*'s narrator appears to mourn the loss of a literary dialogue that she clearly prefers to the trends in post-war literary tradition inflected, as they appear to her, with an isolating political and erotic 'sex consciousness' that seemed to foster sexual difference for the worse. Woolf's conceptualisation of androgyny permits a fantasy that enables the writer to disregard the material realities produced by the cultural regulation of sexual difference: there are obvious differences between the quashed spirit of the Victorian Orlando, which is an attempt to register the effects of nineteenth-century ideologies on the woman writer's imagination, and the livelier romantic exchange that *A Room*'s narrator selectively reads in the poetry of Rossetti and Tennyson. The attempt to redeem that tradition by nostalgically retrieving nineteenth-century literary sensibility as a kind of genteel courtship against the unrestrained expression of sexuality in the twentieth century is arguably re-enacted in the marriage of Orlando and Shelmerdine, a re-enactment that seems as optimistic as it is atavistic.

4
The Second Wave

'The early seventies were a good time to be flat-chested,' Cal recalls, remembering his adolescent girlhood in *Middlesex*: 'Androgyny was in' (p. 304). By the 1970s, androgyny was 'an idea whose time had come' as social scientists 'rediscovered' the concept.[1] It wasn't just social scientists who had rediscovered it, though: within second wave feminism and in literature, androgyny heralded the possibility of 'a much broader range of sex-role possibilities for members of both sexes'.[2] It was also perceived as the expression of 'a psychic unity, either potential or actual, conceived as existing in all individuals'.[3] Androgyny was in the head, on the body, an attitude, a way of being, in the psyche, cosmic, unisex, bisex. The ubiquity of the concept and the ways in which it was deployed have made the term a nebulous one: when we speak of androgyny, when someone is described as androgynous, when androgyny is cited as a particular aspiration, what exactly do we mean by the term, what does it describe, what are we talking about? Even a brief glance at books and articles written between the 1960s and 1990s tells us that androgyny was a protean concept whose function shifted according to the discourse that constructed it. The androgyne could be 'a person who unites certain of the essential characteristics of both sexes and who, consequently, may be considered as both a man and a woman or as neither a man or a woman, as bisexual or asexual'.[4] Alternatively, androgyny is 'a synonym for bisexuality',[5] or else it is 'not bisexuality',[6] androgyny is 'an energy between individuals, rather than a psychic state locked within'[7] or 'the androgyne is a *representation in human form* of the principle of wholeness'[8] or 'it is the blending of *positive* masculine and feminine characteristics within a given person'.[9] Androgyny might be deployed as a useful force within culture: 'Androgynous integrity and transformation will require that women cease to play the role of "complement" and struggle to stand alone as free human beings',[10] or else it is something that we can only imagine: 'It is quite simply an imaginative construct, an idea/ideology that has never existed in the realm of fact.'[11] Or, 'we do not become androgynous; we already are.'[12]

Carolyn Heilbrun's *Towards a Recognition of Androgyny* (1973), a collection of three different but interrelated essays, remains a frequently cited text in discussions about androgyny during this period, even 'a focal point for the emerging field of feminist literary theory',[13] as Catriona MacLeod has suggested. This, despite the fact that, like Virginia Woolf before her, Heilbrun denied any necessary connection between androgyny and feminism.[14] That repudiation partly addresses the broad mythological and literary tradition of androgyny, a tradition that supersedes the political demands of contemporary feminism. Kari Weil suggests Heilbrun also appeared to be writing 'in the face of obvious resistance',[15] not the least of which was Heilbrun's implicit caution about homophobia. Although, historically, there have been clear associations of androgyny with homosexual and bisexual sexuality,[16] Heilbrun was cautious about representing her version of androgyny in this way. That she explored a relationship with bisexuality and androgyny in her essay on the socio-sexual lives of the Bloomsbury Group suggests, perhaps, that the historical and cultural distance of Bloomsbury also gave her a safely permissible space in which to discuss it. But only just: the 'androgynous qualities' of Bloomsbury 'should not be confused with the homosexuality of many of its members'.[17] She stepped warily through potential homophobic and misogynistic minefields when discussing bi- or homosexuality and androgyny in terms of contemporary America: 'Androgyny appears to threaten men and women, even more profoundly in their sexual than in their social roles.'[18] Andrea Dworkin was considerably less reserved: androgyny – and importantly the embodied androgyne – were subversive and counter-cultural for her: '[t]he myth of a primal androgyne survives as part of a real cultural underground: though it is ignored, despised by a culture which posits other values, and though those who relate their lifestyles directly to it have been ostracized and persecuted.'[19] Whilst Heilbrun was pleased with the responses that *Towards a Recognition* attracted, she also claimed that she had been misunderstood, and went on to reiterate the centrality of androgyny to creation myths, noted again the insidiousness of sexual division in contemporary culture, and stressed that her readers had understood androgyny to be aligned with 'homosexual, bisexual, hermaphrodite, feminist, revolutionary or, at the very least, [to be] decidedly peculiar',[20] all of which, she felt, was not necessarily what she had been writing about. (Writing in 1970, Shulamith Firestone noted that 'homosexuality or bi-sexuality [were] so unheard of that when I brought it up several women walked out of the room in protest.'[21])

There could be no question, though, that the promotion of an androgynous ontology was part of emerging feminist debates. Mary Daly, writing at the same time as Heilbrun, argued that androgyny and feminism were crucially linked, stating in *Beyond God the Father* (1973) that radical feminism would give rise to 'an intuition of androgynous existence'.[22] In her introduction to *Women's Studies'* special edition of 'The Androgyny Papers', Cynthia Secor expressed the hope that the collection of writings would 'be a tool for the feminist classroom where we strive collectively to articulate and document the necessarily complex connections between literature and life'.[23] Heilbrun's rejection of androgyny as a feminist concern is a strange myopia (or disavowal) given that *Towards a Recognition of Androgyny* re-read some of the major texts of the western canon through a critical frame that made gender (recalculated as androgyny) central to her interpretive strategies. None the less, it was popular and (more or less) well received. Daniel Harris, though generally critical of androgyny, described *Towards a Recognition* as 'important and provocative'.[24] (It was provocative for Camille Paglia, whose unsigned review, published in the summer of 1973, was excoriating: 'Heilbrun's book is so poorly researched that it may disgrace the subject in the eyes of serious scholars.'[25])

Heilbrun's literary and cultural study invoked androgyny as a liberating (often strategically feminising) ideal which offered recuperation from an overly masculinised culture.[26] In the process of her arguments, she made literature and mythology relevant to contemporary questions and concerns about shifts (actual and potential) in sexual politics.[27] The text was divided to consider three different approaches to contemplating androgyny: in mythology, in literature and as a possible way of life, exemplified for her by bi-sexuality in the Bloomsbury Group. Androgyny could be, she argued, a palliative for an era that she defined as 'an age of manliness'.[28] She stated her thesis with a caution that speaks *sotto voce* to a culture that she portrayed as being entrenched in, and committed to maintaining, sexual division:

> My opinion is easily enough expressed: I believe that our future salvation lies in a movement away from sexual polarization and the prison of gender toward a world in which individual roles and the

modes of personal behavior can be freely chosen. The ideal toward which I believe we should move is best described by the term 'androgyny'. This ancient Greek word – from *andro* (male) and *gyn* (female) – defines a condition under which the characteristics of the sexes, and the human impulses expressed by men and women, are not rigidly assigned. Androgyny seeks to liberate the individual from the confines of the appropriate.[29]

Her argument, an essentially humanist one, suggested that we (women and men) might be our own radical agents of change, and that to embrace the metaphysical ideal of androgyny would then be to engage with the possibility of an androgynous identity that everyone has the capacity to achieve.[30] Mary Daly had also underlined the possibility of the restoration of a full and crucially spiritual humanity in *Beyond God the Father*:

Instead of settling for being a warped half of a person, which is equivalent to a self-destructive non-person, the emerging woman is casting off role definitions and moving towards androgynous being. This is not a mere 'becoming equal to man in a man's world' – which would mean settling for footing within the patriarchal space.[31]

In spite of the evident differences in their respective positions, for Heilbrun, androgyny offers to redeem masculinity by feminising it; for Daly, women needed to reject or transcend entrenched sex-role sociali-sation, and she argued that there would liberating consequences for men, too – both had a vision of androgyny that looked to restore psychic equilibrium and 'wholeness' (later rejected by Daly in *Gyn/Ecology* as 'pseudowholeness'[32]). This would in turn contribute to the social and cultural good (using an implicitly Platonic model) by promising the restitution of a wholeness temporarily fractured by the effects of dominant and aggressive masculinity evident in 1960s and 1970s America, exemplified for Heilbrun in America's war with Vietnam, My Lai and the events at Kent State University.[33] 'This healing process,' Daly argued, 'demands a reaching out toward com-pleteness of human being in the members of both sexes – that is, movement toward androgynous being.'[34]

Heilbrun filtered her re-reading of the western canon through the broadest, though not always most rigorous, conceptualisation of androg-yny. That is to say, Heilbrun tended to state rather than explicate, and in doing so, she constructed, as much as she reflected on, various representations of androgyny. *Wuthering Heights*, for example, is 'the greatest androgynous novel of them all' (p. 62), 'a pure androgynous novel' (p. 79). The index of a redemptive and unifying androgyny in that text seems to be the love of Catherine and Heathcliff, which 'represents the ultimate, apparently undefined, androgynous ideal' (p. 80).

Such description is characteristic of the critical mode adopted by Heilbrun, one that tended to be speculative, even sentimental. Thus, Emily Brontë had imaginatively created 'in art the androgynous ideal which she perceived within herself on the loneliness of those moors' (p. 82). The American novel *par excellence* was *The Scarlet Letter*: 'From that day to this, America has not produced a novel whose androgynous implications match [it]' (p. 63). Heilbrun's use of the term is catholic, and always assumes that androgyny implies a redemptive, restorative and creative power: there are 'androgynous implications' (p. 63), there's 'androgynous energy' (p. 65), the 'androgynous ideal' (p. 65), 'androgynous realization' (p. 70), the 'androgynous impulse' (p. 73). *Vanity Fair* is an 'androgynous novel' depicting an 'anti-androgynous world' (p. 68). The novels of Thomas Hardy, she claimed, are so self-evidently androgynous that they're not worth discussing. George Eliot's mind was 'absolutely androgynous' (p. 76), Austen's 'genius' had an 'absolute androgyny' (p. 76). Coleridge 'was right: great minds do tend to be androgynous' (p. 77). Colette was 'marvellously androgynous' (p. 87). 'Orlando ends with the marriage of the future, a marriage of the androgynous world' (p. 165). Mr Ramsay, after Mrs Ramsay's death, offers his children 'androgyny' (p. 160) much as he might offer them sweets. Whilst Heilbrun refashioned the concept of androgyny,[35] advocating androgynous ontology as a subject position that should be readily available to us, she seemed to follow Virginia Woolf in recuperating it from its earlier twentieth-century associations with perversion and decadence, a point for which Daniel Harris took her to task, accusing her of failing to 'recognize the tradition of negative attitudes' engendered by considerations of androgyny. But even as the term 'androgyny' was re-acquiring greater cultural currency via Heilbrun's work and more generally across the second wave, the increasingly broad use of 'androgyny' and 'androgynous' meant that its application was extensive as the term underwent a series of paradigm shifts.

In *Towards a Recognition of Androgyny*, Heilbrun cast her net wide (Greek tragedy, the Judaeo-Christian tradition, Islam, the Apocryphal New Testament, medieval history, the romance tradition, Shakespeare, the nineteenth-century novel, the New Woman, Bloomsbury), but a general assumption consistently informed her reading: androgyny was, or could be, a liberating ideal. As her reading repeatedly affirmed, its promise was the reconciliation of the internecine sexes and a 'liberation from the confines of the appropriate'. In the words of one feminist critic, Mary Anne Warren: 'To many feminists androgyny has come to represent escape from the prison of gender[36] – that is, from socially enforced preconceptions of ways in which women and men ought to differ in their psychology and behavior.'[37] If androgyny promised a truce between the warring couple, Dworkin envisaged an androgynous ontology that discarded what she recognised as false sexual dichotomy. In *Woman Hating* she wanted to attempt 'however modest and incomplete ... to discern another ontology, one which discards the fiction that there are two polar distinct sexes'.[38] Such a rupture required androgyny as an interim measure until the binary had eroded and 'androgyny' had no signifieds to give it any significant meaning.

Mary Daly, in *Beyond God the Father* (1973), suggested that as women acquired liberation through feminism, men might experience liberation too, so that 'the becoming of the androgynous human persons implies a radical change in the fabric of human consciousness and in styles of human behavior'.[39] In considering the possibility of androgynous identity, Joyce Trebilcot argued that the point of inhabiting an androgynous model of being was 'to break the normative connections between sex and gender by bringing about gender crossing'.[40] Nor were feminist theorists like Trebilcot alone in envisaging 'a hypothetical future society in which masculinity and femininity are no longer normatively associated with sex'.[41]

For Mary Daly, androgynous identity held the promise of transgression and as she described it, feminists were 'breaking the dam of sex stereotyping that stops the flow of being, that stops men and women from being integrated, androgynous personalities'.[42] One comic, parodic response to the idea of the integrated, androgynous personality came in *Myron*, Gore Vidal's sequel to *Myra Breckinridge*. Margot Hentoff, reviewing *Myra Breckinridge* in the *New York Review of Books*, suggested that 'the appeal of *Myra Breckinridge* is that it unwittingly invokes what might be the ultimate shared fantasy of the age – a future of androgynous independence'.[43] That is debatable, as I discuss in chapter 5, but six years later, Vidal demonstrated the often hilarious impossibility of such a prospect. At the end of *Myra Breckinridge*, Myra, involved in a road accident, has been surgically transformed into Myron, marries Mary Ann, Myra's former student, and settles to a life of absolute conformity working in Chinese catering in the San

Fernando valley. *Myron* begins, surreally, inside the television: somehow (via Myra's magical intervention), Myron, who was watching television, finds himself on the film set of *Sirens of Babylon*, an undistinguished film made in 1948, starring Maria Montez and Bruce Cabot.[44] What follows is a comic and ceaseless oscillation between the male and female aspects of a camp and obstreperous psyche, a psychodrama in which Myra and Myron fight for control of the body that they both feel is theirs to possess. Myron is utterly conservative, the embodiment of all that is conventional about the middle-of-the-road American male, whereas Myra is flamboyant and always overtly sexual. To the outsider, 'Myra' appears to be the name and persona that Myron adopts when he wants to pose as a drag queen, a supposition that Myra is quick to dispel: '*Never* use that word to me, because I am *all woman*. Or was' (p. 271). Theirs is an entirely *dis*integrated personality in which one can exist only by suppressing the other. Consequently, Myron wakes up to discover that he's wearing make-up and that Myra has plucked his (her?) eyebrows. Gradually, Myra is able to take over Myron's identity for days at a time, but this only causes confusion: when Maude, a character said to be modelled on Truman Capote, brings Myra new clothes, Myron is furious: 'You thought I was Myra didn't you? ...You're in cahoots with that bitch' (p. 312). At another point, Myron reawakens from being Myra to discover that he's in women's clothes in a room with an actor called 'Steve Dude' who is naked and handcuffed to the bed. Later, Myra gets rid of all Myron's clothes so that he's forced to 'dress up in a pair of women's slacks and a blouse' (p. 384). But what is being satirised? Myron is a figure of such conservative masculinity that much of the humour derives from the contrast between his sententious personality and Myra's flamboyance, but it often seems that the punishment for being so ultra-orthodox is to become an unwilling female impersonator, marking the limits of what the 'real woman', as Myra describes herself, is. At one point, Myra declares war on Platonic androgyny which she rejects as the 'unnatural whole', a vision which she will supplant with her 'truer vision of forcibly divided and forever separated parts. No monist Myra!' (p. 293). As Catharine Stimpson has observed:

Because Myra has been a gay man (Myron the First), mostly but not exclusively a straight woman (Myra), and a boringly normal man at heart but not in body (Myron the Second), her experiences replicate the Western conflict between repressive sex roles and the range of human sexual drives.[45]

That's truer of *Myra Breckinridge* (the text that Stimpson refers to) than it is for *Myron*, which seems to suggest that heterosexual masculinity is a mask for the gay man who really wants to be a woman.

A similar kind of fluctuation to that experienced by Myra/Myron had been explored in Hammer's 1971 production of *Dr Jekyll and Sister Hyde*, directed by Roy Ward Baker and starring Ralph Bates and Martine Beswick as the eponymous Jekyll and his alter ego 'sister', Mrs Hyde. Historical and fictional representations present a slightly bizarre array of figures dislodged from their historical contexts: Jack the Ripper and Burke and Hare share studio space with Robert Louis Stephenson's fictional character. Intent on discovering an elixir that will prolong life, Dr Jekyll inexplicably needs to extract 'female hormones' from recently deceased young women, procured (more or less) honestly at first and then illegally through murder. After drinking the evil scientist's obligatory green potion, Jekyll turns into a woman, and the rest of the film explores the battle that ensues between the essentially evil feminine part of him and the good male part. Hammer's mandatory sexual dynamic is supplied by the other brother and sister of the film, the innocent Susan and the foppish Howard, she in love with Dr Jekyll and he with Sister Hyde. As Jekyll appears to be narcissistically delighted with his new female body, his femininity also allows for the occasional and ostensible gesture to homosexual desire: when Howard enquires after the health of Sister Hyde, Dr Jekyll tells him that he is 'excellent – I am in excellent health' before stroking Howard's face, a sign that Jekyll is losing control of his ability to wilfully change into a woman. The incidence of murder increases as Sister Hyde strives for control of a body that is increasingly subject to an involuntary metamorphosis. In a classic Whitechapel fog scene, Sister Hyde stalks Susan but is prevented from killing her by Dr Jekyll's attempt to reassert control of his now split psyche and body. As he tries to escape the police, he loses his footing on the rooftops, and Sister Hyde's attempt to wrest control of the body ends in their deaths: physically weaker, she cannot hold on to the guttering and falls to the ground, splitting his/her face in a gruesome and distorted mask, offering a tragic dénouement to an evidently cautionary tale. Susan and Howard are left to gaze on the single but duplicitous figure that each of them had loved. Whilst it is unlikely that an exploration of oscillatory androgyny was the impetus behind Ward Baker's film, the vacillations between the evil, sexualised woman and the essentially good and well-meaning man dramatise a cultural representation of men and women that has its origin in Genesis.

Heilbrun, like Mary Anne Warren and Mary Daly, recognised that androgyny could only ever be a temporary solution to the perceived socio-sexual crises highlighted by second wave feminism: 'the word "androgyny",' Heilbrun wrote in her response to *Towards a Recognition*, 'is only to get on with. Without it we cannot break from the stage in which we now are, but with it, I think, we can move into other realms where the term may no longer be either useful or appropriate.'[46] Dworkin imagined a more permanent 'community built on androgynous identity':[47] if androgyny might be seen to reify masculinity and femininity, it also offered the possibility of re-addressing cultural assumptions about masculine rationality or feminine intuition which, subject to feminist scrutiny, would be denaturalised and rendered inoperative.[48] Daly anticipated a point at which androgyny would become meaningless once the androgynous world had been established: 'Before the androgynous world can begin to appear, however (a world in which even the term "androgynous" itself would be rendered meaningless because the word reflects the archaic heritage of psycho-sexual dualism).'[49] In identifying several precise permutations or categories of androgyny within contemporary sociological research and theory, Ellen Cook's 1985 survey of the field reinforced the aspirational points that Daly and Dworkin were making. She identified 'multiplicative' or 'interactive' models, 'developmental models' and 'sex-role transcendence', 'where sex-role standards become irrelevant in determination of behavior, as masculine and feminine qualities are smoothly blended together into a process orientation to life'.[50] Within 'cognitive schema theory', androgynous people had non-sex-related ways of perceiving information. As Cook went on to argue, there simply wasn't a single model of, or perspective on, androgyny within a bewildering burgeoning of sociological categorisations through which androgynous behaviour was seen as exemplifying personality traits, behavioural traits, new cognitive schema or promising a new hybrid model of being. All these categorisations (and more) reproduced androgyny as a label in a methodological practice; androgyny, that is to say, was used as a 'descriptive label to aid in data analysis' rather than signifying 'a unique concept or type of person'. [51]

Following a forum on androgyny held at the Modern Language Association in 1973, the journal *Women's Studies* devoted a special issue, 'The Androgyny Papers', to the topic. Although Kari Weil and Catriona MacLeod have both pointed out that the issue 'contained ... a chorus of denunciations and warnings',[52] the edition included papers that were both for and against androgyny. Heilbrun answered responses to her book, and whilst she defended herself and the concept of androgyny, she still looked forward to the moment 'when we shall have passed from the gravitational field of the old anti-androgynous world, and the word "androgyny" itself will drop from us into that limbo where discarded relics orbit'.[53] Barbara Charlesworth Gelpi tempered her criticism that androgyny tended to be represented by men assimilating femininity in order to complete themselves, by considering contemporary theories of androgyny as 'useful and potentially liberating'[54] and by suggesting that it was 'good for women to begin speculating for themselves on the reintegration of the masculine principle into the feminine psyche ... as a potential which they possess and should use'.[55]

The Modern Language Association's *Commission on the Status of Women in the Profession* prompted the edition, making it clear that androgyny was being vetoed less as a mystical or sexual ideal, and more as a pragmatic and realisable possibility (although Harris reiterated that 'the myth is a purely imaginative construct, unusually malleable because it corresponds to nothing we commonly observe in our experience' and Nancy Topping Bazin and Alma Freeman claimed that epiphanic unity would be available 'after we become androgynous people living in an androgynous society'[56]). '[T]his androgyny business,' as Heilbrun suggested, was blamed whenever claims were made for equal pay. Like Heilbrun, and unlike Dworkin, Cynthia Secor, the guest editor, expressed a conservative concern with the androgyne as a corrupt counter-cultural figure, defined 'solely in terms of whom you fuck, how often, how freely, and without what hang-ups'.[57] And yet, even as she recognised androgyne ontology as somehow hijacked into a pan-sexual culture, she felt, too, that it was a static image 'which cannot take into account the rough going of historical process'[58] even while, as seems clear, second wave feminists were precisely reviving the concept of androgyny to meet their specific aims. As Nancy Topping Bazin and Alma Freeman argued: 'We use a term that has its roots in the past because we too have been shaped by the past, but just as we must go beyond our own past, we must go beyond past definitions of androgyny.'[59] In other words, its historically specific meanings needed to be re-attuned as a motif for, or index of, equal opportunities.

For Dworkin androgynous ontology would not be just social, but sexual too, and whereas Heilbrun stepped gingerly round the sexual and political implications of her arguments, Dworkin waded in: '*androgynous fucking requires the destruction of all conventional role-playing, of genital sexuality as the primary focus and value, of couple formations, and of the personality structures dominant-active ("male") and submissive-passive ("female")*[60] (italics in original). Dworkin signals a notable shift in terminology here too, from 'androgynous' to 'androgyne.' Most discussions in second wave feminism focused on 'androgyny' or the 'androgynous' rather than on the embodied figure of the 'androgyne'. Men and women would not necessarily be re-embodied as androgynes through feminism, but we could be androgynous in our behaviour: one need not be male to be a priest, or female to be a nurturer, as Heilbrun put it. Sexual dissolution or the abolition of sexual difference was never really under discussion, then: we would function as men and women but non-hierarchically, and perhaps importantly, still retain the appearance of 'men' and 'women' whilst all behavioural characteristics might be open to us, not assigned on the basis of our anatomical difference.

For Jan Morris, androgyny was the embodiment of an experience of disunity, rather than unity or completeness, marked by her constant shifting between male and female identities before she underwent surgery. Recalling early sexual experiences with other boys, Morris recalled the dysfunctional experience of those encounters in terms of a Platonic model: 'Our bodies did not cleave' (*Conundrum*, 19). 'Completeness' would come with a realignment of sex and gender: Morris's gender was the most substantial, the most true thing, her male body the thing that was 'wrong' about her (p. 21). As she undergoes hormone treatment, she became a 'chimera, half male, half female, an object of wonder even to myself' (p. 95). As a pre-operative male-to-female transsexual, she recalled that she 'found the androgynous condition in some ways a nightmare, but in others an adventure'.[61] Morris's ambiguous sex and gender meant that she never knew how she was going to be perceived, as woman or as man: one colleague likened her to Shakespeare's Ariel, 'insubstantial, ill-defined and always on the move' (p. 97):

> Reactions to my ambivalence varied greatly from nation to nation, or culture to culture. Among the guileless peoples the problem was minimal. They simply asked. After a flight from Darjeeling to Calcutta, for instance, during which I had enjoyed the company of an Indian family, the daughter walked over to me at the baggage counter when we had disembarked. 'I hope you won't mind my asking,' she simply and politely said, 'but my brothers wish to know whether you are a boy or a girl.' In Mexico, after staring hard for several days, and eyeing my sparse traveller's wardrobe with bewilderment, a deputation of housemaids came to my door one day.

'Please tell us,' they said, 'whether you are a lady or a gentleman.' I whipped up my shirt to show my bosom, and they gave me a bunch of flowers when I left. 'Are you a man or a woman?' asked the Fijian taxi-driver as he drove me from the airport. 'I am a respectable, rich, middle-aged English widow,' I replied. 'Good,' he said, 'just what I want,' and put his hand upon my knee. (p. 97)

In Oxford, she lived 'the role of a woman' (p. 102), and in Wales, with her family, she resumed her life in the role of a man. 'It required no great subtlety,' she commented, 'androgynous as I was' (p. 102). For a while, Morris switched between the two cheerily enough: '"Cheerio, sir," the porter would say at one club, and "Hullo, madam," the porter would greet me at the other' (p. 104). Morris's sense of androgyny was located simultaneously in her body, in the process of transitioning from male to female, and in her oscillation between masculine and feminine gendered identities, but if she perceived them as 'roles', she also affirmed an absolute faith in them as cultural truths. Though Morris lays claim to an androgynous identity, it is only ever a temporary one that exists as the wavering sum of these binary roles that she played out prior to her sex change. Androgyny is a kind of process, a coming to identity, but the chimerical body is also essentially private and, though real enough, Morris describes a kind of detachment from it. An 'equivocal figure', Morris bathed alone in the early morning in the Welsh mountains:

The silence was absolute. There I would take my clothes off, and all alone in that high world stand for a moment like a figure of mythology, monstrous or divine, like nobody else those mountains have ever seen: and when, gently wading through the weeds, and feeling the icy water rise past my loins to my trembling breasts, I fell into the pool's embrace, sometimes I thought the fable might well end there, as it would in the best Welsh fairy tales. (p. 95)

Catharine Stimpson, arguing that androgyny was only 'an idea' as opposed to an achievable and material reality, had criticised it as a flawed concept, even as she invoked an apparently ontological, rational androgyne: 'the androgyne still fundamentally thinks in terms of "feminine" and "masculine." It fails to conceptualise the world and to organize phenomena in a new way that leaves "feminine" and "masculine" behind.'[62] When Morris emerged from his/her androgynous chrysalis to re-encounter the world as a woman ('like a princess emancipated from her degrading disguise', as she put it, p. 126), it was to a world that feminist values seem hardly to have touched, and her androgynous identity seems relegated to the mythical and private scenario of that pool in the Welsh mountains.

> The more I was treated as a woman, the more woman I became. I adapted willy-nilly. If I was assumed to be incompetent at reversing cars, or opening bottles, oddly incompetent I found myself becoming. If a case was thought too heavy for me, inexplicably I found it so myself ... I discovered that even now men prefer women to be less informed, less able, less talkative and certainly less self-centred than they are themselves: so I generally obliged them. (p. 131)

Virginia Woolf's *Orlando* was one of the books Morris recalled being in the family home when she was a child, and it is in descriptive scenes like this that *Orlando* functions intertextually: on her return from Constantinople, having changed from man to woman, Orlando mimics the mannerisms of femininity, exposing femininity precisely as a process of mimicry and imitation that, in becoming naturalised, illustrates the cultural construction of the 'natural'. Morris's point seems more obliquely made but it hardly constitutes a criticism of the then existing relations and expectations between men and women.

In the literary imagination, androgynous *and* androgyne ontology were achieved through the destabilising effects of various literary strategies rather than through realism, either through the genre of science fiction, or through postmodern play. Ursula K. Le Guin explored androgyny as a transient but crucially embodied condition for the inhabitants of the planet Gethen in her much-celebrated *The Left Hand of Darkness* (1969). The novel comprises an interlinked collection of stories, fables, allegories, myths, in which androgyny is constructed either as a fluidly successive (rather than simultaneous) kind of embodied identity, or else marked by asexuality, or non-sexual identity. It is far from a utopian text, as she herself recognised.[63] Gethen (with its semantic echo of Gehenna, or Hell) is corrupt and dangerous. Gethen is ruled by a mad monarch, King Argaven, and Gethen's rival state, Orgoreyn, is founded, as Harold Bloom has noted, 'upon a barely hidden system of concentration camps'.[64] Gethenians are capable of inflicting torture and terror on each other: their archival and foundational national myths comprise stories of murder, suicide, exile, isolation. Though they have no war, they none the less have 'Quarrels, murders, feuds, forays, vendettas, assassinations, tortures, abominations' (*Left Hand of Darkness*,

47). On the other hand, as Catharine Stimpson has noted, Le Guin also explores the positive potential of an androgynous civilisation: sex happens only by mutual consent and desire, there is no rape; there are equal work opportunities; and though she does present a world of intrigue, its culture eschews the military, and tokenistic guards with 'foray-guns' represent 'relics of a more barbaric past' (p. 11).

The Left Hand of Darkness didn't advocate or predict androgyny but worked from a premise that 'if you look at us at certain odd times of day in certain weathers, we already are'.[65] 'I was not recommending the Gethenian sexual setting,' Le Guin wrote in a candidly critical response to her text, 'I was using it. It was a heuristic device, a thought-experiment.'[66] She conceived of the Gethenians as part of a process, 'not questions, not answers',[67] whereby she could think about what it was to be 'simply human', an identity that was somehow outside the male-female polarity and therefore not defined or constrained by cultural prescriptions. Initially, she claimed that she had seen the book not in terms of gender at all, but in terms of broader themes, 'a book about betrayal and fidelity',[68] but later confessed that she had been disingenuous: 'This is bluster. I had opened a can of worms and was trying hard to shut it ...'.[69] It was also a book about the absence of war, an absence threatened once the state opens itself up to capitalism, 'the centralisation of power, authoritarian government, and a secret police'.[70] The novel explores the exploits of Genly Ai, an envoy from a federation of planets called the Ekumen, who has lived on Gethen (also known as Winter) for two years. It is his mission to persuade the Gethenians to join the Ekumen, who rule not through monarchy and hierarchy, but through collective action. His main contact in Gethen is Estraven, a prime ministerial figure (symbolically, Genly Ai tends to be positioned always to the right of Estraven, underlining the masculine/feminine differences between them). Estraven is exiled by Gethen's wilful 'mad' king Argaven, and Genly Ai, mindful of his now perilous position, sets out to leave Gethen. His journey often seems allegorical: he enters dark forests and woods, encounters religious sects that exist without institutional dogma or creed, is captured and placed in a concentration camp, rescued by Estraven, and through their journey over an unforgiving icy wasteland, learns to counter his prejudices about an androgynous condition where men become women. (The alternative oscillation is never explored, helping to shore up later criticisms that the androgyne was really the womanly man.[71]) The condition of his self-knowledge, though, entails cultural dislocation, as it did for Gulliver after his travels. Androgynous metamorphosis is never available to Genly Ai since his physiological makeup doesn't allow it, and when he re-enters the conventional world of sexual division and difference, he feels alienated and disgusted by it. Le Guin later admitted that she showed 'certain timidities or ineptnesses' when she was writing her novel: one was that she had been naively pragmatic in 'quite unnecessarily lock[ing] the Gethenians into heterosexuality'.[72] But she also suggested that what her depiction of androgynous physiology lacked was the presence of an anima or animus, the male and female contra-sexual impulses that, Jung argued, were inherent in men and women. Le Guin's representation of androgynous physiology inadvertently, then, lent itself to a cautious version of androgyny that was sexless and masculine: although she later recognised that the matter of naming *was* important, she said that she had kept male pronouns because she didn't want to 'mangle English by inventing a pronoun for he/she'.[73] Without mangling English, Marge Piercy did invent a new pronoun, 'per', to describe a utopian world of androgynous, bisexual free love.

Marge Piercy's feminist and postmodern *Woman on the Edge of Time* (1976) imaginatively re-engages with many of the aspirations of contemporary feminist politics in positing androgynous sensibilities and embodied androgynes, but does so through a narrative that oscillates, and then collapses the distinctions between, realism and private fantasy, dystopia and utopia. Piercy imagined (as did Le Guin before her) a new anthropological community in which androgynous sensibilities were the norm. Piercy's ideal community of Mattapoisett is not dissimilar to the one Barbara Charlesworth Gelpi identifies when she describes Gabriel de Foigny's *Terre Australe Connue* (*A New Discovery of Terra Incognita Australis, or the Southern World*). De Foigny described the adventures of Jacques Saduer, an explorer who encountered a colony of androgynous beings in Australia, living in 'a perfect Image of the State that man first enjoyed in Paradise. They live a community life, hold all possessions in common, are wise, gentle, and completely free from strife.'[74] Dworkin had proposed an ideal community that abandoned institutionalised sexism as a feminist – and androgynous – goal: 'if we can create androgynous community, we can abandon power altogether as a social reality – that is the final, and most important, implication of androgyny.'[75] Mattapoisett was a world that, akin to Dworkin's aspirations, did away with sexist institutions, sexual taboos, and insisted on the values of community, 'where violence is not the main dynamic of human relationship, where natural desire is the fundament of community, where androgyny is the operative premise, where tribe based on androgyny and the social forms which would develop from it are the bases of the collective cultural structure – noncoercive, nonsexist'.[76] In Mattapoisett, Piercy conjured with the radical possibility that men might be nurturing mothers, that, in Shulamith Firestone's words, '[t]he tyranny of the biological family would be broken' through the mechanical rather than biological reproduction of children. Women like Luciente, a character we are initially invited to perceive as male, appears to be assertive, functioning with a 'brisk unselfconscious authority' (p. 59).[77]

In *Woman Hating*, Dworkin notes that:

> we look at the world we inhabit and we see disaster everywhere; police states; prisons and mental hospitals filled to overflowing; alienation of workers from their work, women and men from each other, children from the adult community, governments contemptuous of their people, people filled with intense self-hatred; street violence, assault, rape, contract murderers, psychotic killers; acquisition gone mad, concentrated power and wealth; hunger, want, starvation, camps filled with refugees.[78]

Marge Piercy's imaginative redress to this description of western civilisation not only underlined the consequences that arose from the dislocation between sex and gender roles in late capitalist culture, but also expressed concern about the environment and about who controlled (or rather abused) technology. In the nightmarish world of the present, depicted in the realist sections of the text, doctors work on the assumption that people, rather than culture, need to be changed, and that technological advances might pacify the apparently irrational violence exhibited by them. The socially dispossessed are not just dehumanised, they are also hybridised, diagnosed as somewhere between human and machine, at least as an authorising medical discourse defines them: 'The focal brain dysfunction we see in this patient has resulted in episodic dyscontrol. We believe this kind of hardcore senseless aggression can be controlled – even cured. In layman's language, something is wrong in the electrical circuitry – some wires crossed in the switchboard of the amygdala' (p. 195). The 'cure' will result in the sinister production of inert cyborgs, passive like *A Clockwork Orange*'s Alex, re-programmed to act in accordance with the normative expectations of the state.

At the centre of her text is the impoverished and brutalised Connie Ramos, who notes that she has 'lived in three cities and seen them all from the bottom' (p. 38). The text traces the punishment and subsequent disintegration of Connie, victim of a racist and misogynistic patriarchal state who is punished by an involuntary incarceration in a mental hospital after attacking her niece's violent pimp. Shortly before and then during her incarceration, she's increasingly visited by Luciente whose status as either an actual material body or as a manifestation of Connie's imaginative (or drug-induced) fantasy depends on whose perspective you're sympathetic to, Connie's or the doctors'. Connie is 'a catcher, a receptive' (p. 34) able to communicate with and visit people from the future in a community called Mattapoisett; she is also heavily sedated with drugs and possibly subject to hallucinatory fantasies. The text is thus divided between the realist world of institutionalised misogyny and racism and a feminist alternative, where roles are redistributed amongst the bisexual and androgynous inhabitants of communities who work collectively. In Mattapoisett, Connie remains outside their more fluid social and sexual ethics, but in the 'real' world, she is on the verge of becoming a nightmarish cyborg (rather than the ironic one that Donna Haraway hypothesised several years later in 'Manifesto for Cyborgs'),[79] a hybrid organism of woman and machine, whose will can be controlled by the medics who install a 'corrective' device in her head. Connie is only the crude prototype for a possible cyborg, part-woman, part-machine, which represents the antithesis of the androgynes of Mattapoisett.

Masculinity is represented as violent and abusive in the text. Geraldo, her niece's pimp, symbolises all men for her: 'he was the man who had pimped her favourite niece ... Geraldo was her father, who had beaten her every week of her childhood. Her second husband, who had sent her into emergency with blood running down her legs. He was El Muro, who had raped her and then beaten her because she would not lie and say she had enjoyed it' (pp. 6–7). She's given an unasked for hysterectomy when the hospital's medical residents need practice. And then she becomes the subject of a new medical development where a chip lodged in her brain will make her entirely subjective to the controlling will of the medics. Anyone who stands outside the legitimising normative frames of mainstream American culture – the Latino Connie, the homosexual Skip, Alice, the white witch – will be subject to forms of control that will render them the inert cyborg agents of the state.

Luciente is the redemptive and idealised androgynous figure, the utopian alternative to Connie's virtual and real nightmare world. Always a mediating, liminal figure, she initially appears to be a 'Young man of middling height with sleek black hair to his shoulders, an Indio cast to his face' (p. 25). Luciente lacks 'the macho presence of men in her own family' (p. 28) and has a voice that's 'high-pitched, almost effeminate' (p. 28). The alternative masculinity that 'he' appears to present is a redeemed one, made attractive by his apparent 'girlish' appearance. Only on the way to Mattapoisett does Connie realise that the muscular, authoritative, confident Luciente is not a man but a woman, though she always remains an oscillatory figure who appears to be male or female at different times. The narrative's own oscillation between the two worlds of the asylum and Mattapoisett lends a delib- erate instability to meaning and perception: definitions and facts are revealed to be perceptions produced by point of view and the shifting trends of cultural sensibilities rather than transcendent and authorita- tive, and Piercy is careful to ensure that everyone in the real world has a counterpart in Mattapoisett, outlining the alternative possibilities that might and should be available. In spite of the apparent lunatic incongruity of this list – sexuality, alternative forms of medical prac- tice, poverty, madness – they are all seen as symptoms of illness that can be cured by the self-legitimating practices of the state. So whilst Skip is being 'treated' for his homosexual desires, Luciente moves freely and non-monogamously between men and women. Madness is break- down in the 'real' world, but a form of private and visionary retreat in Mattapoisett. In the 'holi', a kind of theatrical performance piece per- formed by two of Mattapoisett's inhabitants, Jackrabbit and Bolivar, Piercy dramatises her vision of recuperative androgynous unity:

> The bones lay in the dust. Slowly they put out roots that sank deep in ravaged earth. Slowly the bones burgeoned into sprouting wands. The wands grew to a tree. The oak thrust its taproot deep and out- stretched its massive boughs. The tree became a human couple embracing, man and woman. They clutched, they embraced, they wrestled, they strangled each other. Finally they passed into and through each other. Two androgynes stood: one lithe with black skin and blue eyes and red hair, who bent down to touch with her/his hands the earth; the other, stocky, with light brown skin and black hair and brown eyes, spread his/her arms wide to the trees and sky and a hawk perched on the wrist. (p. 173)

Embracing both earth and sky, these inter-sexed and multiracial figures offer the possibility of regeneration and resurrection. 'Only in us do the dead live,' they intone, making Connie realise that she is the dead, and they are the possibility of her potential (re)incarnation: 'In their real future, she has been dead a hundred years or more; she was the dead who lived in them' (p. 174). The alternative to this restorative vision lies in the dystopian world inhabited by Gildina, in a culture that is recognisably contemporary even as it is pitched as a possible future scenario. Gildina, too, is a hybrid figure, but is a rather differently idealised hybrid, part-masculine fantasy, part-machine.

In Mattapoisett, the regenerative and multiracial androgynes embrace the gamut of the natural world, from earth to sky. In chapter 15 of *Woman on the Edge of Time*, Connie finds herself in a windowless room with Gildina, 'a cartoon of femininity' (p. 281) with her tiny waist, pointed breasts and impossibly small feet. Gildina is entirely cosmetic, 'still on the full shots and re-ops' (p. 282), her skin artificially lightened, she's been '[c]osmetically fixed for sex use' (p. 293). Opposed to the androgynes, the people in this alternative future are either 'Cybo' or 'Assassin', and since everyone has been implanted, they're in complete servitude to the demands of the multinational corporations who now own them overtly: the 'multi', according to Cash, 'is everything' (p. 294), Cash, the pimp-like figure who appears to control Gildina, is almost a 'Cybo', able to 'control the fibers in his spinal cord, control his body temperature. He's a fighting machine' (p. 291). Food is produced on corporate factory farms, the people are subject to total video surveillance and human contact is both minimal and affectless: Gildina converses with a virtual world via the screen of a computer or a TV. The nightmare of postmodern depthlessness against the utopian (and humanist) idealist dream of the androgyne is presented here as a contrast, as though cyborg and androgyne themselves constitute an irreconcilable dualistic tendency. Arguably, the cyborg is similar to the androgyne as image or concept because it represents a way of trying to express the complexity of human intellectual and emotional make-up by a sensationalised/abstracted structural dualism. On the one hand, the cyborg split between human and machine seems to be quite removed from the androgyne split between masculine and feminine, but they both could be read, perhaps, as having their roots in a gendered stereotyping of human characteristics – masculine/rational (which has an instrumental, active component) and feminine/emotional (which is responsive). Lisa Rado has suggested that the post-modern cyborg is the newer incarnation of the androgyne as we witness 'its transfer from (male/female) mind to the vast networks of increasingly human machines'.[80] While the idea of the cyborg is an attempt to imagine and theorise material developments in humanity's interaction with and response to the world, androgyny, for many of those who discuss it, represents an idealist retreat from the material and physical world: the androgyne, unlike the hermaphrodite or the cyborg, is a concept with, at best, a fugitive referent: Cynthia Secor, sceptical about androgyny, declared that androgynes were 'rarer than unicorns'.[81] Once, Huysmans conjured a wavering androgyne without content in *À Rebours*; now, Secor reaffirmed the androgyne as a figure 'devoid of social context'.[82] In *The Left Hand of Darkness*, the androgyne exists only via the capacity of the Gethenians to metamorphose from the non-sexual to male or female embodiment, persistent but transitory and conceivable through the distance engendered by the science-fiction imagination. Piercy's androgynes are theatricalised in the 'holi', and otherwise exist in the private, incommunicable retreat of Connie Ramos's mind. Connie resists the doctors' attempts to implant their mechanism in her brain: one part of the text suggests that's a willed rejection on Connie's part, the successful consequence of her own agency. The realist text implies that it is the body's rejection and has nothing to do with the passive, affectless object of scientific observation. Impelled by the messages that she hears in her head, Connie averts the disaster of a world populated by Gildinas by fatally poisoning the doctors who administer the programme. Thus sabotaged by a patient apparently driven mad by it, the project's funding will be withdrawn and it will fail. Connie, no longer able to communicate with Mattapoisett, faces a lifetime of incarceration. At the historical root of her troubles was the abusive relationship of her niece and her niece's pimp: in Connie's private, essentially incommunicable, fantasy is the androgynous ideal, marking the limits of Piercy's utopian vision of communitarian living.

Whilst critics and writers like Andrea Dworkin argued androgyny myths offered 'nonsexist, nonrepressive notions of sexuality',[83] 'many feminists' also repudiated androgyny precisely for reinforcing sexist and repressive notions of sexuality. Elizabeth Lane Beardsley, questioning the efficacy of androgyny, doubted that the journey to the promised land of 'humanity and personhood' could be accomplished by androgyny, which she described as both 'self-defeating' and 'self-defeated'.[84] Androgyny represented less a liberation from the prison house of gender, then, and more a bolting of the door, since the model also threatened to reify what it sought to release: although representations of androgyny yielded a particular consciousness about the relationship between maleness and masculinity, femaleness and femininity, models of androgyny tended to accept, reinforce, even legitimise the cultural constructions of the sexed body: '[m]asculinity is instrumental/agentic and femininity is expressive/communal in nature'.[85] Catriona MacLeod summarises it well:

> On the one hand, many feminists could and did embrace the unisex fluidity of the 1970s; on the other hand, and this was the difficulty, they detected the polar structures upon which such an androgynous ideal appeared to be premised, definable psychological categories of 'masculine' and 'feminine' that were aligned in a problematic fashion with the biological categories of 'male' and 'female'.[86]

As Daniel Harris had argued, the interest in androgyny could only promote an insidious politics 'perpetuat[ing] the habits of oppression that we seek to reject'.[87]

Virginia Woolf, celebrated by Heilbrun in *Towards a Recognition*, was castigated by Daniel Harris and famously criticised by Elaine Showalter in *A Literature of Their Own*. Harris argued that 'the much-touted vision of androgyny in *A Room of One's Own* is actually a compromise, a retreat from the more radically feminist fury Woolf feared to express'.[88] Showalter's recuperative history of women's writing, *A Literature of Their Own: British Women Novelists from Brontë to Lessing* (1977) developed Harris's criticism in the penultimate chapter, 'Virginia Woolf and the Flight into Androgyny'. Underlying Showalter's criticism was the contemporary critical tendency to denigrate androgyny as repressive rather than radical, but it's worth also taking into account the fact that Woolf herself was becoming ubiquitous during the 1970s. Quentin Bell's two-volume biography of her was published in 1972; Anne Olivier Bell's meticulous editions of Woolf's diaries began to appear in 1977, alongside Nigel Nicolson and Joanne Trautmann's equally meticulous editions of her letters. Joan Russell Noble's *Recollections of Virginia Woolf* was published in 1975, Spater and Parson's *A Marriage of True Minds* in 1977, Woolf's autobiographical *Moments of Being* appeared in 1976, and in 1978, a year after Showalter's text was published, Phyllis Rose published her feminist literary biography of Woolf, *Woman of Letters: A Life of Virginia Woolf*, the same year that Roger Poole's *The Unknown Virginia Woolf* came out. Showalter's critical reading of Woolf's argument for androgyny reads more as a disappointment in her as a failed feminist icon than it does for a more specific or historically focused criticism of the political argument of *A Room of One's Own*.

For Showalter, androgyny somehow functioned as Bloomsbury's serial killer: she drew attention to the 'failures of androgyny; in the suicides of

Bloomsbury satellites like Mark Gertler, Dora Carrington, and, more centrally, Woolf herself. Showalter mounted a sustained critique of what she considered Woolf's flight from femininity into a retreat afforded by the vision of androgyny. Showalter's definition of androgyny, the 'full balance and command of an emotional range that includes male and female elements',[89] is, perhaps, a selective one given the catholic range of definitions that the concept had attracted during the 1970s. Showalter read androgyny biographically as a motif that helped Woolf 'evade confrontation with her own painful femaleness and enabled her to choke and repress her anger and ambition'.[90] In Nancy Topping Bazin's reading (her book was published in 1973), androgyny occupies an over-determined importance in Woolf's life, which speaks more to the resurgence of interest in androgyny during the early 1970s than it answers to a description of Woolf's psyche. Problematically, such criticism re-enacted the repressive models that it also sought to destroy, and in doing so, endorsed the reservations and scepticisms of those who were critical of androgyny. Androgyny was the fulcrum, according to Bazin, on which Woolf's suicide balanced, between despair and faith: 'despair that the androgynous whole would never be established on earth but faith in the existence (in the timeless realm of death) of its mystical equivalent – oneness'.[91] Although Showalter shows some scepticism about Bazin's reading ('to see Woolf's suicide as a beautiful act of faith, or a philosophical gesture towards androgyny')[92] she also seems to collude with such a reading and presents an unproblematic acceptance of some mystical faith in 'androgyny': 'Deprived of the use of her womanhood, denied the power of manhood, she sought a serene androgynous "oneness," an embrace of eternity that was inevitably an embrace of death. In recognizing that the quest for androgyny was Woolf's solution to her existential dilemma, we should not confuse flight with liberation.'[93] Showalter remained critical of the 'serenity' that Woolf appeared to find in the androgynous vision, and she traced a history of Woolf's dilemmas with both writing and with the self up to the moment in which she declares that a great mind should be androgynous: 'Her wish for experience was really a wish to forget experience. In the 1920s, as her fiction moved away from realism, her criticism and her theoretical prose moved away from a troubled feminism toward a concept of serene androgyny.'[94] It is a criticism that is informed by the precepts of contemporary feminism rather than a reading of Woolf's representation of androgyny in the context of *A Room of One's Own*, within the cultural context of literary modernism or within the wider context of constructions of androgyny during the early twentieth century.

In the end, argues Showalter, androgyny helped Woolf to evade the terrible difficulties she had with her own relationship with her body and with womanhood, and with the ideological constraints she felt writing as a woman. In spite of androgyny as a technique to help her evade the realities of the body (however that might work out), Woolf still cannot help herself, invoking the heterosexual practices of the sexual body *even as* she is in the process of evading it: 'Woolf uses a literal sexual imagery of intercourse between the manly and womanly powers of the mind.'[95] In her critique of Woolf's use of pronouns, Showalter argues that 'Obviously Virginia Woolf had not looked at or questioned what she had done in this passage: made the writer male' (p. 288). But that 'obviously' carries an enormous speculative weight, and whilst it is possible that Woolf was oblivious to her slip, it is equally possible that her choice of pronouns were strategic, or that she was following conventions in assuming that 'he' speaks for a universal humanity.[96] Toril Moi went some way towards redeeming Woolf's vision of androgyny from Showalter's biographically-based reading in *Sexual/Textual Politics* (1985), where she argues that Woolf's version of androgyny was a deconstructive one that recognised the 'falsifying metaphysical nature'[97] of masculine and feminine polarity as they are embodied in Mr and Mrs Ramsay in *To the Lighthouse*. It is Lily Briscoe, the figure of the artist, who comes to question the opposition. In the end, though, even Lily's vision is one that the reader, mediating the visual through language, must take on good faith: if Lily's is an 'androgynous' vision, it is an androgyny that sacrifices mimetic representation of the body in favour of a sparsely picturesque geometry. Even if Lily's painting is about the evasion of the body (at least its mimetic representation in painting), Woolf is surely foregrounding issues pertaining to painterly and writerly aesthetics, which is what the androgynous writing mind had been an index of in *A Room*.

Writing in 1976, June Singer thought that the Women's Movement 'may turn out to be the decisive step in the direction of androgyny, inasmuch as it confronts directly some of the obstacles that lie in the path toward androgyny'.[98] Androgyny had functioned as an interpretive model for Ursula Le Guin in *The Left Hand of Darkness*, a model that helped her to conceptualise subjectivity (even though she came to recognise its limitations) and social organisation outside of gender. When Jeanette Winterson's *Written on the Body* was published in 1992, a text that also imagined subjectivity and sexuality denuded of a recognisable or stable gender identity, critical responses, on the whole, declined to read the novel as in any way exemplifying androgyny: Ute

Kauer states categorically on the opening page of her essay on this text that it is not 'an attempt at self-discovery by reviving the androgynous myth of Virginia Woolf's *Orlando*; sexual ambiguity is not the same as androgyny'.[99] Though one might counter her argument by pointing out that historically, sexual ambiguity has been and indeed can be synonymous with androgyny, Kauer's argument is part of a critical consensus that *Written on the Body*'s narrative voice is not an androgynous one, perhaps not that surprising since in the paradigm of the postmodern a moratorium of sorts was issued for androgyny, which came to be regarded as naively optimistic. Chris Straayer regarded the androgynous as obscure, and certainly not radical: 'The transgressive figure of the She-man is glaringly bi-sexed rather than obscurely androgynous or merely bisexual'[100] and the obscurantism that Straayer saw was reinforced by Judith Halberstam: 'When a woman is consistently mistaken for a man, I think it is safe to say that what marks her gender presentation is not androgyny but masculinity.'[101] Recognition of the performative nature of gender, an insecure ontology brought into being each time by the acts that iterate and produce it, inevitably helps to recast androgyny as old-fashioned and misconceived, crudely relying on masculinity and femininity as a metaphysics of presence; as Catherine Belsey notes, '[p]ostmodern writing knows that metaphysics is not an option'.[102]

Lisa Moore's reading of *Written on the Body*'s narrator's attempt to blow up some urinals at the behest of a radical feminist character named Inge leads her to conclude that the narrator's shifting relation to and distance from feminist discourse means that s/he 'is not an androgynous figure, the imprecise claim of some reviewers', an argument that assumes that androgyny must be implicated in feminism. 'Neither,' she argues, 'is the narrator sometimes a man and sometimes a woman.'[103] With no recourse to reified gender, Moore argues that Winterson's narrator is, instead, constituted by 'disparate body parts, desires, identities and histories, put together in a postmodern pastiche'.[104] Certainly, the narrator teases us with the sartorial and institutional markers of gender identity, calling attention to ready assumptions about how roles may (or may not) consolidate anatomy and gender: s/he stays in the Women's Institute in Pimlico (p. 23), on Friday nights and at weekend conferences, it's 'Off with the business suit, legs apart, pulling me down on them' (p. 72), s/he had never been a boy scout (p. 58), feels like 'a convent virgin' (p. 94), settles into a parody of the sporting colonel (p. 77), quivers 'like a schoolgirl' (p. 82), and so on. Like Stephen Gordon in *The Well of Loneliness*, who repeatedly throws binary structures into disarray, Winterson's narrator has a disruptive function in the text: if prosaically s/he breaks up the marriage of Elgin and Louise, s/he is also the translator who dissects the male-female binary and re-inscribes the economy of desire outside the structures that assign men and women to their respective social and sexual places. If the narrative declares a war on clichés, Louise and Elgin are (strategically) constructed in them, underlining how difference works through constructed oppositions – art and science, fluid, fixed, tangible, virtual, but those binaries no longer work (they're no longer needed) since desire is reconfigured between the narrator and Louise. At times, the narrator exhibits a nostalgic desire to transcend difference altogether: recalling a couple s/he knew, the narrator comments, 'Time had not diminished their love. They seemed to have become one another without losing their very individual selves. Only once had I seen it and I envied it' (p. 82). If that's a nostalgia that recalls the recuperative coupling of the Platonic androgyne (re-coupled, they transcend the pain obviated by difference), it also calls to mind Hélène Cixous's desire for the '*other bisexuality*', one opposed to the bisexual (and for her 'neuter') 'fantasy of a complete being'.[105] That fantasy speaks to the neutrality of non-being, since the acquisition of subjectivity entails loss as we recognise and enter language and sexual difference, and to ward off 'castration' is to ward off becoming and being a subject. In 'Sorties', Cixous reclaims bisexuality from 'the fate classically reserved for it in which it is conceptualized as "neuter" because, as such, it would aim at warding off castration',[106] an aim that is evident in Freud's explanation of the fantasy of the hermaphrodite mother in his interpretation of Leonardo's early life. Cixous's reconceptualisation of bisexuality operates outside 'the spurious Phallocentric Performing Theater'[107] – for her, writing is the place that is 'not economically or politically indebted to all the vileness and compromise ... not obliged to reproduce the system', a place that can re-imagine representation.[108] Sexual difference, as Morag Shiach has argued, thus becomes relocated 'at the level of sexual pleasure, of *jouissance*'.[109] What is inscribed is a translation or approximation of unbounded sexuality, the expression of the inexpressible and a self-consciousness about language. Afraid of expressing or naming desire at the beginning of the narrative, the narrator is as much afraid of language as s/he is of emotion, claiming to want '[t]he saggy armchair of clichés' (p. 10) because it is easier. Later, s/he progresses to the 'saggy rented double bed with Gail Right sagging beside me' (p. 144) and right at the end, sits down again in the 'saggy armchair', wondering whether this is the 'proper ending' (p. 188). Of course it isn't: love – and language – are dynamic, not static, and slinging the sun under an arm, the narrator and Louise are either confined by the world and go to explore a space beyond it, or are so expanded by love that such hyperbole gestures to the erasure of boundaries that place any restriction on imagination or expression. What marks the distinction between the 'bisexual' fantasy of unity, on the one hand, and 'bisexual' *jouissance* on the other, is the location or construction of culture which, for Cixous, invalidates 'in advance any conceptualisation'.[110]

Inevitably, the distance we have travelled from second wave to post-feminism means that, accommodating and general as some constructions of androgyny were in the early 1970s, they are, by now, rooted in a specific moment, located in time and place. Andrea Dworkin – like Carolyn Heilbrun – speaks to (even constitutes) a zeitgeist in which the idea of an androgynous ontology enjoyed some currency, however momentary that may have been. Oppositional and counter-cultural, the promotion of androgyny addressed the need for alternative social and sexual identities. In *Woman Hating,* Dworkin argued for the necessity of a 'community built on androgyny' not only to engage with the hierarchical dualism of sex and gender, but also to re-engage with 'our general multisexuality'. In such a scenario she argues, 'the transsexual will be able to expand his/her sexuality into a fluid androgyny, or, as roles disappear ... that energy will be transformed into new modes of sexual identity and behavior'.[111] Her aspiration calls to mind one of Shulamith Firestone's goals in *The Dialectic of Sex*: 'in our new society, humanity could finally revert to its natural polymorphous sexuality – all forms of sexuality would be allowed and indulged.'[112] The desire to reconfigure, rethink, re-experience identity beyond the prescriptive and normalising hetero-normative binary oppositions found expression, for Dworkin in 'androgyny', the 'androgynous' and the embodied 'androgyne'.

It is instructive to compare the idealism of Dworkin's aspirations with Leslie Feinberg's *Stone Butch Blues* (1994). The text's central character, Jess Goldberg, is readable within the terms that Dworkin imagined, at least in the narrative's evident search for 'new modes of sexual identity and behavior'. Jess's interaction with second wave feminism, though, collides with its emphasis on the importance of maintaining sexual difference in order to celebrate being a woman, rather than marking androgynous identity. *Stone Butch Blues* is overtly concerned with the difficulties experienced by those who identify and are identified outside of dominant sex-gender systems. 'Is that a boy or a girl' or 'Are you a boy or a girl' are questions that punctuate the text and gesture to the prescriptive and delimiting choices that Jess must decide upon. But s/he wants to celebrate the 'shades of gender' that constitute hir, a desire that calls to mind Kate Bornstein's criticism of androgyny as a limiting bipolar model:

> Androgyny assumes that there's male stuff on one side of a spectrum, and female stuff on another side of that spectrum. And somewhere in the middle of this straight line, there's an ideal blend of 'male' and 'female'. However, by saying there's a 'middle', androgyny really keeps the opposites in place, By saying that we have a 'male side' and a 'female side', we blind ourselves to all the beautiful shades of identity of which we are capable. Androgyny could be seen as a trap of the bi-polar gender system, as it further establishes the idea of two-and-only-two genders.[113]

When Jess is a child, s/he tries hir father's suit on and enjoys staring at the image reflected back at hir: the girl transfigured by sartorial change is an image of masculine femininity that Jess approves of: 'I liked the little girl looking back at me' (*Stone Butch Blues*, 20). In response to Theresa's affirmation that Jess is a woman, Jess replies, 'I'm a he-she. That's different' (p. 147). As Feinberg commented in *Transgender Warriors*: 'Are you a guy or a girl?' I've heard the question all my life. The answer is not so simple, since there are no pronouns in the English language as complex as I am, and I do not want to simplify myself in order to neatly fit one or the other.'[114] In the preface to *Transgender Warriors*, Feinberg comments that: 'As the overall transgender movement has developed, more people are exploring the distinction between a person's sex – female, intersexual, male – and their gender expression – feminine, androgynous, masculine, and other variations.'[115] In the balance of that list, 'androgynous' becomes the expression of intersexed identity, and because it does not categorically define or construct it, 'androgynous' becomes a general culturally descriptive term rather than a specific or prescriptive one.

'Who was I now,' Jess asks hirself, shortly after commencing a self-administered course of hormone treatments, 'woman or man. That question could never be answered as long as those were the only choices' (p. 222). The hormones give Jess what Dworkin might have described as a more androgynous appearance: 'My body was blending gender characteristics, and I wasn't the only one who noticed' (p. 224). That Jess disrupts the gender binary is perceived as a source of outrage and not least for the emerging feminist activists s/he's in contact with through her lover Theresa. The rise of feminism's second wave, as it is represented in *Stone Butch Blues*, coincides with Jess's dilemma about taking hormones and passing as a man, but feminism and women-centred theories of lesbianism preclude Jess. Whilst feminist activism positively redraws the parameters of Theresa's life, it contracts Jess's by rendering it illegitimate or imitative, and as Theresa celebrates female difference, the feminist movement also teaches her that the dynamics of their butch-femme relationship is a repressive one and that the butch simply masquerades as a fake man: rather than gender blending or supporting androgyny, it's difference that feminism is represented as celebrating.

In *Woman Hating*, Dworkin called for a community that could be redefined through the dissolution of rigidly codified gendered and sexual identities in order to freely accommodate those who cannot and do not identify themselves within 'normative' structures. Jess's trajectory is a restless one that moves from hir birthplace in the desert to New York, and from a culture that perpetrates racial and sexual segregation to one that promises a greater toleration: at a gay pride rally in New York Jess has a voice and is able to speak on hir own terms and eventually finds a tentative love with Ruth, a male-to-female transsexual who also embodies the 'shades of gender' that constitute Jess. The historical overlap between Dworkin's desire for an androgynous ontology that would involve the dissolution of the male-female binary clashes with Feinberg's representation of the sexual politics of second wave feminism which celebrates sexual difference by insisting on women's fundamental difference from men. But the 'gendered contradiction'[116] that Jess embodies is one that never achieves androgynous resolution: reading a passage marked out for hir in a book that s/he's given, s/he reads 'about two souls, two thoughts, two unreconciled strivings; two warring ideals in one dark body' (p. 178). These factions *appear* to recognise an irreconcilable internecine division, although souls, thoughts, strivings and ideals also promise redemption. In *Stone Butch Blues* specific categories are recognised and proliferated: he-she, stone butch, butch-femme, drag queen, transgender, transsexual. It is the existence of this always extending and visible series of categories that Dworkin appeared to have anticipated in *Woman Hating* and which sheltered under the general (and generalising) category of androgyny. In 1974, when discourses of androgyny were themselves in proliferation, Jess, and hir community may well have figured androgynous possibility for Dworkin. Within the terms of Dworkin's rubric, then, androgyny was not a blurring or assimilation or evacuation of sexual difference, but a constant reconfiguring of it, mapped through evolving cultural change. That evolution constructed androgyny as both a realisable ontology and an impossible, flawed, even pernicious ideal. But whereas feminism's exploration of androgyny sincerely imagined cultural transformation, postmodern literary imagination, itself product and agent of cultural transformation, also parodied idealised androgyny and emphasised its symbolic, rather than material, status.

5
Myra Breckinridge and *The Passion of New Eve*

There is a revelatory moment in Gore Vidal's *Myra Breckinridge* (1968) when the detectives, Flagler and Flagler (a portmanteau name that surreptitiously conflates fag with flag), confirm Uncle Buck's suspicions: Myra Breckinridge is an impostor. Myron Breckinridge, contrary to Myra's story, didn't drown in an accident on the Staten Island Ferry, as Myra had claimed. Spluttering his disbelief, Buck records Myra's cool response: 'she stands up and hikes up her dress and pulls down her goddam panties and shows us this scar where cock and balls should be' (p. 190). It's a moment that appears to confirm the triumphant policing of identity and affirms the illegitimacy of Myra's claim to a share in Buck's Academy of Drama and Modelling. In a sense, though, the revelation comes too late, since Myra has already made clear her singular, privileged and

> profound grasp of philosophy and psychology to trace for man not only what he is but what he must become, once he has ceased to be confined to a single sexual role, to a single person ... once he has become free to blend with others, to exchange personalities with both women and men, to play out the most elaborate dreams in a world where there will be no limits to the human spirit's play. (pp. 186–7)

It sounds like the utopian aims of second wave feminism's ideal of androgyny, but to compare Myra's aggrandising aims for humanity with those of feminism's wish for social transformation is to trace a movement from sincerity to parody and camp. Myra concerns herself less with feminism and more with the 'realignment of the sexes' in her search for a new creation myth. 'I must bring back Eden,' Myra grandly

126

declares (p. 200). Perceiving herself as the hieratic saviour of a debased culture, she was, in her turn, read as the epitome of all that was corrupt about it: 'The transsexual Myra is ... the radical figure of our cultural impotence and spiritual sterility, and as the archetypal pervert, she is the image of a debased and debauched society.'[1]

Angela Carter's *The Passion of New Eve* (1977) shares the desire to make a new creation myth. If Myra wants to bring back Eden, Evelyn, temporarily cast as a migrant trespasser in the desert, is recreated as the new 'daughter of Beulah'.[2] Since he once felt 'all the ghastly attraction of the fall' (p. 25), he has an apparently momentary identification with Adam, before Carter recreates him as his 'Other', making Eve central to the creation of a new, if empty, world, as she sails away from the New World itself. Androgyny tends to be central to creation myths, but Myra considers it only in order to reject it: 'No monist Myra!' she tells us, dismissing Plato as 'that dumb Greek' (*Myron*, 291). When Tristessa and Eve copulate on the flag of the United States (another reclamation of the iconography of nation), it's as though, as Eve later recalls, they recreate 'the great Platonic hermaphrodite', experiencing a momentary ecstasy before they are violently separated by the boys of the Children's Crusade. The violence endemic in America not only destroys redemptive and consolatory union, but also supplants one mythology with another, the dream turned evident nightmare of corporate culture which adorns and seeps into the bodies of the boys from the Disney watches they wear to the Coca Cola they drink. It's self-perpetuating: the American Dream sows and reaps the seeds of an implosive, self-destructive violence and destroys the powerful ideals that another myth imagines but fails to inaugurate. What a myth of sexuality might redeem, the politics of nation corrupts and kills.

Myra Breckinridge

Myra Breckinridge is structured from the beginning around the notion of impersonation: Myra presents herself to her 'uncle' Buck Loner, as the widow of Buck's nephew Myron, much to Buck's surprise, since he recalls his nephew, 'a sissy kid' as a 'fag' (p. 20). She keeps us guessing as to her 'real' identity throughout: 'Did Myron take his own life, you will ask? Yes and no is my answer. Beyond that my lips are sealed' (p. 13). Having inveigled her way into Buck's academy, Myra proceeds to teach courses in Posture and Empathy. Buck's narrative, apparently recorded and transcribed from tape, is interspersed with Myra's grandiose narrative, and he remains suspicious of her throughout.

Planning to realign the sexes, she chooses the ordinary boy and girl next door, Rusty and Mary Ann. Representative of the heterosexual and anatomically differentiated couple, Myra re-orders their sexual orientations and preferences whilst she attempts to take over Buck Loner's film academy and to complete Myron's book, *Parker Tyler and the Films of the Forties*. In the end, it is revealed that Myra was formerly Myron, Buck's 'fag' and 'sissy' nephew, and Myra – 'I am Woman' – Breckinridge is, in the end, turned back into Myron, through the force of his personality and through reconstructive surgery as the forces of conservatism proclaim their wilted triumph.

For the young people around Myra, metamorphosis amounts to little more than a change of clothes and the affecting of speech mannerisms appropriated from what they see on television, and Myra's own difference to that is marked by the changes that are made to her body, though that is never immune to the affectation that she condemns and is mediated not just through television and cinematic history, but through mythology as well. But TV represents a depleted kind of masculinity for Myra, and she goes on to argue that, without Clark Gable, there'd have been no defeat of Hitler, as though there's a connection between the kind of masculinity one learns, introjects and then projects into the 'real', or other, material world. Indeed, the present seems denuded of the kind of heroic masculinity that Myra appears to treasure. Contemporary masculinity doesn't measure up and she is bent on unmasking that:

> it is costumes that the young men now wear as they act out their simple-minded roles, constructing a fantasy world in order to avoid confronting the fact that to be a man in a society of machines is to be an expendable, soft auxiliary to what is useful and hard. (p. 59)

Only the cinema can represent – and preserve – authentic masculinity: 'Since Brando, there has been nothing except the epicene Peter O'Toole, the distracted Mastroianni, and the cheerfully incompetent Belmondo. The roof has fallen in on the male and we now live at the dawn of the age of Woman Triumphant of Myra Breckinridge' (p. 59).

In *Myra Breckinridge* the oscillation between masculinity and femininity is conceived as an opportunity for release from a stifling male embodiment. Myra's embodied self is the flamboyant Myron's cultural fantasy and the conservative Myron's nightmare: like Carter's New Eve (Eve is the embodiment of Evelyn's old masturbatory fantasy), Myra's type of femininity constitutes Myron's projected fantasy, presented in the text as an amalgam of celluloid women. Myron, formerly a film critic, now embodies and lives out the topics of his former critical and cultural analysis as Myra Breckinridge. Rejecting totality and unity, Myra is always a compelling but also a potentially grotesque assemblage of disembodied fragments, a kind of celluloid *bricolage* that, like Frankenstein, assembles the best possible physical features into a grotesque embodiment. She is Fay Wray in three-quarter profile (to look, to appear, is at the heart of the confirmed ontology of the simulacra). Myra's breasts are like those of Jean Harlow in *Hell's Angels* 'seen at their best four minutes after the start of the second reel' (p. 5). Hers is a narcissistic narrative; in love with her own body, she has, she tells us, 'lovely feet with a high instep and naturally rosy heels, fit for any fetishist' (p. 12). Her voice is modelled 'on that of the late Anne Sheridan (fifth reel of *Doughgirls)*' (p. 13). Or again, Myra's voice is low and croaks, 'not unlike ... that of the late Margaret Sullavan' (p. 14). When she goes to work, she wears a false hairpiece and uses a light Max Factor base like the one used by Merle Oberon. To be a film star is her 'dearest daydream' (p. 25). Regretting her lapse in dignity at a party (she smokes marijuana and is involved in an orgy) she thinks she would prefer to be Greer Garson (p. 52). When she speaks to Rusty, she is 'stern but pleasant, like Eve Arden' (p. 59). She laughs like a good sport, like Carole Lombard (p. 86), and has a sweet tone 'not unlike Irene Dunne in *The White Cliffs of Dover*' (p. 87). She directs the Academy like 'Rosalind Russell efficient girl executive' (p. 196). In *Myron*, Myra is 'Kay Francis in *Four Hills in a Jeep*' (p. 272). Myra, like Carter's Eve, dramatises the possibility of becoming the object of one's narcissistic fantasies where film functions like the mirror, except that the spectator's body is not reflected back: only its idealised and fetishised image and Myra/Myron explicitly engages with the idea that we take on body image as we take on identity.

In an early critical study of Vidal, *The Apostate Angel*, Bernard Dick suggested that 'Vidal has despaired of anyone's understanding *Myra* without the aid of the Classics, particularly Plato's *Symposium* and Petronius' *Satryricon*'.[3] 'Myra's tragedy,' he suggested, 'was her attempt to live the role of the original androgyne; and halved androgynes, according to the myth, are doomed to heterosexuality, which is her ultimate fate.'[4] This misreading of Aristophanes' myth (it is the united male and female who make the androgyne, not the divided parts) sits awkwardly with Myra's avowed intention to reject the Platonic myth of the androgyne in order to create a new one. In his reading of *Myra Breckinridge*, Bernard Dick suggests that the androgyne and the transsexual can be conflated – that the 'transsexual operation is a metaphor for androgyny'[5] (an argument sustainable only within the imagined world of *Myra Breckinridge*) and he gives androgyne identity an ontological status – 'It is strange that the more civilized we are, the more we claim to be androgynous; yet our acts belie our claim, and we literally settle for half.'[6] In the end, Myra doesn't settle for half: as Myron, he settles for marriage with Mary Ann, but it's hard to see what Vidal was trying to say in an anti-climactic dénouement – as though it wasn't clear where else Myra could go or what else Myra could do. In an interview, Vidal claimed that 'there is no activity more classically masculine than sex with your own kind. Those men who change their sex through surgery or like to live *en travestie* are something else again. A small category of misplaced identities.'[7] But the cultural milieu of *Myra Breckinridge* is constituted precisely by misplaced identities, so that what is 'misplaced' is actually the cultural norm.

The sexual is insistently polymorphous in this text and is a rejoinder to the psychiatrist's normative practices: if psychoanalytic theory and practice constitute a grand narrative, *Myra Breckinridge* questions its totalising and teleological assumptions. It is tested out through Clem Masters' orgy, which appeals to Myra: 'Myron sometimes enjoyed the company of four or five men at the same time but he did not believe in mixing the sexes. I of course do' (p. 87). Her own theories of sexuality gesture towards bisexuality, which she would like to reinstate as the normal mode of polymorphous sexual behaviour:

> Although I am not a Lesbian, I do share the normal human response to whatever is attractive physically in either sex. I say *normal* human response, realizing that our culture has resolutely resisted the idea of bisexuality. We insist that there is only one *right* way of having sex: man and woman joined together to make baby; all else is wrong. Worse, the neo-Freudian rabbis (of whom Dr. Montag is still one despite my efforts at conversion) believe that what they call heterosexuality is 'healthy,' that homosexuality is unhealthy, and that bisexuality is a myth despite their master Freud's tentative conviction that all human beings are attracted to both sexes. (p. 90)

Myra's narrative develops into an account of the nature and identity of American history and culture through an account of its representation of masculinity and femininity in film, exploring how film services myths of heroism to lay the foundations of modern America. Rusty is an atavistic kind of male figure, typifying modern American masculinity. Myra perceives him as constructed from the shadows of the films of the 1940s, anachronistic now in the era of television:

> In a sense, Rusty is a throwback to the stars of the Forties, who themselves were simply shadows cast in the bright morning of the nation. Yet in the age of the television commercial he is sadly superfluous, an anachronism, acting out a masculine charade that has lost all meaning. That is why, to save him (and the world from his sort), I *must change entirely his sense of himself.* (p. 122)

The historical, cultural and sexual are negotiated through the relationship of Myra and Myron. It's a novel that seems at once sincere in its criticisms of contemporary America and also parodic in its nostalgic recuperation of a golden age whose cultural superiority is measured against the supposedly debased cultural currency of the present day. If Myra/Myron are the index of an age of cultural supremacy and the promulgation of idealised heroism through celluloid images, Rusty and Mary Ann are the contemporary versions, the boy and girl next door representing the old order of sexual polarities. Rusty and Mary Ann are the apparently uncomplicated embodiments of an orthodox masculinity and femininity, and it is Myra's job not only to unsettle that binary, but to break down the 'masculine principle' that she sees embodied in Rusty. As though to parody second wave feminism's adoption of androgyny, Myra tells Mary Ann that the role of femininity is changing. Though Mary Ann would willingly sacrifice her career for Rusty's, Myra tells her that the relationships between the sexes are changing so rapidly that women are now becoming more aggressive and men more passive (p. 78). At this stage in the text, Mary Ann proclaims her dislike for bisexuality ('I hate these boys who just drift around taking pot and trips and not caring if – well, if it's a boy or a girl they're with. It's just so terrible the way so many are now, and I guess that's why I'm so hung up on Rusty. He's all man', p. 78). Mary Ann echoes precisely a distaste for androgynous sexuality as counter-cultural and pan-sexual, defined, as Cynthia Secor put it 'solely in terms of whom you fuck, how often, how freely, and without what hang-ups'.[8] Rusty and Mary-Ann between them also endorse conventional heterosexuality at the dinner that Myra has with them. At this they want to affirm that 'a woman should act like a woman and a man should act like a man, and that's that' (p. 124). That proper or authentic manliness and womanliness is to be acted only affirms the imitative nature of gendered identity, drawing attention to their constructedness. It's at this point that Myra begins to tell them about sexual customs all over the world, rendering their certainties uncertainties as they are revealed not to be transcendently true, but culturally provisional: there is, after all, a world outside of southern California.

Whilst Mary Ann and Rusty speak for an atavistic masculinity and femininity, Dr Montag is offered as a parody of the psychiatrist, inviting questions about the function of analysis in the text. Myron's 'death', in the context of Dr Montag's correspondence with Myra, suggests that Myron's resurrection functions like the return of the repressed. His letter to Myra cheers her up: 'He warns against depressions of the sort I have been prone to since Myron's death and so he proposes, rather obviously, that in lieu of analysis I must keep busy' (p. 57). Dr Montag interprets Myron to Myra, but consolidates particular constructions of the homosexual man as having repressed femininity (one of the tentative suggestions in Roy Ward Baker's *Doctor Jekyll and Sister Hyde*), as though Myron was the androgynous womanly-man. Myra, then, was the symbolic, but is now the material, embodiment of an aspect of Myron Breckinridge:

> Myron's polymorphism (quite exceptional even by contemporary standards) was coupled with a desire to surrender entirely to the feminine side of his nature, symbolized by you. Yet I cannot help but believe that his masculinity was of great intensity, as you knew best, while the sadomasochistic proportion was quite evenly balanced. That is to say, he was apt to beat up trade as be beaten up.' (p. 80)

But Myra knows best and displaces the authority of the psychiatrist/ dentist's verdict. Myra understands Myron's sexual desires as being about power, which oscillated between wanting to fuck (a repressed desire) as much as he wanted to be fucked, and it is only in the triumphant evolution of Myra, the dominant, but formerly the repressed aspect of Myron, a kind of host body now displaced, that the repressed desire can be articulated and performed. Myron didn't want to be penetrated but was easily abused: to penetrate, for Myra/Myron, is to retain power, to be penetrated is to renounce it. And it is whilst she is discussing this sex-power dynamic that she announces that, in spite of Dr Montag's intentions, she will never marry – 'Dr Montag still believes that each sex is intended to be half of a unit, like those monsters mentioned in Plato's

Symposium' (p. 82). In *Myron*, it's this Platonic union that Myra is committed to overthrowing and this sexual repression that she wants to redress: Myra as Myron's vigilante. It's Myra's desire, then, to find a different creation myth, to reject Plato's myth of the androgyne. Trapped inside the TV set, the location for the action in *Myron*, Myra sees a young man and imagines the inversion of Plato's androgynous 'beast': 'Those gorgeous hemispheres, crying out to be wrenched apart in order that one might create the opposite to Plato's beast by substituting that dumb Greek's trendy ideal of the unnatural whole to my truer vision of forcibly divided and forever separated parts. No monist Myra!' (p. 291) Myra's denial of duality is undermined by the relentless oscillation between the two, an oscillation that appears to resist resolution, as the last chapter's mirror writing affirms: '*!sevil aryM*' (p. 440).

But what does Myra want to do? It's secure masculinity that Myra is keen to unmask. When Rusty comes to her room, 'downright defiant, even contemptuous of me, so secure did he think himself in his masculine superiority' (p. 58), it's clearly hubris that precedes his downfall. Her plans to tame the male principle go badly wrong, though, and it prefaces her eventual undoing as Myra and presages the resurrection (or reconstruction in this secular age of technology) of Myron. For Myra the rape has a cathartic function – 'I shall be free of all guilt toward Myron and for Myron. I shall be a new woman, literally new, something unique under the sun' (p. 174). But she has turned Rusty from a gentle lover into a violently abusive one: 'Wanting to tame for all time the archetypal male, I have created something ten times as masculine in the classic sense as what I started with. All in all, not the desired effect but perhaps like Columbus, I have stumbled on a new world' (p. 183). And then there's another turning point for her: as she seduces Mary-Ann, she tells Myra that she would love her if only she were a man, if only there had been a man like Myra – which of course there had been and still, potentially, is: 'This froze me, turned me to stone' (p. 183). This second transformation – from Myron to Myra to Myron again – comes about, as Vidal argues, as an act of love for Mary Ann.

Towards the end of Myra's narrative, Myron returns to re-inhabit the body. The victim of a car accident, Myra ends up in hospital and is appalled to discover that an encroaching masculinity threatens to occlude her feminine self. Myron then returns to repossess the now male body, and the period in which he lived as Myron Breckinridge is repressed. *Myron* begins with the return of the triumphant Myra – history has apparently demanded Myra's return so that she can resume her mission to save civilisation from its current cultural and political impoverishment: 'If ever anyone was needed, I am needed at this crossroads in human history' (p. 301).

The condition of the existence of each of them seems to rest on the repression of the other. In a surreal twist, Myra has returned to haunt Myron and has pushed him into the TV screen onto the film set of a dire B movie called *Sirens of Babylon*. By moving back in time, Myra plans to sabotage the film, which bankrupted the studio that made it in order to recuperate film and to save it – and America – from the deleterious effects of television. As Catharine Stimpson elegantly put it: 'Like that of many contemporary writers, Vidal's catalogue of narrative possibilities is a tough-minded elegy for literary culture composed in a visual culture that reads little or nothing, that writes little or nothing except its autograph.'[9]

But what is the condition of her possibility? It is as though Myra exists as the repressed homosexual's fantasy of possessing and inhabiting the female body – like Carter's Tristessa, Myron makes of himself the perfect emblem of a fetishised femininity. Myra, in *Myron*, *is* the fetishised female – the woman with a penis. Each chapter, and within chapters, Myra and Myron wrest control from a body that is also increasingly in the process of transformation, sartorially and somatically. Myra admits to having 'insufficient control over the mutilated body I am forced to share with Myron Breckinridge' (p. 247). Myron's body, then, is the site of alienation for Myra, and a disavowal: '*Hair* grows down my – no, not my: *his* ugly chest' (p. 261). If projection is a defence mechanism whereby the subject's ego disowns undesirable impulses by attributing them to someone else, Myra *is* the projection of Myron, a defence against his homosexual impulses.

Between them, Myra and Myon offer an exploration of embodied and disembodied sexuality. The material, embodied self is insisted upon even as it is negated through a recognition of a different 'real', mediated through a depthless visual culture. What this text offers, it also retrieves: the material body is interchangeable with the sign; unity is interchangeable with fragmentation; one myth (Plato's myth of the androgyne) is replaced with another (Myra's realignment of the sexes).

The successive androgyne, always in the process of exchange, becomes an emblem of the simulacra and the image without referent is portrayed in a series of endless exchanges in *Myra* and *Myron* and is embodied in the figure of Tristessa, 'so like her own reflection on the screen'. (*Passion of New Eve*, 118) The oscillation between sexes in Vidal's texts, triumphant as well as cantankerous, suggests a parody not just of the idealised androgynous couple. Rather like Woolf's

Orlando, Myra and Myron end up vacillating between one sex and the other, but it's a mercurial, often comic oscillation, particularly in *Myron*, where vacillation is never offered as a liberating possibility, but rather as the defeat of the modern American male by the phallic woman: as with Carter's English Evelyn, the modern American woman ends up eclipsing both the English and the American man. *Myra Breckinridge, Myron* and *The Passion of New Eve* all render *un*certain received ontological and epistemological certainties: in the America of these novels, the Age of Reason is over, and political commitment evaporates before the cultural vulgarity of the television and the appeal of the big screen. Many of those certainties are to do with how masculinity and femininity is idealised and maintained through capitalism, as Myra notes: 'few men are anything but slaves to an economic and social system that does not allow them to knock people down as proof of virility or in any way act out the traditional male role' (*Myra Breckinridge*, pp. 94–5). If androgynous ontology in the 1970s might be said to constitute the most positive aspects of maleness and femaleness, then Vidal's Myra and Myron comprised, if not the worst, then at least a pretty combustible misalliance.

Susan Sontag claimed the androgyne as 'one of the great images of Camp sensibility',[10] but in claiming that, she elaborated different kinds of androgynous representations, embodied and disembodied. One kind lay in the 'corny flamboyant femaleness of Jayne Mansfield, Gina Lollobrigida, Jane Russell, Virginia Mayo; the exaggerated he-manness of Steve Reeves, Victor Mature. The great stylists of temperament and mannerism, like Bette Davis, Barbara Stanwyck, Tallulah Bankhead, Edwige Feuillère'.[11] Movie criticism itself, she suggests, was 'probably the greatest popularizer of Camp taste today, because most people still go to the movies in a high-spirited and unpretentious way'.[12] This positions Myra as securely inside camp since she is *entirely* serious about cinema and the cultural myths of masculinity that it promotes: the Breckinridge orthodoxy decrees that '*in the decade between 1935 and 1945, no irrelevant film was made in the United States*' (*Myra Breckinridge*, p. 13). Sontag argues that there was camp in 'such bad movies as *The Prodigal* and *Samson and Delilah*'.[13] In *Myron*, Myra wants (camply?) to rescue Victor Mature, star of *Samson and Delilah*, from 'his subsequent decline into camp' (p. 299), as though camp were somehow debased and debasing. But Sontag's definition also positions Myra within the iconography of the camp androgyne: Myra's femininity is always hyperbolic and flamboyant, her immediate task 'is to impress upon you how disturbingly beautiful I am' (p. 7).

The view from Myra's window overlooks the Château Marmont Hotel, 'where Greta Garbo stays on her rare visits to Hollywood' (p. 8). Garbo is never a model for Myra, and nor is she, tenuous as she sometimes seems, someone that Myra ever sees (although in *Myron*, Myra imagines that she's Dietrich or Garbo in butch mood when she's forced to wear Myron's clothes, p. 287). That ghostliness, or emptiness, is what defines Garbo as androgyne for Sontag, for whom she was 'the great serious idol of camp taste'.[14] What Sontag admired about Garbo was 'the haunting androgynous vacancy behind [her] perfect beauty'.[15] Bewitching, absorbing, wraithlike: 'androgynous vacancy' implies a fascination for representation without content and lacking context. For Sontag, the pleasure of the androgyne as camp spectacle was the sense of antagonism that it engendered, the 'going against the grain': 'What is most beautiful in virile men is something feminine; what is most beautiful in feminine women is something masculine'.[16] It is not Eve who embodies this antagonism or paradox, of course, in *The Passion of New Eve*: it's Tristessa, the most beautiful woman in the world, who is revealed to be an anatomic (often priapic) male, exemplar too, had Paglia chosen to make her one, of the 'apollonian androgynes', the antithesis of the chthonic Mother (also the corrupter of the natural) that Eve is in flight from.[17]

The Passion of New Eve

The Passion of New Eve is a text that begins twice: once, conventionally, on its opening page, and then again, less conventionally, on its closing page. It begins with an Englishman, Evelyn, watching his childhood heroine, Tristessa, in the darkened cinema, and ends on the ocean with Eve, the Englishman surgically reconstructed as a woman through the intervention of American feminism, embarking on a journey on (rather than back to) the place of birth. 'I think it was Balzac,' Carter said in a documentary made towards the end of her life,

> who said all fiction was symbolic biography. Well of course it is. Because, basically, when one writes a story, you know, you start at the beginning, you go on till the end. It's the story, obviously, of life. And this may sound complicated – we project this as a passage forward – in fact, of course, it's both a passage forwards and a passage backwards at the same time.[18]

Like Vidal, Carter was interested in exploring social fictions and performative gender as these are projected and internalised by the big screen. The hierarchical distribution of gender identity is re-examined and relocated somatically, performatively *and* symbolically as Carter re-examined, or framed, an exploration of performative gender within a series of symbols derived from alchemical practice. As Heather Johnson has noted, alchemy is one of the major tropes in this text.[19] The abyss, amber, the Bird of Hermes, chaos, use of colours (particularly black, red, white, yellow, gold, silver), the crucible, the journey from the East to West Coast, the egg, feathers, flowers, the fortified city, glass, the hermaphrodite, laundry, sheets, nigredo, peace, strife, salt, sulphur, mercury, the sea and water, sperm, sun and shadow, tears, the theatre, the unicorn, the uroborous – the emblems and descriptions in *The Passion of New Eve* are routinely informed by the emblems of alchemy, the science of transformation in which base metals can be purified and turned into gold. Alchemy, the process by which matter is transformed 'to the perfection of its own nature',[20] not only engenders androgynous reconciliation between the male and female, but describes the trans-gendered transformation perfected by Tristessa. Abrams points out that the chemical union of alchemical process was 'equated with a sexual coupling; and the culmination of the entire physical *operatio* was frequently imaged as the *coniunctio*, or "chymical wedding", of the prototypical male and female opposites'.[21] It is from the chymical wedding, the union of oppositions – sulphur and mercury, fire and air, earth and water – that the philosopher's stone comes into being, a stone which, as Abrams says, 'figured as a "rebis," or androgyne, who reunites the two sexes into the unitary form they had exhibited before their separation'.[22]

Eve's trajectory also follows other, familiar patterns consonant with narratives of androgyny. Describing androgyny in Romanticism, Diane Long Hoeveler identified characteristic stages that came to constitute the romantic hero's rather problematic androgynous assimilation, the merging with a 'chthonic Great Mother', the narcissistic search for a second self in which he will be mirrored. 'As an "adult",' Hoeveler says, 'the hero faces three transformations of the feminine: He can pursue the woman as beloved, the woman as castrating *femme fatale*, or the woman as mentor/muse. But no clear demarcations exist between these forms of the female; they often overlap in ways that suggest that for the male psyche all women are ultimately the same one.'[23] Carter's Evelyn follows a similar trajectory in his picaresque journey. His merger with the chthonic Great Mother in the underground caverns of Beulah is unasked for and unwanted, but is the consequence of his seduction by Leilah in her guise as *femme fatale*.[24] Narcissism characterises another stage of Eve's journey: his/her relationship with Tristessa, the Hollywood screen idol, is predicated on self-love: partly fashioned after the image of Tristessa, Eve sees her self-image vacantly, terrifyingly, reflected back to her:

> I went towards you as towards my own face in a magnetic mirror ... (p. 110)

> I want to fall; I must not fall into the chasms of her eyes where I see myself reflected twice ... The abyss on which her eyes open, ah! it is the abyss of myself, of emptiness, of inward void. (p. 125)

Clear demarcations *do* exist, though, between the different stages of Eve/lyn's journey, that takes him/her from England to Manhattan to the desert to Zero's ranch, Tristessa's glass palace and finally to the cave, the scene of dramatic rebirth at Eve's journey's end. Though Hoeveler argues that androgyny, within Romanticism, involved the subsuming of the female into the male, that is hardly the case in *The Passion of New Eve*, where Eve repeatedly recognises herself, as Alison Lee suggests, as 'both self and other',[25] and also because the postmodern dynamic of this text throws into question what constitutes 'female' and 'male'. That is to say, a notional 'male' and 'female' are negotiated in this text not through a reifying metaphysics of presence but restlessly through myth, alchemy, the simulacra and the performative. Sex, the very ontological foundation of the androgyne, is recognisable, but only ever as a bewilderment of fragments in *The Passion of New Eve*.

During the course of Eve's narrative, we come to understand that the penis no longer functions as the sign or the guarantee of masculinity: the material referent is also, insistently, metaphorical. When the new Eve looks at her reconstructed embodiment in the mirror, it is, after all, 'the cock in [her] head' that prompts a narcissistic arousal. The fractured phallus outside Beulah is the emblem of a broken symbolic order now turned over to a new (if parodic) semiotic rhythm in the otherwise efficiently rationalised matriarchal community. How we might understand the body, then, is not through its materiality or even its psychology, but through its cultural signification, and in the absence of any totalising grand narrative, signification, as Eve recollects of Tristessa, is false, and 'all of metaphysics' as Baudrillard puts it, 'is lost. No more mirror of being and appearances, of the real and its concept.'[26]

Angela Carter said of *The Passion New Eve*, 'I do put everything in a novel to be *read* – read the way allegory was intended to be read, the way you're supposed to read *Sir Gawayne and the Grene Knight* – on as many levels as you can comfortably cope with.'[27] And so, alchemy intersects with postmodernism, mythology with technology. These are not, though, set out as relational terms in a binary schema, but rather as terms within a dialectic that require, rather than define, each other, or that exist in metonymic relation to each other: 'all myths,' she said in 'Notes from the Front Line, 'are products of the human mind and reflect only aspects of material human practice'.[28] If she offers us allegory, it's as a mirror to, rather than an escape from, the real of culture. Fiction, as Carter knew, is not divorced from fact: it constitutes it and is constituted by it. She recognised the summer of 1968 as a moment of self-consciousness or awareness about her own self in culture, about 'the nature of my reality as a *woman*. How that social fiction of my "femininity" was created, by means outside of my control, and palmed off on me as the real thing.'[29] The 'social fiction of femininity' is explored throughout *The Passion of New Eve*, a text conceived by Carter as 'a feminist tract about the social creation of femininity, amongst other things'.[30] That social creation, or social fiction, is dramatised in the character of the trans-gendered Tristessa, in the creation of Mother and, of course, in the transsexual Eve herself, although Carter's representation of femininity has led feminist critics to question the 'anti-feminist caricature' of Mother, sometimes read as 'a grotesque parody of the maternal'.[31] Carter was, she's famously said, 'in the demythologising business' and *The Passion of New Eve* was, for her, an 'anti-mythic novel'. Mythology, that is to say, should be read as inseparable from the 'real', and as one of the means we have of confronting and negotiating it.[32]

Evelyn's self-discovery begins when the university ends. Literally and symbolically defunct, the location of knowledge signals, as the Czech alchemist Baroslav understands, the end of the Age of Reason and the advent of the Age of Chaos in the metropolis. It's a city whose apparently postmodern inhabitants are without morality and without affect, 'estranged even from their own fear' (p. 11) in a permanent carnival of chaos and misrule which Evelyn comes to see as the 'alchemical city' of chaos and dissolution (p. 16). Carter's consideration of alchemy constitutes a series of thematic and consistent concerns in this text that announce transformation but also become readable through historical retreat as a form of engagement with the real. That is to say, everyone seems in flight from the historical process in this text, not least Baroslav: marked by Nazi violence (tied to a tree, he was a helpless onlooker when they and raped and dismembered his wife),[33] he finds consolation in alchemy, a philosophical science that was itself, as Jung comments, 'incompatible with the spirit of enlightenment'.[34] With the Age of Reason at an end, Baroslav can return to the quest for knowledge that preceded it. It is Baroslav who shows Evelyn 'pictures of bleeding white birds in bottles' (p. 13), an image that comes to haunt him in the desert, when he encounters the dying Bird of Hermes, shot by the intransigent Zero ('the sign for nothing,' as Carter says in *The Sadeian Woman*)[35] who inadvertently engineers reconciliation when he presides over the marriage of Eve and Tristessa. The death of that bird is also redeemed after Eve has sex with Tristessa (Tristessa's hair is 'like shed feathers of birds', p. 147) and again at the end of Eve's journey when she finds the 'feather of a bird' trapped in the alchemist's alembic, one of several alchemical treasures she finds in the cave of her mythical, insistently symbolic rebirth. It is Baroslav, too, who shows Evelyn the figure of the hermaphrodite, calm and comprehensive, carrying a golden egg, a possible reference to Plate 9 in Salomon Trismosin's *Splendor Solis*, which depicts a clothed hermaphrodite holding a golden egg. At that moment in the text, the dual sexed figure seems fated to remain preserved in the texts of antiquity, interpretable only by a figure for whom alchemy is both a practice and a refuge from the violence of contemporary culture. And yet, the hermaphrodite turns out to have a broader significance, functioning within a highly symbolic but redemptive schema that re-reads the chaos and disintegration of modernity.

Heather Johnson has pointed out that the narrative shape of *The Passion of New Eve* loosely follows the stages of alchemical theory or process. Eve intimates as much; in this retrospective narrative, Evelyn's experiences are mediated through the wisdom and experience of Eve, who plots her trajectory but also offers to interpret it for us. As Evelyn, his sexual encounters with Leilah function as part of the text's critique of a culture that imbricates violence and sex. But even as Eve relates Evelyn's experiences, she also interprets them (towards the end of her narrative, she's not just in the desert with Tristessa, they're 'in the heart of that gigantic metaphor for sterility', p. 148). Leilah, we learn later, is also Lilith, Adam's apocryphal first wife and created as his equal rather than his other.[36] She later resurfaces as a resistance fighter, and as the daughter of Mother. None of these incarnations is more 'real' than another[37] since the text never moves progressively from allegory to realism, and never privileges one rhetorical or narrative mode over another; rather, it makes them part of an interrogative dialectic, although, as Christina Britzolakis asks, 'Are we, then, to read Lilith the activist as the revelation of Leilah's true self?'[38] The protean Leilah can be incarnated to suit the text's (or Eve's) discursive purpose, but she's broken down (and not unproblematically) as symbol too: Eve recalls Evelyn giving the gift of alchemical gold to Leilah, 'a girl all black in colour – nigredo, the stage of darkness, when the material in the vessel has broken down to dead matter. Then the matter purifies. Dissolution. Leilah.' (p. 14) 'Nigredo' is the first stage of the 'opus alchymicum', as Lyndy Abraham describes it:

> in which the body of the impure metal, the matter for the stone, or the old outmoded state of being, is killed, putrefied and dissolved into the original substance of creation, the prima materia ... The alchemist, along with popular seventeenth century belief, held that there could be no regeneration without corruption.[39]

That corruption, or defilement, is also symbolised by Leilah's soiling of the sheets, a 'revenge' as Eve/lyn interprets it, for being manacled to the bed for hours at a time (later, when she resurfaces as a freedom fighter, she, too 'was part of the purging', p. 176). Michael Maier's 'wonderfully illustrated *Atalanta Fugiens*' (p. 13) represents the blackening and staining of white sheets which must be cleansed in order to lead on to the stage called 'albedo', symbolised by whiteness, as does Plate 21 of Trismosin's *Splendor Solis*, both texts that Baroslav shows to Evelyn. Much later, when Eve enters Tristessa's glass palace, her exploration takes her through the laundry room, suggestive of the necessary next stage for the transformation, that of cleansing and purification. The interpretive frame offered by alchemical symbolism indicates that during the first stages of her journey, Evelyn must sin in order for reparation to be made, must be corrupt in order for regeneration to redeem the old and decaying order. In Evelyn's case, he abandons Leilah after her botched abortion and, admitting to needing 'pure air and cleanness', he goes to the desert where 'the primordial light ... would purify me' (p. 38) It does, but not quite as he imagined.

In the desert, Evelyn encounters the Bird of Hermes, the philosophical bird born from the philosopher's egg. The putrefying corpse of the bird suggests the destructive purposes of Zero, who shot it, rather than the impossibility of purification, for when Evelyn enters Beulah, described as a crucible (p. 49), it's clear that Evelyn himself is the object of transformation who must understand the nature of his sins by embodying and experiencing the violence that he had once perpetrated upon women. Beulah represents sterility rather than purity, though, and Eve must experience defilement and filth as a woman in the ranch of Zero before undergoing marriage to Tristessa in the glass palace. Glass symbolises the alchemical vessel and, as Lyndy Abraham points out, 'the alchemical couple, philosophical sulphur (male, hot, active) and argent vive (female, cold, receptive), must be united at the chymical wedding to produce the philosopher's stone.'[40] The chymical wedding itself is the unification or reconciliation of opposites, resulting in a final purification, where, as Jung describes it, the 'supreme opposites, male and female ... are melted into a unity purified of all opposition and therefore incorruptible'.[41] Eve experiences something of that unity and dissolution in the desert, after her marriage to Tristessa and shortly after they had 'made the great Platonic hermaphrodite together' (p. 148) when '[t]he lateral beams of the setting sun melted the gold; it turned to alchemical gold' (p. 150). As the sun sets, the moon gives enough light 'to let a regiment of alchemists perform the ritual of the dissolution of the contents of the crucible, which, Baroslav, the Czech, had told me, may only be taken in polarised light' (p. 150). At that moment of metamorphosis and apparent purification, night is not the opposite of the day but interrelated with it, 'a cool day itself, without colours' (p. 150) just as masculinity and femininity are 'correlatives which involve one another' (p. 149).

At the glass palace, it's as though time has frozen, and the present itself is embalmed: the glass sculptures outside the house give the appearance of quiescent tears, preserving the moment, 'as in a passion of grief' (p. 111). Tears are also multifunctional within alchemy, as expressions of sorrow for the death of the Hermetic Bird or for the hermaphrodite couple after they have been united in the Chymical Wedding (prophetic in the case of Tristessa and Eve). Zero's violence frees the glass tears from their petrified state, just as it frees Tristessa from 'a non-life of intermediate stasis', as Eve describes it. (Petrifaction surfaces as an index of fear intermittently: Eve's narrative contains at least three allusions to Lot's wife, turned into a pillar of salt as a punishment for her disobedience and, of course, her curiosity, pp. 24, 140, 180.) The intrusion of outsiders into this becalmed scene violently ruptures it and Tristessa (not unlike Miss Havisham) is forced to enter time once more and (unlike Miss Havisham) is made to marry. The revelation that Tristessa was, after all, anatomically male precipitates a scene of disintegration rather than clarity. 'He, she – neither will do for you', Eve comments (p. 143), before claiming him as almost a second or extended self that observes an essential duality: 'We are Tiresias' (p. 146).

In 1975, Angela Carter wrote an observational piece, 'The Wound in the Face', the result of what she mockingly termed a 'hallucinatory weekend', during which she had been cutting out women's faces from glossy magazines. Then in vogue in *Vogue* was the retro 1930s face, 'the iconographic, androgynous face of Dietrich and Garbo, with heavily emphasised bone structures, hollow cheeks and hooded eyelids'.[42] Fashionable and influential, too, she noted, were 'Warhol's transvestite superstars', gracing the pages of his magazine, *Interview*. Tacky, kitsch and fake, these images had, she understood, a 'profound influence' on women's transvestite representation: 'fashionable women now tend to look like women imitating men imitating women, an interesting reversal'.[43] There is some overlap between those observations, at least in terms of contemporary (or recent) iconographic appropriation of androgynous appearance that, if not kitsch like the 'transvestite representation', had come to be defined as camp.[44]

The wedding scene in which Tristessa and Eve are married, far from the ritualised observation of institutionalised norms, is a scene of carnival that works itself into a climactic frenzy around the performance of the primal scene – the brief and rapid coitus of Eve and Tristessa, witnessed by Zero and his group of seven women. Eve, costumed as the cross-dressing George Sand, marries Tristessa, costumed in a wedding dress s/he'd first worn in a film adaptation of *Wuthering Heights*. Far from the reinstatement or consolidation of gender roles, the wedding scene initiates their dizzying collapse: a woman, who was a man, now dressed as a man, wearing the costume of a woman who cross-dressed as a man, played by a man who cross-dressed as a woman, marries a man, now dressed as a bride. The wax mannequins, the *memento mori* of Hollywood legends, have been broken down and re-assembled by Zero's women, but not in an order that observes coherency: Ramon Navarro's head sits on Jean Harlow's torso and has the arms of John Barrymore Junior and Marilyn Monroe as though to embody the complex configurations now enacted by Tristessa and Eve in their 'double wedding' in which 'both were the bride, both the groom' (p. 135). Binaries are not broken down so much as proliferated, rupturing the hierarchical order of what Butler refers to as 'the illusion of a symmetrical difference which consolidates the metaphysical economy of phallogocentrism, the economy of the same'.[45] But it's an economy that's plundered rather than bankrupted or spent: maleness and femaleness are still 'ineradicable', even if they are protean; the mask of gender, if lifted, reveals only another mask, also gendered, underneath, and though Eve makes a distinction between mimicry and becoming

('I only mimicked what I had been; I did not become it', p. 132), mimicry itself *is* a form of becoming, as the text dramatises. It's as if they're wedged inside a form (somatic and generic) that is confining and petrifying. Eve recognises that Zero expects closure through marriage, the formal conclusion of the pastoral, but this is necessarily corrupted as the permutations of gendered identity riotously ricochet back and forth in an apparently endless, and so rather stultifying, oscillatory movement – from man to woman to man again.

In the 'real', Tristessa attempts to 'coincide with [the] model of simulation' (as Baudrillard describes it): evidently discomposed by Zero and his group of women following their invasion of the glass palace, she recomposes herself by re-enacting the other real of the screen, as '[t]ouchingly ... she tries to put herself to rights' (p. 124). The resumption of this particular masquerade is violently disrupted by Zero and his group of women, intent as he is on unmasking the masquerade, a revenge on the woman who, he believes, 'magicked the genius out of [his] jissom' (p. 91). But as Eve comes to realise, 'this masquerade was more than skin deep' (p. 132) and the mask only conceals another mask underneath, one no less 'real' than the other. Tristessa has been read as a relatively conservative figure ('a male appropriation of femininity, not a radical form of gender-bending'),[46] as has Eve, interpreted as an androgynous figure who threatens the erasure of femininity, and therefore of sexual difference ('the perfect woman constructed according to an androgynous blueprint').[47] Paulina Palmer has suggested that Tristessa is 'modelled on Greta Garbo'[48] and, whilst Carter never explicitly describes or names Tristessa as 'androgynous', the bone structure, hollow cheeks and hooded eyes *are* often the signatures of an essentially dual figure, timelessly preserved in celluloid but also subject to time, divine and mortal, essential and depthless, the 'female man' as Eve describes her, never entirely certain which pronoun to settle on (p. 128). Whatever else Tristessa signifies (falsity, says Eve at the beginning of her reminiscences), as an androgyne, s/he is also the mark of stasis, death and failure. Described by Leilah as the uroborous (p. 173), sometimes regarded as the perfect emblem of the circular androgyne, but now dismissed as 'a vicious circle, the dead end' (p. 173), Tristessa is also hailed (by Eve) as the mythical unicorn, emblem of androgyny in alchemy.[49] But Tristessa is also the index of an aspiration that failed: the individual, we should infer, cannot singly embody the androgyne, not least because the androgyne is the trope of a union made redemptive through love, as Eve's narrative demonstrates: completion, as Louisa Agnew comes to realise in *The Chymical Wedding* 'was not merely a matter of singularity: it must inhere *between*'.[50] From their ecstatic consummation in the desert, Eve observes that it is as if they had

> made the great Platonic hermaphrodite, the whole and perfect being to which he, with an absurd and touching heroism, had in his own single self, aspired; we brought into being the love who stops time in the self-created eternity of lovers. (p. 148)

Of course, they do not stop time, and their reverie is broken by the boys from the Children's Crusade, marking time with their Mickey Mouse watches as the symbols of corporate America and a confused culture of machismo (the boys are both violent and vulnerable). These boys destroy the figures who, in any case, thought they were dying in the desert, and the triumph of one mythology annihilates the redemptive possibility of another. The pleasurable and private consummation of their desire for one another has been read as an atoning, reconciliatory moment,[51] but the violent intrusion of the Children's Crusade suggests that such reconciliation is locked into a moment of being that cannot extend beyond the limits of its own solipsism and that has no resonance within a broader cultural understanding.[52] As a private retreat from the demands of culture, it is, though, evidently liberating. Ideal femininity, we learn, is constructed by masculine desire (Leilah comes into being as Evelyn watches her, Tristessa embodies what he most desires) and comes into being via the axis of the gaze. As Alison Lee comments, Eve 'learns to be a woman from the way she is looked at'.[53] In the desert, though, there is no one there to see, and when that happens, gender might be rewritten outside of culture, which is to say, the self might be reconceived outside gender, just as it can only be reconceived within it at the spectacle of the wedding. But such a self is also a non-self, constituted outside language's social and symbolic order. At the point of orgasm, Eve

> would find myself moving through a succession of rooms which appeared to me with all the vividness of actuality, and then they would dematerialise under the stress of those fleshly impressions that require another language, not speech, a notation far less imprecise than speech, to log them. (p. 149)

A profoundly pleasurable moment, a kind of *jouissance*, it offers an apparent recuperation of an earlier moment of fearful alienation,

experienced during her sadistic life as Evelyn. Enticed by the preda-
tory Leilah, he entered her apartment block 'with its many, many
rooms, all tenanted by strangers' (p. 25). At that moment (the equivalent of the alchemical 'nigredo') Evelyn equates his 'atavistic panic'
with anteriority; like Adam, he felt 'all the ghastly attraction of the
fall' (p. 25), clearly linked here to the temptation of female sexuality.
This is chaotic, dark, mysterious, and Evelyn's response to it is an
explicitly phallic one: he takes 'the quickest way down', he 'plunged',
his existence 'was now gone away into my tumescence; I was nothing
but cock' (p. 25). The symbols of an explicitly phallic sexuality and
culture are eventually damaged (they're never entirely destroyed) their
potency re-imagined as part of a system of mutual exchange through
an 'interpenetrating, undifferentiated sex' which gestures to the
Platonic iconography of the androgyne as it is enacted in the sexual
coupling of Eve and Tristessa (p. 148). When Eve revisits the 'house'
the experience is reclaimed as an entirely pleasurable one, but it's a
pleasure that can only be experienced, never communicated.[54] The
'interpenetrating, undifferentiated sex' is possible: but it happens
where language fails.

Familiar cultural scripts become unreadable and unspeakable. Trying
to describe the smell of female sex is impossible: '[Tristessa] rummaged
in a forgotten word-hoard of metaphor but was at last forced to
abandon imagery, since it was inadequate' (p. 148). Identity is modu-
lated as they become 'aspects of being, ideas' (p. 148) and kaleido-
scopic: 'I beat down upon you mercilessly with atavistic relish, but the
glass woman I saw beneath me smashed under my passion and the
splinters scattered and recomposed themselves into a man who over-
whelmed me' (p. 149). It's only when culture intrudes, in the form of
the boys from the Crusade, that Tristessa is recast once more into 'his
female aspect' (p. 156) and Eve becomes the nurturing mother who, in
an act of self-preservation, escapes the boys and enters the final stages
of her journey where she declares that she both has, and has not 'come
home' (p. 186). It's a stark choice: Mother, maternity, the maternal, is
what she's always in flight from, but what she's also fated to experience. Language is, of course, gendered, the product of a cultural system
that is itself profoundly gendered. The experience or possibility of
androgyny appears to shrivel language at the point of utterance, but
when Eve embarks on the final stages of her journey, it is to re-embrace
the emblems of alchemy possibly because they offer a way of thinking
that is directed towards the unity of opposing elements held in balance
– rather than the conflict of opposing elements, one trying to overwrite

the other. After all, the events of Eve's journey are concerned with the restitution of myth over history.

Eve's journey takes her, in the end, to a beach whose sole occupant is an old woman. She cuts an anachronistic figure, her festering flesh a cruel contradiction to the desire that she sings about. She is also the masquerade unmasked: wrinkled, ravaged, sagged, dirty, chipped, scratched, her face immobile, 'stiffened as it was by the mask of cosmetics and grime' (p. 178). She is a sexless figure, 'old enough to have been either man or woman' (p. 190), elaborately made up, she has an 'Adam's apple, prominent as that of an old man' (p. 178). She is also a fusion of alchemical colours – white face, yellow hair, red (or scarlet) lipstick – even her sandals are silver: when Eve gives her the gold ingot produced by Baroslav's successful alchemical endeavours, it seems as though purification is complete and the new Eve will be able to repopulate the world with the child of her androgynous union.[55] Eve's journey through the cave takes her through a succession of small ordeals; each one relates to the symbols of alchemy, although their purpose is never altogether clear. Thus, she is immediately drenched and frozen when she enters the first of the caves, first drenched with water, then with sweat – tears, sweat, rain, dew or gum are all cleansing agents within alchemy. In one cave, she experiences a 'scarcely tolerable stench of sulphur' (p. 181), symbolically allied to the soul, and she's aware of light that is red, a cloth that's white, colour symbolism that alludes to the King and Queen of the androgynous Chymical Wedding. She tears a photograph of Tristessa into four pieces (a prefiguring of the four elements that she cites at the end of her journey), which float like boats, 'or white feathers' (p. 182). Alchemical instruments are in the cave – the alembic, a chunk of amber (synonymous, in alchemy, with gold). Though it does not turn into gold, it does undergo a process of liquefaction, signalling 'the dissolution ... of the impure metal or matter of the Stone'.[56] From the damp of one cave, Eve walks into a dry cave, which becomes progressively more viscous, or gummy, and which suggests the interior of a womb. This is a rather different journey to anteriority; there, Eve sees the archaeopteryx, the transitional, intermediate creature that marked the evolutionary stage between bird and dinosaur, a 'being composed of the contradictory elements of air and earth' (p. 185) When she emerges into darkness, the 'sound of the sea becomes omnipresent' (p. 186). She has come, then, to the sea, the point of origin, one of the images for the alchemists' obscure *prima materia* or 'chaos of mutable substances'.[57] 'Time and again,' says Jung, 'the alchemists reiterate that the *opus* proceeds from the one and leads back to the one',[58] an iteration that seems apposite for a text with two beginnings.

If alchemy slowly 'perished in its own obscurity',[59] it seems an odd choice, perhaps, for Carter to engage with, and to decode the text as simply a re-articulation of its symbolism seems, in the end, a reductive endeavour. In reality, the ultimate goal of the philosopher's stone receded further, not unlike the androgynous union or unified self. Alchemy itself was an unstable practice: 'hardly two authors are of the same opinion regarding the exact course of the process and the sequence of its stages.'[60] The apparent precision of alchemical formulae didn't necessarily yield any consistent result, in spite of Baroslav's ability to manufacture it: 'he made me gold for me – yes; he did' (p. 14), says Eve, acknowledging our incredulity. Heather Johnson has argued that for a writer like Carter, 'the attraction of alchemical imagery lies in its wealth of colourful images, emblematic scenes and baroque myths'.[61] Potentially, that attraction privileges myth and style over the social and political substance of her text, returning us to a binary that keeps them opposed rather than integrated or interrogatory.

Though there is political action in *The Passion of New Eve*, the ideological aims of the civil war are never made clear, and its politics are caught up in the field of their own unwieldy logic, lacking an organising telos. Once the Age of Reason is declared over, America seems to collapse in on itself in a series of factions and civil wars: 'Was it arson?' Evelyn asks: 'Were the blacks responsible, or the Women? The Women? What did they mean?' (p. 11). In these texts, America is the epicentre of an entirely self-regarding, narcissistic and sometimes tragic world where subjectivity is secured via projection, as phantasmagoria, and as a form of mimicry which confirms the simulated self. Gazing into the eyes of Tristessa, a figure with 'no ontological status, only an iconographic one', p. 129), Eve sees 'all the desolation of America ... all estrangement, our loneliness, our abandonment' (pp. 121–2). Femininity and masculinity are scarcely reified in Carter's and Vidal's texts: their essential nature is reconceived less through the institutional apparatus that produce and define us, and more via projection, fantasy and the mediated and depthless image of the simulacra. The fantasy elements, as well as the postmodern strategies of these texts, stage a sufficient distance from the 'real' in order to dramatise, exaggerate, distort and parody the present. Catharine Stimpson, arguing that the androgyne was only 'an idea' as opposed to an achievable and material reality, had criticised it as a flawed concept, even as she invoked an apparently ontological, rational androgyne: 'the androgyne still fundamentally thinks in terms of "feminine" and "masculine." It fails to conceptualise the world and to organize phenomena in a new way that leaves "feminine" and "masculine" behind.'[62] These texts gesture less to the possibility of a newly realised and material androgynous identity, and more to concerns with how representation is mediated visually and in language. The androgyne, or the possibility of androgyny, is insistently fictionalised as though to remind us that it belongs in the realm of the imaginary (as Francette Pacteau has argued),[63] and that it is always mediated, temporal, and never transcendent.

6
Alchemy and *The Chymical Wedding*

> [H]er concern was only with the sacred marriage of spirit and matter, the chymical wedding of the androgynous human soul.(*The Chymical Wedding*, p. 361)

Lindsay Clarke's Whitbread Prize winning *The Chymical Wedding* explored androgynous union by revisiting alchemy, and in doing so, offered a representation of androgyny as an achievable event within a profoundly symbolic schema. The chymical wedding was the 'ultimate phase'[1] of the alchemical process that purportedly transformed base metals to gold, in the elusive pursuit of the philosopher's stone. In *Alchemy: Ancient and Modern*, H. Stanley Redgrove distinguished two kinds of alchemists: those interested in material alchemy and the possibility of making cheap gold, and those concerned with mysticism, who believed that 'the writings of alchemists must not be understood as dealing with chemical operations, with furnaces, retorts, alembics, pelicans and the like, with salt, sulphur, mercury, gold and other material substances, but must be understood as grand allegories dealing with spiritual truths'.[2] The literal production of the philosopher's stone must be read simultaneously as one that is also (perhaps more truly) symbolic or allegorical: '[m]etaphysically,' Lyndy Abraham explains, 'the chemical wedding is the perfect union of creative will or power (male) with wisdom (female) to produce pure love (the child, the Stone)'.[3] The chemical or chymical wedding represents the unification of opposites as these are figured within alchemical imagery: sun and moon, king and queen, red and white, sulphur (fire and air) and argent vive (earth and water). The Philosopher's Stone, symbolised as the 'rebis' or hermaphrodite or androgyne, 'is the perfect integration of male and female energies'.[4] 'Chemical union,'

M.H. Abrams explains, 'was equated with a sexual coupling; and the culmination of the entire physical *operatio* was frequently imagined as the *coniuncto*, or "chymical wedding," of the prototypical male and female opposites.'[5] As Louisa Agnew comes to understand in *The Chymical Wedding*, the study of (generic) 'Man' is central to alchemy, 'the true laboratory of the Hermetic Art. He is its subject, he the alembick, he the Stone; and true Self-knowledge is the motive, mode and object of the Work' (p. 296).

The scientific precursor to chemistry, alchemy was the science that failed: '[c]hemistry became natural science, whereas Hermetic philosophy lost the empirical ground from under its feet'.[6] It survived in the arcane workings of Hermetic philosophy and eventually in psychology: 'the psychic part of the work,' said Jung, 'did not disappear'.[7] Alchemy, as hermetic philosophy and as the symbolic location of psychic wholeness, resurfaces in *The Chymical Wedding*'s interweaving of two different but insistently connected narratives. Its movement between the nineteenth and twentieth centuries recognises the interrelatedness of people and events: what was disparate becomes reconciled and apparently linear histories are rendered as though circular, so that the possibility of reconnection is always available. The trajectory of events, though loosely following a linear pattern, is always revealed through both nineteenth- and twentieth-century histories. When Alex is introduced to the carving of Gypsy May at the end of the first chapter, he experiences uncertainty about whether to gasp or laugh, but it's not until the end of the second chapter, when the narrative revisits the carving, that we finally see what it is that makes Alex uncertain, through the eyes of the nineteenth-century curate, Edwin Frere: 'the image squatted, high on the church wall, naked with drooping dugs, and both hands holding open the organ of her sex, as though she were about to drop a child in labour, or as though she might engorge a man' (p. 36). In chapter 2, Louisa picks up a tarot card, the figure of the hanged man, the same card that Alex picks up in chapter 3. The slow disintegration of the Frere marriage at the end of chapter 4 is underlined by a reminder of the breakdown of Alex's marriage at the beginning of chapter 5, and the accelerated disintegration of the Frere marriage is paralleled with Louisa's new understanding of what the chymical wedding must entail in chapter 8 as the content that maps dissolution is matched by a narrative structure that plots to reunite disintegration. Louisa Agnew's arrival at the Decoy Lodge at the end of chapter 6 is followed by Alex's arrival at the Decoy Lodge at the beginning of chapter 7. When Laura asks Alex, 'Why did you have to come?'

(p. 312) she echoes Louisa's more affirmative 'You have come' (p. 360) when Frere arrives at the Lodge, and so on. More significant than these structural connections, though, is the centrality of the chymical wedding itself, an event that both Alex and Louisa are privileged to see in a dream. The dream reveals Sir Humphrey Agnew, Louisa's ancestor, and his 'mystic sister' Janet Dyball, in the process of transforming base metals to gold and Alex watches them apparently metamorphose into Laura and Edward. Louisa has that dream, too, but her dream takes her back to the beginning of time, 'until it was high summer at Easterness, the sun and the moon stood in the sky together, and she knew herself returned to the golden age of alchemy' (p. 291). In her dream, she gazes at 'two figures who were bent at work before a furnace sweating in the heat as they fed charcoal to its flame' (p. 291). She recognises the man as Sir Humphrey, who had supposedly made the elusive philosopher's stone, and the woman as his mystic sister, Janet Dyball, whose face then metamorphoses into Louisa's – '[s]he and Janet were one and the same' (p. 292). But this dream is also anticipatory and so confuses linearity as a progressive trajectory, rendering time circular: what goes around, comes around. Louisa is, in part, the returning shade of her grandfather, and Laura and Alex (not Edward, as in Alex's dream) will work with a similar intensity before a roaring furnace, although in a much more pragmatic endeavour, engaged as they are in firing pots. This pursuit is itself described by Edward as 'a sort of practical alchemy', in which Laura crafts the pots 'from earth and water and then deliver[s] them over to the mercies of fire and air' (p. 230). The achievement of the philosopher's stone in Louisa's dream is followed by a vision, ostensibly of Sir Humphrey and Janet, but anticipatory too of Laura and Alex's sexual meeting; Louisa sees the alchemist and his mystic sister in a redemptive Edenic coupling: 'naked as angels, white among green shade; and such laughter echoing from tree to tree, as though the knowledge of sin had never been conceived, and both knew now only the dazzling appetite to meet' (p. 293). Once Alex tells Edward and Laura his dream, he has to decide whether or not to help them with their quest to discover the lost secret of the Agnews, a decision that forces him to realise that

> it was possible that everything appeared subtly interfused. For an instant I saw it was possible that everything – each one of us – is the condition by which all else exists. I saw that reality might not be a fixture – crudely, inescapably *there* – but a continuing, spontaneous enterprise of the imagination. It might be shaped, remade, revalued,

again and again, through each act of perception, each inventive
gesture of relationship. (p. 172)

Androgyny was employed, throughout the twentieth century, as a
means of representing sexuality or social equality, as an ideal, a perversion, or as an embodiment. In Clarke's text, although androgyny is
explicitly named only once (in the 'chymical wedding of the androgynous human soul'), it draws on the complex semiotics of alchemy to
become a dynamic symbol expressive of the union of 'contraries',
including but not limited to the cultural opposites of masculinity and
femininity. Edward Nesbit, a poet whose gift has failed, none the less
believes in the efficacy of symbolism, and alchemy functions as a compensation for his failure with poetry: 'Infatuated by our own clever
minds, we turned our backs on the old redeeming symbols. We forgot
the *symbolic* is that which holds together' (p. 160). When Louisa
Agnew proposes to work alone in a self-contained building known as
the Decoy Lodge in order to write her prose narrative *An Open
Invitation to the Chymical Wedding*, she none the less affirms the necessity of poetry (ratifying her father's poetic opus in the process). The
hermetic vision, she acknowledges, can only be relayed truthfully
through verse since prose falsifies, or 'depletes' it, as though the truth
of it must remain necessarily noumenal, the 'breathless apprehension
of the mystery in things' as Louisa describes the sexual union of the
chymical wedding.

Chymical union is also deemed necessary to revitalise sexual relations between men and women (as Frere notes despondently, 'life as
meeting always eluded their grasp', p. 355) *and* as a necessary
unification of two systems of belief: Hermetic philosophy and
Christianity. Louisa intersects all these aspirations, working towards
the goal that Edward articulates: 'How to realize a whole vision of life?'
(p. 155). This unity is predicated on a reconciliation of oppositions:
matter with spirit, heart with mind, and female with male. The chymical wedding is the key to redeeming the social malaise of the twentieth
century, just as it had appeared to offer redemption from the social
malaise of the nineteenth. In keeping with other representations of
androgyny, though, its existence is predicated on secrecy, on a retreat
from the social world rather than an engagement with it. To engage
with the social, with its system of obligations and cultural construction, is to invalidate the wedding, as we see in the disastrous coupling
of Louisa and Edwin Frere, and then in the failed but ultimately
hopeful aftermath of Alex and Laura's sexual encounter.

There are two versions of the doctrine of alchemy, as Louisa Agnew comes to realise. One is the dry and scholarly vision of her father, whose commitment to versifying alchemy speaks to his fear of life or of confronting the real or the sexual (he is at one point depicted allegorically as 'Contemplation', p. 291). The other version is fashioned by Louisa, who unites oppositions within herself (her virginal self with her debauched grandfather, the Hermetic mystery with the Christian Church), and also sees them united within Frere; a realisation that prompts her to wish for a dynamic intellectual and sexual communion with him, one that must match learning with experience. She realises that it is not perfection that she should be striving for, but completion, 'at the very heart of the *Coniunctio*' (p. 282), a completion that she achieves (albeit momentarily) with Frere. The diabolic, signified by her dissolute and ostracised grandfather, must be incorporated into the symbolic: the sexual cannot be denied, and its worst excesses can be redeemed: to deny the existence of the dissolute (and therefore of the potential for it) is to deny what exists in the self, a denial that her father is guilty of. As she debates with herself and her grandfather she comes to validate the alchemical system as '*a divine order rich with meaning*', in which sexuality has its appointed place, in contrast to the world without it, '*an insane jumble of atoms in which nothing is forbidden*' (p. 289).

There are two quests at the heart of this narrative. One is pursued by the Agnews but also lost to them: Sir Henry's vision – and his poetic gifts (if he ever had them) – fail him and Louisa's achieved mystical 'wedding' is doomed to failure after Edwin's violent revolt from it. The second quest is that of Edward Nesbit, Laura and Alex. What they cannot discover, what must be concealed from them, is the very thing they look for, and what they discover is not a mystical secret but an appalling act. Edward tells Alex that the Agnews were the keepers of 'the alchemical inner secret', which they held 'while the rest of the world plunged into blind materialism' (p. 157); but that secret, of necessity, can never be revealed since the alchemist must never reveal it. The real secret of the book, for the reader, is the revelation of Frere's self-inflicted fate, and it is towards the symbolic redemption, or at least assimilation, of that horror that the chymical wedding is invoked.

Atomisation and fissure characterise the modern era in this novel: 'you're a man in pieces with none of the pieces in their proper place,' Edward tells Alex (p. 161). Events take place against the political background of Campaign for Nuclear Disarmament meetings, at which Alex listens 'to the clash – the old, endless, point-counter-point failure to meet' (p. 337). It is through his involvement with CND that Alex comes to re-engage with his place in the 'real' world, away from the magical one that he inhabited with Edward and Laura, and begins to see the threat of nuclear war as overwhelming the comparatively footling work of poring over the old Agnew man-uscripts. The locations of alchemy, compared to this contemporary milieu, are always in worlds of retreat: the woods, the Decoy Lodge, the study in the Agnew home. The location of androgynous union, that is to say, is apart from the social, encrypted in the often inscrutable symbols of alchemical practice, and existing in dreams. And yet, the novel seems to hold out a hope for the possibility of reconciliation and redemption, of trying to translate 'a private spiri-tual vision into social action' (p. 196). In learning the lessons of alchemy, Alex also realises that if we are capable of inflicting great evil, we are also capable of perpetrating great good: the 'law of con-traries' underlying alchemy decrees that much. Within the closed, hermetic world of the text, reality *is* 'shaped, remade, revalued again and again' as the narrative follows two groups of people, apparently separated by history, each in their own time seeking to replace isola-tion and incompletion with unity. *The Chymical Wedding* traces the consequences of psychic fracture, for individuals and for systems of faith, but also imagines what the implications might be of their attempts to achieve a renewed unity.

The narrative begins with the failure of a wedding, or rather, of a marriage. Alex Darken, a poet whose marriage has ended, has been invited to spend time in his publisher's cottage in the quiet Norfolk village of Munding. There, he meets another poet, Edward Nesbit, and his much younger girlfriend, Laura, a potter who is also deeply attuned to the continued ghostly existence of Louisa Agnew, an adherent, in the nineteenth century, of Hermetic philosophy. Both Edward and Laura believe that Louisa and her father, Sir Henry, had uncovered an important secret that might help salvage the social fractures of the late twentieth century. Clarke's split time frame allows him to produce a credibly sympathetic engagement with androgynous union through the alchemical 'chymical wedding' in which opposites are 'melted into a unity purified of all opposition and therefore [are] incorruptible',[8] and in a distinctly less fantastic space than the one that Carter had envisaged for Eve and Tristessa in *The Passion of New Eve*. Daniel Harris, writing in the 1974 edition of the 'Androgyny Papers' had been sceptical of contemporary representations of androgyny, and was equally scathing about the practice of alchemy:

> the alchemical tradition is bleakly reactionary; renewed and sympathetic interest in alchemical speculation on the part of white middle-class intellectuals makes the exposure of its insidious substratum imperative at the present time. It should not surprise us that the alchemists and their illustrators, while professing to seek a magical marriage of male and female elements, a balanced and harmonious fusion of opposites, envisage their work from a predominantly male perspective; although they can sanction male transvestism (Mercurius as Virgo), they cannot admit the possibility of a female androgyne.[9]

Though alchemy was not originally the practice of white middle-class intellectuals (the word derives from the Arabic *alkimia* and was developed and practised in China, Greece and the Middle East) it does become the practice of white aristocratic and middle class intellectuals in *The Chymical Wedding*. As if in reply to Harris, however, one of the mysteries that Alex Darken and Edward Nesbit confront in *The Chymical Wedding* is the cryptic meaning of '*Frater mysticus meus*' – my mystic brother. 'There's no precedent for it,' Edward tells Alex: 'The female assistant was known as the mystic sister, but the man was always the Adept, the Master, Magister' (p. 222). Clarke's novel re-imagines that tradition by shifting perspectives or reversing roles: Louisa is the Adept, Frere the mystic brother who fails: he comes to think that Louisa embodies both male and female principles, but that he embodies neither: '*As I now am empty and without form, and therefore neither idea nor mystery, neither male nor female*' (p. 429). Frere's act of self-mutilation is a nihilistic act of union: he elides difference, not through the redemptive and inviolable sacrament of the chymical wedding but by a destructive eradication of the physical signs of gender, in castrating himself: 'Priest to both God and Goddess now, never to be the lover of Louisa Agnew, he had become and would for ever remain, her mystic brother' (p. 450).

The world of the social, of political consciousness, is figured as being in retreat too, represented by a man in retirement, the ex-psychiatric nurse Bob Crossley, a member of CND. The possibility of nuclear annihilation hangs over the novel mainly as a reminder that the world has gone (or has the potential to go) catastrophically wrong. The novel engages with the rather contrived notion that a faith in alchemical practices might somehow have saved us from the worst (as Louisa knows, the world is indifferent to the quest or the vision of the individual). Alex voices the scepticism of the reader, suggesting that alchemy was fraudulent, 'an eccentric quirk of history' (p. 152), but Edward, the poet, insists on reading alchemy symbolically, and as 'the effort to heal the split in consciousness' (p. 153). Saving humanity from the worst was Sir Henry's quest in the nineteenth century: working on his metrical epic of the Hermetic Mystery, he feels that 'Daily the crisis of the age cried out for it' (p. 71), and that the figure who will help him work this out is his mystic sister, his daughter Louisa. In the twentieth century, the crisis of the age is the threat of nuclear catastrophe: in the nineteenth, as Sir Henry sees it, it lies in the triumph of capitalism over spiritualism, as we learn from a letter that he writes to his more worldly son: 'The vision of a golden world will be cashed in for muck and brass' (p. 118).

For Louisa, it is 'vital for the contraries to meet again' (p. 386). These 'contraries' are symbolic, spiritual and sexual, as she explains to Edwin that Hermetic philosophy needed Christianity, and vice versa – one was powerless without the other: 'Without the social strength of Christianity, Hermeticism lay in chains; without the regenerative power of Hermetic knowledge, Christianity was moribund' (p. 386). That reconciliation is also figured for Louisa in her relationship with Frere: 'He was the true spirit of the Christian church; she the handmaid of the Hermetic mystery' (p. 386). That's something that Frere, too, comes to realise: '*As Idea knows itself in man, and man knows himself through Idea, so Mystery knows itself in woman, and woman knows herself in Mystery. Male and female they were created; for the idea divested of mystery is empty, and mystery unshaped by idea is formless*' (p. 429).

Frere's first appearance in the narrative is an unpropitious one, his initial conversation with Sir Henry stumbles uncomfortably round the very thing that Frere needs to repress: the sexual. As a young curate in India, he had been tempted into sex by a temple prostitute; it was this fall, from spirituality to sexuality, that drove him to a nervous breakdown. His predecessor had died *in flagrante*, a fact evidently embarrassing to Frere, and then his Christian beliefs are challenged by Sir Henry, who, like his daughter, believes in both Hermetic philosophy and Christianity: 'All the evidence proclaims that the work of redemption remains incomplete. It is up to us now. We were created in the Divine Image, Mr Frere, and a residual germ of that divinity remains occulted within us even in the fallen state' (p. 27). The amalgamation of these two systems of belief could result in a redemption from the Fall, as

Alex later comes to understand: 'If one knew how to go about it the Fall was reversible' (p. 208) and the alchemical process of turning metal to gold was the 'paradigm of this sacred task' (p. 208). Whilst Sir Henry and Edwin Frere discuss Hermetic philosophy and Christianity, Louisa Agnew and Emilia Frere discuss Anne Brontë's *The Tenant of Wildfell Hall*. This conversation, ostensibly about literature and marriage, tests the limits of an understanding about what men and women are capable of (Emilia thinks the book is written by a man, Louisa thinks it is written by a woman). It also reinforces the vulnerability of marriage: the failure of the Huntingdon marriage in *The Tenant of Wildfell Hall*, though not precisely mirrored in *The Chymical Wedding*, produces, still, a thematic consistency since the Frere marriage is also set to fail ('no true marriage', Louisa later thinks of it, 'no irrevocable meeting of souls', p. 365), stimulated by the growing chasm between Emilia's boredom and Edwin's sincere sense of Christian charity, her commitment to social pleasure, his to Christian duty. The discussion that ensues about *The Tenant of Wildfell Hall* only serves to emphasise sexual difference: 'Can one be quite certain that the novel is a man's work?' 'Do you not feel a woman's sensibility in its insights?' (p. 22). Later, Sir Henry, bored by the discussion, 'felt it high time the sexes took their separate ways' (p. 23). The relative crudity of that binary schema is later belied by the more complex one that the narrative strives to instate: all 'contraries', that is to say, must be resolved and even transcended, as Louisa suggests to Edwin: 'And you my dear, are more than male, as I myself am more than female now' (p. 428). Emilia (ironically, as it turns out) suggests that marriage vows are the most sacred vows of all, but since the religious beliefs that they are founded on are later demonstrated to be insufficient (Christianity, it is suggested, is spiritually moribund without Hermetic philosophy to inform it), Christian marriage is destined to fail.

The failure of the marriage is coterminous with the collapse of Frere's faith: as Easter approaches, and with his wife gone, Frere knows that intellectually he should be able to take consolation from the Easter message but cannot. Indeed, Frere's dream shortly after his arrival in Munding (one that sits on the exposed border of public locution and private fear) invokes, only to reject, Genesis and the story of the beginning of sexual difference. In the dream, Sir Henry looks bored: '*How long*, the bored smile seemed to say, *will you detain us with this pap?*' (p. 31). If his Christian understanding of difference is disconcerted by a scenario that seems prompted by Sir Henry's discussion about the merits of Hermetic philosophy and Christianity, it is further unsettled by Louisa herself, whose persistent questioning about his unspoken anxiety over the carving of Gypsy May makes him wonder at her apparently fluent reversal of the gender roles.

Louisa's own understanding of her 'reversal' of gender roles is based on a belief that she harbours the spirit of 'Mercurius' within her, a figure of 'a duplicitous and antinomian nature' (p. 66), partly a vital figure for her, but also a 'prankster and deceiver' (p. 66). That is to say that, in social interaction, 'Mercurius' can only find expression as a mischievous and mildly anarchic figure, but in her private work as a Hermetic philosopher, he occupies a much more important function which is to do with the translation of the private vision to social – and also sexual – interaction. As she comes to realise, 'The powers of this spirit were immense and impersonal. Unassimilated, they might one day wreak havoc in her life' (p. 282). The dissolute is as death-dealing as the virginal, and it is the reconciliation of these opposing states, as they determine her family history, that Louisa wishes to achieve. It is in his capacity as 'prankster and deceiver' that Mercurius prompts Louisa to step outside the bounds of conventional femininity by persuading Frere to discuss his misgivings about the pagan carving of Gypsy May. This figure, insistently symbolic (through her, says Edward Nesbit, 'We come alive again to the tremendous symbolic dignity of things', p. 49), is also resolutely sexual, as Louisa recognises: 'there is knowledge between us that we have both looked upon the private parts of Gypsy May and I have impudently advised him to take her to his bosom' (p. 67).

Whilst Louisa is obliged to think about her lapse in social propriety, that particular fissure, the small ingress she makes into Edwin Frere's consciousness, begins to be matched with the slow severance of the Frere marriage, personal crises that do not yet figure in Sir Henry Agnew's increasingly isolated understanding of 'the crisis of the age', that of the 'beleaguered human soul' (p. 116). When the lake freezes over and the villagers are able to skate on it, Frere is a revelation to Louisa. In a scene that offers up its symbolism overtly, Louisa, a relatively poor skater, is helped across the ice by Frere, the sincere man of faith, and by the local doctor, Tom Horrocks, the cynical man of science. Horrocks effectively blasphemes in front of Louisa, claiming that he needs a glass of mulled wine if he is to race with Mercury (Frere has proved himself to be a skilled and graceful skater). She starts at the too casual mention of Mercurius's name, cast here not only as the androgynous spirit that exists inside her, but also as the 'tutelary deity of the Hermetic Art – a slippery, ambiguous figure who was, according to that great master Gerhard Dorn, "the true hermaphrodite Adam"' (p. 180).[10] The words of Dorn are in her mind as she gazes at Frere: 'In this moment all contraries seemed reconciled in him – shyness and strength, awkwardness and grace, the spirit bright within the balanced body, his parson's black against the white of the distant drifts' (p. 181). Aesthetic, balanced and spiritual, the scene is a turning point in the narrative: Louisa's realisation that Frere seems to embody the reconciliation of a series of oppositions is matched by the break-down of his marriage, precipitated by his wife's miscarriage on the edge of the lake. Emilia's subsequent withdrawal from her marriage begins when she is recuperating at the Agnew home, whilst the narra-tive increasingly draws together its disparate components. As Edwin sends an ill-fated letter to Emilia's Cambridge home, Louisa's dissolute grandfather, 'Madcap' Agnew, appears to her in a vision whose sexual nature is so diabolical that it fills her with fear. This resolutely sexual vision brings her to a sense of the *prima materia* – the unspecified chaotic material that the alchemist first works with, as she gazes at the lake, once frozen, now the site of a potential rebirth: 'Here like the mingled waters of a flood, was the first chaos of things. It was the dead sea of being female. Here one drowned' (p. 271). But here, too, she 'wanted to feel the world real around her again ... wanted to touch and be touched' (p. 271). In the Decoy Lodge, she experiences a kind of breakdown which is also a breakthrough: frightened at the sight of her reflection in the glass, Louisa seems a figure first divided (the reflected image fails to confirm identity, but rather dissociates it) and then reconciled to a sense of purpose that she realises will have profound personal repercussions for herself. It is no good repressing the vision, or the history of her grandfather, since 'He was here because she was here herself. In part at least, she was his returning shade, and that shade was clamouring now to be embraced' (p. 281). Her book, she thinks, will have nothing to say until her grandfather's misspent energies have been redeemed: she herself must embody the chymical wedding:

> It was the reconciliation of *Sol* and *Luna* after the violence of their strife, the chymical wedding of Sulphur and Quicksilver, the meeting of dark and light in close embrace from which the golden stone was born. She had known this all along, but she knew it with a different knowledge now. It was more than an intellectual com-prehension; and to write of it she must strive to become that meeting. She must submit to its ordeals. (p. 283)

That ordeal takes the form of a strange encounter with the shade of her grandfather, a shade whose presence is so powerful that it appears to be material. As she progresses with her work, she comes to realise its – and her – limitations: marked by intellectual blindness and her own sexual inexperience. Her work is about the sexual, she comes to realise, a thing she has never had direct experience of. Whilst her grandfather had purportedly visited the Lodge for sexual purposes, an even more remote ancestor, Sir Humphrey, had been a magician and 'had consorted with a witch hereabouts' (p. 258). Sex, witchcraft, magic and madness lie in the hinterland of a childhood memory that come to mythologise the Lodge for her – these are the histories that the mature Louisa rewrites, and in so doing redeems: 'Was it only lovelessness then that made an evil of the flesh? For in the Hermetic Art – symbolic though its language was – the mating of Sol and Luna was a moment of great joy and exaltation. It was the healing of ills, the great *mysterium*' (p. 260).

When a dishevelled Frere finally comes to see Louisa at the Decoy Lodge, his tested faith seems to regain some of its former strength, shocked as he is by her suggestions. For her, Gypsy May is the symbol that completes the Christian Church, but for Frere, she represents a tempting female sexuality. Though she believes that his arrival at the Lodge is fated, he is more pragmatic: he feels as though he is losing his mind. But as she tries to explain her creed to him, he recoils in horror, and his lapsing faith returns, executed in pious if halting rhetoric: 'As a Christian ... clergyman ... I cannot admit' (p. 369). He persistently misreads her, as though hers are the ramblings of a frustrated spinster, or a child who still grieves the loss of her mother and finds some consolation in the carving of a figure that is both maternal and sexual. The Church, consecrated as it is to the Father, is, she tries to tell him, half a Church: it needs the pagan carving of the Magna Mater to complete it: 'She is completion, Edwin. Without her we are less than ourselves' (p. 370). For him, the oppositions integral to alchemy are heretical, a denial of the Christian faith as he understands it. Louisa, on the other hand, has worked out her own complex and individual understanding of reconciliation that brings together Pagan and Christian, spiritual and sexual, and at the centre of that are herself and Frere. Her endeavour is to redress the wrongs of an historical moment when – as she sees it – a dreadful fissure occurred and the Church failed 'to wed its spiritual vision with the natural magic of alchemic lore. For a moment, there at the height of Renaissance humanism, Trismegistus might have been preferred over Aristotle as the cornerstone of Christian philosophy' (p. 386). But he wasn't, and that was the moment of division which saw the privileging of mind over body as femininity was made outcast: 'The female knowledge of the heart was ever more mistrusted and reviled; and where it might have been made whole – the consciousness of man shattered between the tragic contraries' (p. 386). Hermetic philosophy needed the 'social strength' of Christianity just as Christianity required 'the regenerative power' of Hermeticism. That reconciliation might be embodied by Edwin, 'the true spirit of the Christian church', and Louisa, 'the hand-maid of Hermetic mystery' (p. 386). As though to confirm the proper alliance of those two systems of faith, the eventual sexual union of Frere and Louisa appears to bring with it an uneven promise of redemption: he is like Adam 'shown the garden after his own fall' as though he is permitted re-entry: 'astoundingly, the gate stood open' (p. 409). But when he looks at her again, he is struck by terror and presumably by the unassailable demons of his now stricken conscience. The idea of the chymical wedding always gestures to a social and sexual ideal beyond its scientific provenance as it symbolises the unification of two people to make one. But in the end, the wedding fails just as alchemy failed, and the attempt at a newly redemptive union leads to disaster when Edwin Frere castrates himself. That castration might be read as the achievement of a negative or sexless androgyny: at any rate, he embodies sexual neutrality and the 'chymical wedding of the androgynous human soul' is not realised as a triumphant embodiment, but rather signals a failure or lack. And yet, the apparent circularity of time in *The Chymical Wedding*, embedded in the narrative structure, suggests that there must be redemption because there is always, as the book is plotted, reconciliation.

The event of the castration in the nineteenth century and the discovery of the castration in the twentieth occur almost simultaneously in the narrative structure. The second quest of the book, as I suggested above, is that of Edward, Laura and Alex, who are set on unearthing the secrets held by the Agnews, one that would allow them to find spiritual renewal from the crass materialism Edward sees as endemic of late twentieth-century cultural capitalism. Alex, in retreat from marital breakdown and social obligation, comes to realise that his marriage had dissolved because he was denying part of himself to himself (his own femininity he concludes, after reading Blake). But Alex is privileged to experience a visionary dream in which he sees Sir Humphrey Agnew and Janet Dyball produce the philosopher's reconciliatory stone, and on the strength of that dream he agrees to help

Laura and Alex with their quest to discover the secret of the Agnews. Like Sir Henry Agnew, Edward Nesbit disdains the contemporary age as one that has slipped from myth to materialism, hence his faith in the secrets of alchemy. The structural parallels established in the narrative suggest, also, that each figure has a counterpart: Edward, the failed poet, is coupled with Sir Henry, the failed alchemist, both fated to profound disappointment when the alchemical mystery fails to yield itself or turns out to be no mystical secret at all; but the necessary engagement with the past, the recovery of buried (and repressed) secrets, offers a redemption of sorts. Sir Henry dies from his disappointment, but Edward, following a heart attack and near-death experience, is given a second chance, and he lives. Laura might be paired with Louisa, Alex with Edwin Frere. Whilst sexual union leads to disaster rather than regeneration or recuperation in the nineteenth-century strand of the narrative, it does promise a resolution for Alex and Laura as they enact the sexual union that Louisa once dreamed of and which was ultimately denied to her. Laura feels a restoration of self, a connectedness with the world and the life around her, and Alex comes to an understanding of alchemy and what its practical application might be. He does this through a dream in which a woman knows how to solve the world's apprehension about the threat of nuclear war by taking keys from a group of jaded old men. She gives the keys to the Pope and he tells her that 'The Quakers shall hold the keys' (p. 378). When Alex finally comes to understand the symbolism of the dream, he sees it as one 'elegantly structured around the tension of opposing forces' in which the 'key to the explosive condition of the world ... could only be done by holding contraries together. That *was* the key' (p. 395).

Though *The Chymical Wedding* offers an apparently different approach to conceptualising and representing androgyny, the problem of its incommunicability still arises: the androgynous spirit of Mercurius is a presiding one, a tutelary deity that makes itself manifest in trivial and profound ways, but its profundity can only be realised away from the prescriptive demands of social obligation. Read in the context of social paradigms, Louisa's masculine spirit functions as a transgression of a strictly codified femininity. Read in the terms of a symbolic schema that can only operate privately, away from the prescriptions of the social, it offers fulfilment and completion. The chymical wedding fails when Alex and Laura have sex because he can never finally abandon his social self, just as Frere can never discard his sense of Christian obligation. The narrative remains alert to the improbability and contrivance of chymical union as the key to preventing apocalypse, but its ambition for forms of reconciliation is sincerely held – between men and women, between the historical past and the demands of the present, which is also a way of addressing what is consciously accepted and what is unconsciously denied. The embodied androgyne invites if not a second look, then a quizzical, puzzled one that speaks to the irresolution that it fosters: neither – or both – a man and a woman, defined by sexuality, or not sexed at all. Androgyny, or symbolic union, is not contested in *The Chymical Wedding* but fulfils its function within a highly schematic system of thought. With this representation, we must look and look again, not at an embodiment that disturbs, but as a symbol that invites us to exhume as many meanings as we can from what we see and read; androgyny, the goal of union within the chymical wedding, is insistently a symbol within a finely wrought set of classifications, one that fails in the social or the real, but that paradoxically thrives – even as a necessary melancholy – in literary imagination.

Notes

Introduction

1 Cal's narrative is told retrospectively, and from the vantage point of the male identity he adopts.

2 Jeffrey Eugenides, *Middlesex*, London: Bloomsbury, 2002, p. 41. See also Kimbrough: 'much of the recent literature on androgyny has been confused and muddled because of the simple inability to distinguish between the fact that *androgyny is a mythic concept* which represents an inner, psychic state of experience available to all human beings, whereas hermaphroditism is an objective, physical state of being forced on a limited few.' Robert Kimbrough, *Shakespeare and the Art of Humankindness*, New Jersey: Humanities Press, 1990, p. 20. See also Mary Anne Warren: 'Androgyny, in this feminist sense, has nothing to do with physical hermaphroditism, a biological anomaly in which a person's body fails to develop in an unambiguously feminine or masculine manner.' 'Is Androgyny the Answer to Sexual Stereotyping?' in Mary Vetterling-Braggin, *'Femininity', 'Masculinity', and 'Androgyny': A Modern Philosophical Discussion*, New Jersey: Littlefield, Adam and Co., 1982, p. 170.

3 Eugenides, *Middlesex*, p. 489.

4 See Kari Weil, *Androgyy and the Denial of Difference*, Charlottesville and London: Virginia University Press, 1990, p. 10. Comparing Ovid to Plato, Weil suggests that Ovid's 'myth ... presents the union of male and female as forever incomplete, two bodies competing with, rather than complementing, each other'.

5 Hélène Cixous, 'Sorties', *The Newly Born Woman*, Minneapolis and London: University of Minnesota Press, 1986, p. 84. Although both narratives describe dual-sexed bodies, critics have pointed out the differences between them. For the psychoanalytic critic Francette Pacteau, Aristophanes' story describes 'the desire ... for union and re-union' ('The Impossible Referent: Representations of the Androgyne', in Victor Burgin et al., eds, *Formations of Fantasy*, London and New York: Routledge, 1986, p. 66); whereas in Ovid, 'In the myths of Caenis and Caeneus and Hermaphroditus, it is the rape, respectively of the woman and the man's body, which provokes the metamorphoses. The injury made to a body that wants itself whole is repaired through the abolition of the other. Hermaphroditus and Salmacis become one ...' (ibid., pp. 69–70). Weil debates the differences between androgyny and the hermaphrodite extensively in *Androgyny and the Denial of Difference*, reminding us again that 'they have different histories and different psychical effects having to do primarily with the status of the body', p. 9.

6 Jeffrey Eugenides in interview with Geraldine Bedell, *The Observer*, 6 October 2002, p. 17.

7   See, for example, Michael Joyce, in *The Collected Dialogues of Plato*, ed. Edith
     Hamilton and Huntington Cairns Bollinger, Series LXXI, Princeton, NJ:
     Princeton University Press, 1963; and Walter Hamilton, *The Symposium*,
     Harmondsworth: Penguin, 1951. Both translate the male-female figure as
     hermaphrodite. P.B. Shelley, Benjamin Jowett, R.G. Bury, Kenneth Dover
     and Robin Waterfield all translate the same figure as androgynous.

8   Weil distinguishes the terms by seeing 'Aristophanes' description of the
     androgyne as the original, harmonious and ideal state of man in the
     Symposium against Ovid's myth of Hermaphroditus in the *Metamorphoses*,
     wherein hermaphroditism itself constitutes the fallen state.' *Androgyny and
     the Denial of Difference*, p. 12.

9   Earl Lind, writing his autobiography, is the notable exception as I explore
     in chapter 2.

10 Catriona MacLeod, *Embodying Ambiguity: Androgyny and Aesthetics from
     Winckelmann to Keller*, Detroit: Wayne State University Press, 1998, p. 11.

11 I am grateful to Zowie Davy for the Hedwig reference.

12 Olive Schreiner, *Woman and Labour*, London: Virago, 1978, pp. 250–1.

13 Diana Collecott, *HD and Sapphic Modernism 1910–1950*, Cambridge:
     Cambridge University Press, 1999 p. 94.

14 Havelock Ellis, *Studies in the Psychology of Sex*, vol. II, Philadelphia: F.H.
     Davies, 1917, p. 311.

15 D.H. Lawrence, *Women in Love*, Harmondsworth: Penguin, 1995, p. 201.

16 Ibid.

17 Thomas Hardy, *Tess of the d'Urbervilles*, London: Macmillan, 1974, p. 72.

18 *The Letters of John Cowper-Powys to Frances Gregg*, ed. Oliver Marlow
     Wilkinson, assisted by Christopher Wilkinson, London: Cecil Woolf, 1994,
     p. 97.

19 Jacques Lacan, 'From Love to the Libido', in *The Four Fundamental
     Concepts of Psychoanalysis*, ed. Jacques Alain Miller, trans. Alan Sheridan,
     Harmondsworth: Penguin, 1977, p. 197. Note his addition, though: 'I
     will try'.

20 Catharine R. Stimpson, 'The Androgyne and the Homosexual', in *Where the
     Meanings Are*, New York and London: Methuen, 1988, p. 56.

21 Pacteau, 'The Impossible Referent', p. 74.

22 Ibid., p. 62.

23 Ibid.

24 Hari Kunzru, *The Impressionist*, London: Hamish Hamilton, 2002, pp. 92
     and 256.

25 Philip Roth, *The Human Stain*, London: Vintage, 2001, p. 156.

26 Weil, *Androgyny and the Denial of Difference*, p. 2.

27 Ibid., p. 3.

28 Edward and Eleanor Marx-Aveling, *The Woman Question*, London: Swan
     Sonnenschein, 1886, p. 7. They also claimed that 'There are approximately
     equal numbers of men and women, the highest ideal seems to be the
     complete and harmonious, lasting blending of two lives', p. 15.

29 Camille Paglia, 'The Beautiful Boy as Destroyer: Wilde's *The Picture of Dorian
     Gray*', in *Sexual Personae*, New York: Vintage Books, 1991, pp. 512–30.

30 Angela Carter, in 'Angela Carter's Curious Room', *Omnibus*, BBC1,
     15 September 1992.

1 Classical to Medical

1 Linda Dowling, *Hellenism and Homosexuality in Victorian Oxford*, Ithaca, NY and London: Cornell University Press, 1994, p. 77. Oxford undergraduates were first examined on Plato in 1847.
2 Ibid., p .xiii.
3 E.M. Forster, *Maurice*, Harmondsworth: Penguin, 1985, p. 50.
4 John Addington Symonds, in *The Memoirs of John Addington Symonds*, cited in Anne Herrmann, *Queering the Moderns*, Basingstoke: Palgrave, 2000, p. 148.
5 'The "Love that dare not speak its name" in this century is such a great affection of an elder man for a younger man as there was between David and Jonathan, such as Plato made the very basis of his philosophy.' Cited in Richard Ellmann, *Oscar Wilde*, London: Hamish Hamilton, 1987, p. 435.
6 Edward Carpenter, *My Days and Dreams*, London: Allen & Unwin, 1916, p. 196.
7 Beverley Thiele, 'Coming-of-Age: Edward Carpenter on Sex and Reproduction', in *Edward Carpenter and Late Victorian Radicalism*, ed. Tony Brown, London: Frank Cass, 1990, p. 100.
8 Mary Shelley, letter to Leigh Hunt, October 1839, cited in James Notopoulos, *The Platonism of Shelley: A Study of Platonism and the Poetic Mind*, Durham, NC: Duke University Press, 1949, p. 389.
9 See James D. Steakley, '*Per scientam ad justitiam*: Magnus Hirschfeld and the Sexual Politics of Innate Homosexuality', in Vernon Rosario, ed., *Science and Homosexualities*, London: Routledge, 1997. Steakley notes that Hirschfeld produced a 26-page brochure entitled *What Should the People Know About the Third Sex?* 'The title,' he says, 'hearkened back not only to the use of the term "third sex" to designate homosexuals in Plato's *Symposium*.' The 'third sex' did not, though, refer to the male-male pairing, but refers to the heterosexual androgynous pairing.
10 Jowett, pp. 530–1.
11 Xavier Mayne (pseud.), *The Intersexes: A History of Similisexualism As a Problem in Social Life*, [Rome]: privately printed, 1908, p. x.
12 Ibid.
13 Steakley, '*Per scientam ad justitiam*', p. 144. See also Hubert Kennedy, 'Karl Ulrichs First Theorist of Homosexuality', in Rosario, *Science and Homosexualities*. Kennedy also notes that Magnus Hirschfeld 'published prolifically on the full spectrum of human sexual "intermediacy", which he held to comprise hermaphroditism, androgyny, homosexuality, and transvestism', p. 15.
14 Metatropism comprised 'homosexuality and bisexuality as intersexual variants of sexuality' and Tranvestism was 'an intersexually mixed form of other psychological qualities'. Steakley, '*Per scientam ad justitiam*', p. 144.
15 Mayne, *The Intersexes*, p. 19.
16 Ibid.
17 Ibid., p. 18.
18 Ibid., pp. 256–7.
19 Michel Foucault, *History of Sexuality: An Introduction*, trans. Robert Hurley, Harmondsworth: Penguin, 1990, p. 43.

20 Kari Weil, *Androgyny and the Denial of Difference*, Charlottesville and London: University of Virginia Press, 1992, p. 3.

21 Sigmund Freud, 'The Sexual Aberrations' (1905), in *On Sexuality*, Pelican Freud, Vol. 7, Harmondsworth: Penguin, 1987, p. 46.

22 Weil, *Androgyny and the Denial of Difference*, p. 3.

23 M.H. Abrams, *Natural Supernaturalism: Tradition and Revolution in Romantic Literature*, New York: W.W. Norton, 1971, p. 155. See also Andrea Dworkin, *Woman Hating*, New York: Plume, 1974, pp. 167–73 for other accounts of Judaic, Hindu, Egyptian, Australian, African, Tibetan and Indian creation myths. Dworkin found Aristophanes' myth to be a corruption of earlier androgyne creation myths: 'Plato, repeating a corrupted version of a much older myth, describes in *Symposium* 3 types of original human beings: male/male, male/female, female/female. These original human beings were so powerful that the gods feared them and so Zeus, whose own androgynous ancestry did not stop him from becoming the Macho kid, halved them', pp. 168–9. And see Wendy Doniger, 'The Evolution of the Androgyne in India', in *Women, Androgynes, and Other Mythical Beasts*, Chicago and London: University of Chicago Press, 1980, pp. 310–30. See also Edward Carpenter, *Intermediate Types Among Primitive Folk*, London: George Allen, 1914.

24 Cited in Mircea Eliade, *The Two and the One*, trans. J.M. Cohen, London: Harvill Press, 1965, p. 104.

25 Weil, *Androgyny and the Denial of Difference*, p. 18.

26 Barbara Charlesworth Gelpi, 'The Politics of Androgyny', in *Women's Studies* 2 1974, pp. 151–60 at p. 152.

27 In his commentary on Aristophanes' speech, Rowe notes that 'it may or may not be relevant to this part of Aristophanes' story that we evidently find an *Eros* with two genders and two or more things in Orphism'. Plato, *Symposium*, ed. and with intro., trans. and commentary C.J. Rowe, Warminster: Aris and Phillips, p. 154.

28 M.H. Abrams, *Natural Supernaturalism: Tradition and Revolution in Romantic Literature*, Oxford: Oxford University Press, 1971, p. 155.

29 See, for example, Norman O. Brown: 'Original sin is connected in the first instance with division into sexes and the Fall of the androgyne, i.e., of man as a complete being'. Cited in Warren Stevenson, *Romanticism and the Androgynous Sublime*, London: Associated University Presses, 1996, p. 16.

30 Theodor J. Faithfull, *The Mystery of the Androgyne: Three Papers on the Theory and Practice of Psycho-Analysis*, London: Forum Publishing Company, 1938, p. vii.

31 Ibid., p. 2.

32 Freud, 'The Sexual Aberrations', p. 45.

33 Francette Pacteau, p. 66. In *The Mystery of the* Androgyne, Theodore J. Faithfull read the two types of Uranian and Pandemian love in terms of Freud's hypotheses about instinctual love and hunger – one is extraverted and male, the other is introverted, subjective and creative, which he took to be versions of the Uranian and Pandemian, p. 5.

34 Foucault, *The History of Sexuality*, p. 56.

35 Charles Darwin, *The Descent of Man*, cited in Bram Dijkstra, *Idols of Perversity: Fantasies of Feminine Evil in Fin-de-Siècle Culture*, New York and

Oxford: Oxford University Press, 1986, p. 171. See also Steakley, *'Per scientam ad justitiam'*, p. 143, who cites Darwin, 'We thus see that in many, probably all cases, the secondary characters of each sex lie dormant or latent in the opposite sex, ready to be evolved under peculiar circumstances' (Charles Darwin, *The Variation of Plants and Animals Under Domestication*, 2 vols, London: John Murray, 1868, 2:52).

36 Ellis, *Studies in the Psychology of Sex*, p. 314. See also Judy Greenway, who argues that Edward Carpenter used evolutionary theory to posit 'a spiritual stage beyond gender and sexuality'. 'It's What You Do With it That Counts', in Doan and Bland (eds), *Sexology Uncensored*, p. 34. Harry Oosterhuis also suggests that Krafft-Ebing was influenced by Darwin ('Richard Krafft-Ebing's "Step-Children of Nature": Psychiatry and the Making of Homosexual Identity', in Rosario, ed., *Science and Homosexualities*, p. 71). See also Margaret Gibson, 'Clitoral Corruption, Body Metaphors and American Doctors' Construction of Female Homosexuality 1870–1900', in Rosario, ed., *Science and Homosexualities*: 'Perhaps the most common use of evolutionary theory with inversion was the assumption that homosexuality represented a regression to a "bisexual" past, in which hermaphrodism was the rule.' She cites James G. Kiernan, Secretary of the Chicago Academy of Medicine: 'The original bisexuality of the ancestors of the race, shown in the rudimentary female organs of the male, could not fail to occasion functional, if not organic, reversions when mental or physical manifestations were interfered with by disease or congenital defect' (1888, p. 115).

37 Ellis, *Studies in the Psychology of Sex*, II, p. 313, cited in Diana Collecott, *HD and Sapphic Modernism 1910–1950*, Cambridge: Cambridge University Press, 1999, p. 52.

38 'These long-familiar facts of anatomy lead us to suppose that an originally bisexual physical disposition has, in the course of evolution, become modified into a unisexual one, leaving behind only a few traces of the sex that has become atrophied.' 'The Sexual Aberrations', in *Three Essays on the Theory of Sexuality*, p. 52.

39 See Foucault, *The History of Sexuality*: 'It will be granted no doubt that relations of sex gave rise, in every society, to a *deployment of alliance*: a system of marriage, of fixation and development of kinship ties ...', p. 106.

40 'These bisexual varieties may manifest themselves in very various ways, in most cases in gynandry or androgyny is purely spiritual, and finds expression only in association with particular tendencies, especially fetichistic [sic] tendencies', Iwan Bloch, *The Sexual Life of Our Times in its Relation to Modern Civilization*, trans, M. Eden Paul, London: Rebman, 1908, p. 541.

41 Ibid., p. 539.

42 Ibid., cited in Bland and Doan, eds, *Sexology Uncensored*.

43 Siobhan Somerville, cited in ibid., p. 202.

44 Wayne Andersen, Freud, *Leonardo da Vinci and the Vulture's Tail: A Refreshing Look at Leonardo's Sexuality*, New York: Other Press, 2001, p. 4.

45 Jutta Birmele, 'Strategies of Persuasion: The Case of *Leonardo da Vinci*', p. 130 in Sander L. Gilman et al. eds, *Reading Freud's Reading*, New York and London: New York University Press, 1994.

46 Ibid., p. 133.

47   Freud, 'Leonardo da Vinci', p. 190. He also writes in the conclusion of his study, again disparagingly, 'The tendency of biological research to-day is to explain the chief features in a person's organic constitution as being the result of the blending of male and female dispositions, based on [chemical] substances', p. 229.

48   'Nessuna cosa si può amare nè odiare, se prima non si ha cognition di quella', ibid., p. 163.

49   Letter to Carl Jung, 17 October 1909, cited in Andersen, *Freud, Leonard da Vinci*, p. 3.

50   See editor's note: 'A prominent part is played by Leonardo's memory or phantasy of being visited in his cradle by a bird of prey. The name applied to this bird in his notebooks is *"nibio"*, which (in the modern form of *"nibbio"*) is the ordinary Italian word for *"kite"*. Freud, however, throughout his study translates the word by the German *"Geier"*, for which the English can only be *"vulture"*. His mistake originates from some of the German translations that he used.' As the editor points out, 'Freud's psychological analysis of the phantasy is not contradicted by this correction but merely deprived of one piece of corroborative support', p. 148. See also Arthur Scherr, 'He notoriously overstates the significance of a passage in Da Vinci's writing that describes his infantile memory of a vulture opening his mouth with its tail and repeatedly striking against his lips', 'Leonardo da Vinci, Sigmund Freud, and Fear of Flying', *Midwest Quarterly: A Journal of Contemporary Thought*, 42:2, 2001, p. 123. Andersen has written exhaustively in *Freud, Leonardo da Vinci*, that, in fact, Freud's translation *was* apposite: 'Any European of the late nineteenth-century with knowledge of Latin could have translated Leonardo's *nibio* into kite, hawk, vulture, griffin, or griffin vulture' (p. 49). And in terms of its historical moment, Freud's psychoanalytic interpretation of the androgyne still offers an important intervention in the history of androgynous representation.

51   Freud names Strabo, Plutarch, Marcellunis, Horapollo Nilus and Hermes Trismegistus, the 'founder' of alchemy. 'Leonardo da Vinci', p. 179.

52   *The Hieroglyphics of Horapollo*, trans. George Boas, Princeton, NJ: Princeton University Press, 1993: 'When they mean a mother, or sight, or boundaries, or foreknowledge, or the year, or the heavens, or pity, or Athene, or Hera, or two drachmas, they draw a vulture. A mother, since there is no male in this species of animal. And they are born this way: when the vulture hungers after conception, she opens her sexual organ to the North Wind and is covered by him for five days. During this period she takes neither food nor drink, yearning for child-bearing. But there is another species of vulture which conceives by the wind, their eggs are fertile. The vulture stands for sight since of all other animals the vulture has the keenest vision', pp. 49–50.

53   Birmele, 'Strategies of Persuasion', p. 132.

54   Scherr, 'Leonardo da Vinci, Sigmund Freud, and Fear of Flying', p. 126.

55   Andersen, *Freud, Leonardo da Vinci*, p. 48.

56   Freud wasn't alone in seeing the painting of the *Mona Lisa* as androgynous. See Richard Dellamora, *Masculine Desire: The Sexual Politics of Victorian Aestheticism*, Chapel Hill and London: University of North Carolina Press, 1990, for further discussion: 'French critic Charles Clément has argued that

the *Saint John* is a transvestite portrait,' Gautier suggested; Dellamora says that 'the clue to the painting's "secret" exists in its androgynous male beauty' (p. 143); Gautier also describes the angel, supposedly by Leonardo in Verrocchio's *The Baptism of Christ* (Uffizi, Florence) as a 'hermaphrodite céleste' (*Guide* to the Paris Exhibition of 1867, p. 65). Pater speaks of the 'so-called Saint John the Baptist ... whose delicate brown flesh and woman's hair no one would go out in the wilderness to seek' (p. 143). Dellamora also suggests that 'When Marcel Duchamp later put a moustache on a copy of the portrait, he simply made explicit Pater's earlier suggestion that the *Mona Lisa* is a transvestite self-portrait' (p. 144). Andersen cites Bernard Berenson who 'referred to Leonardo's *St. John* as 'a fleshy female leering out of darkness' (p. 93). See also Mario Praz: 'The Androgyne is the artistic sex *par excellence*, realized in the creations of Leonardo.' In *The Romantic Agony*, trans. Angus Davidson, Oxford: Oxford University Press, 1933, p. 334.

57 Walter Pater, 'Leonardo da Vinci', in *The Renaissance: Studies in Art and Poetry*, Oxford: Oxford University Press, 1986. See also Andersen, who suggests that 'Leonardo had become an icon for the emerging nineteenth-century of a third sex ... Surely the writings by such purveyors of romantic thought as Walter Pater and Oscar Wilde contributed to Freud's linkage of Leonardo's homosexuality to the sublime status of genius thwarted by social norms.' *Freud, Leonardo da Vinci*, p. 93.

58 Ralph Werther, Jennie June and Earl Lind were all used as pseudonyms or alternative names. Chauncey refers to him as Ralph Werther in *Gay New York*, but in consonance with the name he gives on the title page of the autobiography, I am using 'Earl Lind'. In his second book, *The Female-Impersonators*, Lind shifts to 'Ralph Werther'. He called himself Earl because it rhymed with 'girl' and Lind after the celebrated singer Jennie Lind; see Herrmann, *Queering the Moderns*, p. 156.

59 See George Chauncey, *Gay New York: Gender, Urban Culture and the Making of the Gay Male World 1890–1940*, New York: HarperCollins, 1994.

60 See Foucault, *The History of Sexuality*, p. 71: 'And we must ask whether, since the nineteenth century, the *scientia sexualis* – under the guise of its decent positivism – has not functioned, at least to a certain extent, as an *ars erotica*.'

61 Alfred W. Herzog, Introduction to Earl Lind, *The Autobiography of an Androgyne*, New York: Medico-Legal Journal, 1918, p. ii.

62 Ibid., p. xi. Herzog was an editor of *The Medico-Legal Journal*.

63 Ibid., p. vii.

64 Ibid.

65 Foucault, *The History of Sexuality*, p. 43.

66 Ibid.

67 See also Jonathon Katz: 'the Victorian concept of "true" mechanically linked biology with psychology. Feelings were thought of as female or male in exactly the same sense as penis or clitoris: anatomy equalled psychology, sex physiology determined the sex of feelings', cited in Rosario, *Science and Homosexualities*, p. 29.

68 Lind, *The Autobiography of an Androgyne*, p. 6. Harry Oosterhuis notes that *Psychopathia Sexualis*, which first appeared in 1886, was followed by new and expanded editions, 17 in all, between 1886 and 1924. It was also translated into several languages, in Rosario, *Science and Homosexualities*, p. 70.

69 Herrmann, *Queering the Moderns*, p. 148.
70 Karl Heinrich Ulrichs developed 'four distinct domains of sexual intermediacy: (1) Hermaphroditism as an intersexual formation of sex organs, (2) Androgyny as an intersexually mixed form of other bodily qualities, (3) Metatropism, homosexuality, and bisexuality as intersexual variants of sexuality, (4) Transvestism as an intersexually mixed form of other psychological qualities'. In Steakley, *'Per scientam ad justitiam'*, p. 144. See also Hubert Kennedy, 'Karl Ulrichs First Theorist of Homosexuality', in Rosario, *Science and Homosexualities*. Vernon A. Kennedy notes that Magnus Hirschfeld 'published prolifically on the full spectrum of human sexual "intermediacy", which he held to comprise hermaphroditism, androgyny, homosexuality and transvestism', p. 15. See also Harry Oosterhuis on Krafft-Ebing, who describes hermaphrodism, androgyny and transvestism as 'radically separate phenomena', in Rosario, *Science and Homosexualities*, p. 71.
71 Dijkstra, *Idols of Perversity*, p. 273.
72 Richard von Krafft-Ebing, *Psychopathia Sexualis*, trans. Jack Hunter, New York: Creation Books, 1997, p. 171.
73 Ibid., p. 169.
74 Ibid.
75 His use of medical terminology and promulgation of medical beliefs does also, though, suggest a reliance on them to understand and construct his sense of physiological, biological and sexual self. See, for example, Steakley, *'Per scientiam ad justitiam'*: 'Such early observers as Ulrichs and Caspar, having determined that the male homosexual manifested a discordance between body ("male") and sexual drive ("female")', had "deduced – what could be more obvious – that one ought to seek the central location of these drives and traits ... in his soul" (Hirschfeld, 1914c, 348). At work a generation later, after considerable process in the field of neurology, Hirschfeld firmly biologized their hypotheses by locating the homosexual drive in the "central nervous system" (1914c, 385), specifically in a "brain constitution characterized by a special mixed relation of male and female hereditary matter" (1914c, 394)'; in Rosario, *Science and Homosexualities*, p. 142.
76 Lind, *Autobiography of an Androgyne*, p. 6.
77 Ibid., p. 8.
78 Francette Pacteau, 'The Impossible Referent: Representations of the Androgyne', in Victor Burgin et al., eds, *Formations of Fantasy*, London and New York: Routledge, 1986, p. 74.
79 Ibid.
80 Herrmann, *Queering the Moderns*, p. 149.
81 Lind, *Autobiography of an Androgyne*, p. 41.
82 Camille Paglia, *Sexual Personae: Art and Decadence from Nefertiti to Emily Dickinson*, New Haven, CT: Yale University Press, 1990, p. 402
83 Maurice Barrès, Introduction to Rachilde, *Monsieur Vénus*, 1889, p. 2.
84 Mircea Eliade, 'Mephistopheles and the Androgyne or the Mystery of the Whole', in *The Two and the One*, p. 99.
85 Praz, *The Romantic Agony*, p. 346.
86 Julia Epstein, *Altered Conditions: Disease, Medicine and Story Telling*, London and New York: Routledge, 1995, p. 6.

87 Eliade, 'Mephistopheles', p. 100.
88 Diana Holmes, *Rachilde: Decadence: Gender and the Woman Writer*, Oxford and New York: Berg, 2001, p. 119.
89 Praz, *The Romantic Agony*, p. 350.
90 *Swinburne Replies: Notes on Poems and Reviews*, ed. Clyde Kenneth Hyder, Syracuse, NY: Syracuse University Press, 1966, p. 28.
91 As Pacteau argues in 'The Impossible Referent: Representations of the Androgyne': 'Androgyny cannot be circumscribed as belonging to some being; it is more a question of a relation between a look and an appearance ... I do not encounter an "androgyne" in the street; rather I encounter a figure whom I "see as" androgynous', p. 62.

2 Despised and Rejected

1 Edward Carpenter, 'The Intermediate Sex', in *The Intermediate Sex*, London: George Allen & Co., 1912, p. 26.
2 Ibid., p. 37.
3 Stephen's governess, Puddle, says, 'Why, just because you are what you are, you may actually find that you've got an advantage. You may write with a curious double insight – write both men and women from a personal knowledge' p. 208. Ulrichs is the first named sexologist in *The Well of Loneliness*, and it is in his work that Sir Philip finds the prototypes of Stephen: 'and reading, Sir Philip's eyes would grow puzzled; then groping for a pencil he would make little notes all along the immaculate margins' (*The Well of Loneliness*, London: Virago, 1990, p. 23).
4 *Intermediate Sex*, p. 14. Carpenter repeats the point: 'The instinctive artistic nature of the male of this class, his sensitive spirit, his wavelike emotional temperament, combined with the hardihood of intellect and body; and the frank, free nature of the female, her masculine independence and strength wedded to the thoroughly feminine grace of form and manner; may be said to give them both, through their double nature, command of life in all its phases, and a certain freemasonry of the secrets of the two sexes which may well favour their function as reconcilers and interpreters', ibid., p. 38.
5 Ibid., p. 30.
6 Ibid., pp. 30–1.
7 *Despised and Rejected*, opposite original title-page.
8 Carpenter, *Intermediate Sex,* p. 32.
9 Ibid., p. 33. This connection is also made by other historians and clinicians. In Xavier Mayne's (pseud. Edward Irenaeus Prime Stevenson) *The Intersexes: A History of Similisexualism as a Problem in Social Life* (privately printed, 1908), he claims that music is 'Doubtless ... pre-eminently the Uranian's art. His emotional nature goes out to it and in it, as in no other', p. 395.
10 Laura Doan, *Fashioning Sapphism: The Origins of a Modern English Lesbian Culture*, New York: Columbia University Press, 2001, p. 155.
11 'The Place of the Uranian in Society', in *Intermediate Sex*, p. 111. The term 'Urning' was coined by Karl Ulrichs.
12 Iwan Bloch, *The Sexual Life of Our Times in its relation to Modern Civilization*, trans. M. Eden Paul, London: Rebman, 1908, p. 501.

13 Daniel Pick, *The War Machine: The Rationalisation of Slaughter in the Modern Age*, New Haven, CT and London: Yale University Press, 1993. In context, Pick was describing William James's attempt to define the relation of war to peace.
14 Philip Gibbs, *Realities of War*, London: Heinemann, 1920, p. 24.
15 Their status as 'women' was further underlined by the fact that conscientious objectors were also disenfranchised. Women in Britain received the franchise subject to specific property, age and status qualifications in 1918, and full enfranchisement was given in 1928. See Joanna Bourke, *Dismembering the Male: Men's Bodies, Britain and the Great War*, London: Reaktion Books, 1996, p. 78. In fourth-century BC Athens, the androgyne came to serve as a term of reproach for men who proved themselves cowardly in battle. Kenneth Dover points out that the comedy by Eupolis known as *The Astrateutoi* (men who haven't done their military service) was also known as *The Androgynoi*. The passive homosexual was also, within Ancient Greek culture, regarded as an 'androgyne', an antecedent that Lind would draw on in his autobiography, first published in 1918, and entitled *Autobiography of an Androgyne*.
16 See for example Bourke, *Dismembering the Male*, esp. chapter 3. See also Paul Fussell, *The Great War and Modern Memory*, Oxford: Oxford University Press, 1977; Samuel Hynes, *A War Imagined: The First World War and English Culture*, London: Pimlico, 1990; Sandra Gilbert and Susan Gubar, *No-Man's Land: The Place of the Woman Writer in the Twentieth Century*, London and New Haven, CT: Yale University Press, 1989. Xavier Mayne also argues in *The Intersexes* that the homosexual prostitute soldier was a common enough sight in London's parks at the turn of the century. His own novel of homosexuality, *Imre: A Memorandum*, was set against a background of Magyar soldier life. See also John Addington Symonds, 'Greek love was in its origin and essence, military. Fire and valour, rather than tenderness and tears, were the external outcome of this passion' (*A Problem in Greek Ethics Being an Enquiry into the Phenomenon of Sexual Inversion Addressed Especially to Medical Psychologists and Jurists*, London: privately printed, 1901, p. 8).
17 Samuel Hynes, *A War Imagined: The First World War and English Culture*, London: Pimlico, 1990, p. 234.
18 Cited in Luc Brisson, *Sexual Ambivalnce: Androgyny and Hermaphroditism in Graeco-Roman Antiquity*, Berkeley: California University Press, 2002, p. 61. Brisson also points out that in Book III of the *Laws*, Plato thought that suitable punishment for the man who ran away from battle would be a metamorphosis from male to female.
19 Mayne, *The Intersexes*, p. x.
20 Mayne suggests that Andersen was also homosexual: 'The pederastic homosexuality of that charming fabulist and mystic, Hans Christian Andersen was recently the subject of a close and affirmative study', ibid., p. 387.
21 See Hynes, *A War Imagined*, p. 17.
22 Antoinette is, at times, like Stephen Gordon, who seems blind to the obvious fact that her governess, Puddle, is an 'invert' too; no matter how many hints Dennis (necessarily) coyly drops, Antoinette understands neither him nor her own sexuality for quite some time.

23 Probably the most infamous example of such an alliance is Otto Weininger's influential and extremely popular *Sex and Character*, London: William Heinemann, 1906, which both feminises and anglicises the Jew. Mayne's *The Intersexes*, an attempt at producing a more understanding history of the 'intersexes' none the less rehearses the same assumptions: 'Show me a Jew and you show me an Uranian.' A like statement might run 'Show me a musician and show me a homosexual', p. 395.

24 Mayne, ibid., p. 87.

25 Susan Kingsley Kent, *Making Peace: The Reconstruction of Gender in Interwar Britain*, Princeton, NJ: Princeton University Press, 1993, p. 94.

26 Beverley Nichols, *The Sweet and Twenties*, London: Weidenfeld and Nicolson, 1958, p. 104.

27 Symonds, *A Problem in Greek Ethics*, p. 71.

28 'Una read aloud about congenital sexual inverts, from *Studies in the Psychology of Sex* by Havelock Ellis, *A Manual of Sexual Science* by Magnus Hirschfeld and *Psychopathia Sexualis* by Richard Krafft-Ebing. Radclyffe Hall took the bits that suited her, mixed them with Catholicism, spiritualism and her own ideas on endocrinology and came up with a theory of lesbian identity about as empirically reliable as the paternity of Jesus Christ or Mabel Batten's whereabouts on sphere three.' Diana Souhami, *The Trials of Radclyffe Hall*, London: Virago 1999, p. 155.

29 Doan, *Fashioning Sapphism*.

30 Judith Halberstam, *Female Masculinity*, Durham, NC and London: Duke University Press, 1998, describes *The Well of Loneliness* as 'the best record we have of masculine inversion in women', p. 95. See also Jay Prosser, *Second Skins: The Body Narratives of Transsexuality*, New York: Columbia University Press, 1998.

31 Susan Kingsley Kent, '*The Well of Loneliness* as War Novel', in *Palatable Poison: Critical Perspectives on the Well of Loneliness*, ed. Laura Doan and Jay Prosser, New York: Columbia University Press, 2001, pp. 216–31 at p. 227.

32 Laura Doan, 'The Outcast of One Age', in *Palatable Poison*, ed. Doan and Prosser, p. 168.

33 Judith Butler, *Gender Trouble: Feminism and the Subversion of Identity*, London and New York: Routledge, 1990, p. 111.

34 *The Well of Loneliness*, p. 49. See also Brhyer's *The Heart to Artemis: A Writer's Memoir*, London: Collins, 1963. In her autobiography, Bryher also discusses having the 'energy and frankness' of a boy, and feeling constrained by the high-necked Edwardian blouses she had to wear. Like Stephen, she's a disappointment to her mother as a child, and later to both her parents 'All their friends had liked me as a child but here I was with the raw aggressiveness of a boy', pp. 156–7. See also Helen Corke, *Neutral Ground: A Chronicle*, London: Arthur Baker, 1933, in which Ellis Brooke, always attracted to other women, turns out to be a disappointment to her mother.

35 See Doan, *Fashioning Sapphism*, for an account of sartorial style in the 1920s. See also Erin G. Carlston, 'Female Homosexuality and the American Medical Community', in Vernon A. Rosario, ed., *Science and Homosexualities*, London: Routledge, 1997: 'during the 1920s a new model of *heterosexual* womanhood appeared in the person of the flapper, who was thin-hipped and small-breasted, wore androgynous clothes and bobbed her hair,

smoked, drank publicly, and enjoyed sports – who, in other words, closely resembled many of the old stereotypes of the invert', p. 178.

36 Kent, *Making Peace*, p. 227.

37 Souhami, *The Trials of Radclyffe Hall*, pp. 159–60.

38 Terry Castle, *Noel Coward and Radclyffe Hall: Kindred Spirits*, New York: Columbia University Press, 1996.

39 Ibid., p. 30. She points out that Gluck's 1937 painting of herself and Nesta Obermer, *Medallion* (once used as the cover of Virago's edition of *The Well of Loneliness*) was a duplicate of a 1924 photographic portrait of Coward and Gladys Calthrop.

40 See, for example, Lisa Rado, *The Modern Androgyne Imagination: A Failed Sublime*, Charlottesville and London: University Press of Virginia, 2000, which explores Woolf, Joyce, Hemingway and Faulkner. Diana Collecott in *H.D. and Sapphic Modernism 1910–1950* and Susan Stanford Friedman in *Penelope's Web* and *Psyche Reborn* have both drawn attention to tropes of androgyny and bisexuality in relation to HD. Emile Delaveney has argued (speculatively) for the influence of Carpenter in D.H. Lawrence.

41 Aldous Huxley, *Point Counter Point*, London: Flamingo, 1994, p. 65.

42 Doan, 'The Outcast of One Age', p. 172.

43 Richard von Krafft-Ebing, *Psychopathia Sexualis*, Case 166, trans. Jack Hunter, New York: Creation Books, 1997, p. 196. Raised as a boy, Sandor/Sarolta was passionate about sport, was, like Stephen, a skilful fencer, and, consonant with Stephen's attraction for Angela Crossby, was drawn towards actresses. She was also a gifted writer.

44 See Collecott, *HD and Sapphic Modernism*, for a fuller account of HD's interest in the figure of the hermaphrodite and in bisexuality.

45 Bryher, letter to HD, 20 March 1919, in *Analyzing Freud: Letters of H.D., Bryher, and Their Circle*, ed. Susan Stanford Friedman, New York: New Directions Books, 2002. I am grateful to Fiona Philip for directing me to their letters.

46 HD, letter to Bryher, 18 March 1933, in ibid.

47 Bryher, letter to HD, 20 March 1933, cited in Joanne Winning, ed., *Bryher: Two Novels*, Wisconsin: University of Wisconsin Press, 2000, p. xxviii.

48 HD is 'KAT', 'Cat', 'Mog', 'Kat, N', whilst Bryher is 'Fido', 'Griffon', 'small dog'.

49 Daphne du Maurier to Ellen Doubleday, cited in Margaret Forster, *Daphne du Maurier*, London: Chatto and Windus, 1993, pp. 221–2.

50 Ethel Mannin, *Young in the Twenties: A Chapter of Autobiography*, London: Hutchinson, 1971, p. 141.

51 Margaret Forster, *Daphne du Maurier*, London: Chatto and Windus, 1993, p. 222.

52 Ibid.

53 Ibid.

54 Ibid., p. 276.

55 John Worthen, D.H., *Lawrence and the Idea of the Novel*, London and Basingstoke: Macmillan, 1979, p. 126.

56 'The Study of Thomas Hardy', p. 60.

57 Carpenter,'The Intermediate Sex', p. 19.

58 Ibid., p. 20.

59 Ibid., p. 38.

60 'The Sexual Aberrations', in *Three Essays on Sexuality*, p. 49.

61 Edward Carpenter, 'The Homogenic Attachment', in *The Intermediate Sex*, p. 47.

62 Carpenter, 'The Intermediate Sex', p. 27.

63 D.H. Lawrence to William and Sallie Hopkin, *Letters*, Vol. II, 25 September 1915. See also Emile Delavenay, *D.H. Lawrence and Edward Carpenter: A Study in Edwardian Transition*, London: Heinemann, 1971. Delavenay argues extensively, hypothetically and over-determinedly that Lawrence was influenced by Carpenter. He suggests that Lawrence was 'attentively and perhaps repeatedly' reading *The Intermediate Sex* between 1914 and 1916 and that he had 'probably' read *Intermediate Types Among Primitive Folk*; see p. 206.

64 D.H. Lawrence, *Fantasia of the Unconscious*, New York: Thomas Selzer, 1922.

65 But see Mark Kincaid-Weeks, who suggests that Lawrence's interest in his new 'metaphysic' or philosophy of writing was implicated in both his marriage to Frieda and what Kincaid-Weeks calls the '[b]ravest of all' recognitions – 'the acceptance of bisexuality in himself'. *D.H. Lawrence: Triumph to Exile*, Cambridge: Cambridge University Press, 1996, p. 162.

66 His slipperiness, his lack of a centre, is referred to again: 'Her uncle Tom was always more or less what the other person would have him. In consequence, one never knew the real uncle Tom, only a fluid, unsatisfactory flux with a more or less consistent appearance' (p. 271).

67 Anne Fernihough, Introduction to D.H. Lawrence, *The Rainbow*, Harmondsworth: Penguin, 1995, p. xvii.

68 Michael Squires, Introduction to D.H. Lawrence, *Lady Chatterley's Lover*, London: Penguin, 1994, p. xxii.

69 Collecott, *H.D. and Sapphic Modernism*, p. 99. In *Bid Me To Live*, London: Virago, 1984, p. 62, Julia/HD is critical of Rico/D.H. Lawrence: 'What did Rico matter with his blood-stream, his sex-fixations, his man-is-man, woman-is-woman? That was not true.'

70 Unsigned comment, 'Famous Novelist's Shameful Book', *John Bull*, 20 October 1928, xliv, 11, cited in *Critical Heritage*, p. 278.

71 Victoria Glendinning, *Vita: The Life of V. Sackville-West*, Harmondsworth: Penguin, 1984, p. 206.

72 Jane Marcus, 'Sapphistory: The Woolf and the Well', in Karla Jay and Joanne Glasgow, eds, *Lesbian Texts and Contexts: Radical Revisions*, London: Onlywomen Press, 1992, pp. 164–78.

73 Virginia Woolf to Desmond McCarthy, 27 January 1930, *Letters*, Vol. 4.

74 Virginia Woolf to Ethel Smyth. 26 August 1936, *Letters*, Vol. 6.

75 Lawrence, *Fantasia of the Unconscious*, pp. 89–90.

76 Cited in Linda Ruth Williams, *Sex in the Head: Visions of Femininity and Film in D.H. Lawrence*, Detroit: Wayne State University Press, 1993, p. 125.

77 Ibid., p. 150.

78 Fiona Becket, 'Lawrence and Psychoanalysis', in the *Cambridge Companion to D.H. Lawrence*, ed. Anne Fernihough, Cambridge: Cambridge University Press, 2001, p. 220.

79 Walt Whitman, *Studies in Classic American Literature* (final version), p. 150.

80 D.H. Lawrence to Arthur McLeod, 2 June 1914, *Letters*, Vol. II, ed. George J. Zytaruk and James T. Boulton, Cambridge: Cambridge University Press, 1981.

81 Kincaid-Weeks, *Triumph to Exile*, p. 158.
82 Halberstam, *Female Masculinity*, acknowledging the work of Martha Vicinus, suggests that the 'androgyne' 'represents some version of gender mixing, but this rarely adds up to total ambiguity; when a woman is mistaken consistently for a man ... what marks her gender presentation is not androgyny but masculinity', p. 57. She goes on to 'propose that we consider the various categories of sexual variation for women as separate and distinct from the modern category of lesbian and that we try to account for the specific sexual practices associated with each category and the particular social relations that may have held each category in place', p. 57.

3   Virginia Woolf

1 Jane Marcus, 'Sapphistory: The Woolf and the Well', in Karla Jay and Joanne Glasgow, eds, *Lesbian Texts and Contexts: Radical Revisions*, London: Onlywomen Press 1992, p. 167.
2 From the manuscript drafts, cited in ibid., p. 173.
3 Jane Marcus '"Taking the Bull by the Udders": Sexual Difference in Virginia Woolf – a Conspiracy Theory' in Jane Marcus, ed., *Virginia Woolf and Bloomsbury: A Centenary Celebration*, Bloomington: Indiana University Press, 1987 p. 166.
4 Michèle Barrett, *Virginia Woolf: Women and Writing*, London: The Women's Press 1979.
5 Morag Shiach, Introduction to Virginia Woolf, *A Room of One's Own*, Oxford: Oxford University Press, 1992, p. xvii.
6 Stephen Heath *The Sexual Fix*, London: Macmillan, 1982, p. 114. Showalter made a similar point: 'Obviously Virginia Woolf had not looked at or questioned what she had done in this passage: made the writer male.' Elaine Showalter, *A Literature of Their Own*, London: Virago, 1986, p. 288.
7 Lamb is a contradictory figure, too. He compares favourably with Max Beerbohm (p. 6), but he is also included in her list of writers who 'never helped a woman yet' (p. 69) but he is also androgynous, along with Shakespeare, Keats, Sterne, Cowper and Coleridge, and, like Thackeray, is 'delightful to the ear' (p. 84).
8 'Women and Books', *Times Literary Supplement*, 31 October 1929; and M.E. Kelsey, 'Virginia Woolf and the She-Condition', *Sewanee Review*, October-December 1931, in *Virginia Woolf: The Critical Heritage*, ed. Robin Majumdar and Allen McLaurin, London: Routledge and Kegan Paul, 1975, pp. 255–6 and 260–2.
9 Vita Sackville-West, in ibid., p. 258.
10 6 August 1937, *Diary*, Vol. 5; Letter to Lady Robert Cecil, 18 June 1938, *Letters*, Vol. 6.
11 'Professions for Women', reproduced in *The Pargiters*, ed. Mitchell Leaska, London: Hogarth Press, 1978.
12 Ibid., p. xxxviii.
13 Ibid., p. xxxix.
14 Virginia Woolf to Vanessa Bell, 22 May 1927, *Letters*, Vol. III, London: Hogarth Press, 1977.

15 HD, 'Vision is of two kinds – vision of the womb and vision of the brain'. *Notes on Thought and Vision* and *The Wise Sappho*, London: Peter Owen, 1988, p. 20.

16 Critics have described Hewett as an androgynous figure. See Stella McNichol, *Virginia Woolf and the Poetry of Fiction*, London and New York: Routledge, 1990, p. 9. Diane Filby Gillespie, 'Virginia Woolf's Miss La Trobe: the Artist's Last Struggle Against Masculine Values', *Women and Literature*, 5:1, 1977, pp. 38–9. In her introduction to the 1992 Penguin edition of *The Voyage Out*, Lorna Sage suggested that Terence 'develops a kind of androgynous insight into women's experience', p. xxv.

17 Kathleen Raine, *The Land Unknown*, cited in *Virginia Woolf Women and Fiction: The Manuscript Versions of A Room of One's Own*, transcribed and ed. S.P. Rosenbaum, Oxford: Blackwell, 1992, p. 22.

18 See, for example, Linden Peach, *Virginia Woolf*, Basingstoke: Macmillan, 2000. p. 151 See also Laura Doan, *Fashioning Sapphism: The Origins of a Modern English Lesbian Culture*, New York: Columbia, 2001, for a more comprehensive account of boyish femininity during the 1920s. See also Ellen Carol Jones, 'Figural Desire in *Orlando*', in *Virginia Woolf: Emerging Perspectives*. Selected papers from the Third Annual Conference on Virginia Woolf, ed. Mark Hussey and Vara Neverow, New York: Pace University Press, 1994.'As Carrol Smith Rosenberg points out, the second generation of New Women of the 1920s adopted the rhetoric of various theories of sexuality to represent the 'New Woman as social and sexual hermaphrodites, as an 'intermediate sex' that existed between and thus outside of the biological and social order" a strategy to overturn patriarchal hierarchies of power' (p. 109). See also Kari Elise Lokke, who suggests that *Orlando* embodies the political and aesthetic theories of *A Room* and challenges the dualisms at the heart of 'the traditional sublime aesthetic', in 'Orlando and Incandescence: Virginia Woolf's Comic Sublime', *Modern Fiction Studies*, 38:1, 1992, p. 236. And see Elena Gualtieri, *Virginia Woolf's Essays: Sketching the Past*, Basingstoke: Macmillan, 2000. 'As an attempt to write social history under the guise of fiction, *Orlando* forms a close couple with *A Room* (1929), Woolf's other main historiographic text' (p. 116).

19 Lisa Rado, *The Modern Androgyne Imagination: A Failed Sublime*, Charlottesville and London: Virginia University Press, 2000, p. 4.

20 Carrol Smith Rosenberg has argued that *Orlando* 'lampoons the sexologists' obsessive linking of cross-dressing and biological determinism', in Ellen Carol Jones, 'Figural Desire in *Orlando*', *Virginia Woolf: Emerging Perspectives*, pp. 108–14, at p. 109.

21 Makiko Minow-Pinkney, *Virginia Woolf and the Problem of the Subject: Feminine Writing in the Major Novels*, Brighton: Harvester Press, 1987, p. 131. Catharine R. Stimpson also describes Vita Sackville-West as 'a sequential rather than a simultaneous androgyne', in 'The Androgyne and the Homosexual', *Where the Meanings Are*, New York and London: Methuen, 1988, p. 56.

22 Hermione Lee, *Virginia Woolf*, London: Chatto & Windus, p. 510.

23 Ibid., p. 511.

24 Woolf, 3 February 1927, *Diary*, Vol. 3.

25 23 October 1929, ibid.

26 In Victoria Glendinning, *Vita: The Life of V. Sackville-West*, Harmondsworth: Penguin, 1984, p. 242.
27 Mary Campbell to Vita Sackville-West, 10 November 1932, cited ibid., p. 253.
28 Ibid., p. 286.
29 Ibid., p. 405.
30 Freud returned to this view, first rehearsed in 'The Sexual Theories of Children', in one of his case studies, the 'Psychogenesis of the Case of Homosexuality in a Woman' (1920–22), in which he argued that 'every human being oscillates all through his life between heterosexual and homosexual feelings, and any frustration or disappointment in the one direction is apt to drive him over into the other' (Standard Edition, Vol. XVIII, p. 158). Edward Carpenter similarly characterised the Uranian temperament in 'The Place of the Uranian in Society' (in *The Intermediate Sex*): 'the Uranian temperament (probably from the very fact of its dual nature and the swift and constant interaction between its masculine and feminine elements) is exceedingly sensitive and emotional' (p. 109).
31 D.H. Lawrence, *Fantasia of the Unconscious*, New York: Thomas Selzer, 1922, p. 87.
32 Sarah Annes Brown, *The Metamorphoses of Ovid: From Chaucer to Ted Hughes*, London: Duckworth, 1999, see esp. 'Intertextuality: Virginia Woolf's *Orlando*', pp. 201–16. I am grateful to Liz Hodson for pointing this reference out to me.
33 Ibid., p. 205.
34 20 December 1927, *Diary*.
35 22 March 1928, *Diary*.
36 Nancy, in Bryher's *Two Selves*, p. 46, also longs for liberation from the present age and to return to the clarity of the Elizabethans.
37 Carl Jung, 'Anima and Animus', in *Aspects of the Feminine*, trans. R.F.C. Hull, London and New York: Ark, 1989, p. 99.
38 Isobel Armstrong, *The Radical Aesthetic*, Oxford: Blackwell, 2000, p. 239.
39 Maria di Battista, *Virginia Woolf's Major Novels: The Fables of Anon*, New Haven, CT and London: Yale University Press, 1980, p. 129.
40 See Rado, *The Modern Androgyne Imagination*, who argues that to confront the body is to evade or dislodge the safe refuge of a disembodied androgyny; and Makiko Minow-Pinkney, who suggests that 'he projects on to her his *own* sexuality, from which he then recoils', *Virginia Woolf and the Problem of the Subject: Feminine Writings in the Major Novels*, Brighton: Harvester Press, 1987, p. 124.
41 Krafft-Ebing, Case Study 129, 'The autobiography of a transsexual', *Psychopathia Sexualis*, pp. 130–1.
42 *The Schreber Case*, p. 34.
43 'Ironically, Freud's psychoanalytic story of the development of heterosexual femininity parallels Orlando's in that it involves a passage through an initial period identical with boyhood before this is lost with the turn towards what will become femininity. Femininity for Orlando is the point of opening up from which places and identities come to be more mobile, and this outcome could be inferred from Freud's account; he states for instance that 'in the course of some women's lives there is a repeated alternation between periods in which masculinity or femininity gains the upper

hand'. Rachel Bowlby, ed., *Orlando*, Oxford: Oxford University Press, 1992, pp. lxiv–xlv. See also Karen Lawrence: 'The Freudian pre-Oedipal child is bisexual; the little girl a little man until she "falls" into sexual division, a trajectory comically revised in Orlando's psycho-sexual development', *Modern Fiction Studies*, 38:1, 1992, pp. 253–77, at p. 255.

44 Ibid., p. 269.

45 'The Psychogenesis of the Case of Homosexuality in a Woman', p. 384.

46 See also Rosemary Dinnage's Introduction to *The Schreber Case*: 'One has to agree with Jung that as an interpretation this was very limited ...When Schreber in his isolation began to believe that the whole world had been devastated, with only himself chosen by God to repopulate the world from his womb, he was surely representing his own life's devastation rather than expressing a homosexual wish' (p. xiv).

47 Suzanne Young, 'The Unnatural Object of Modernist Aesthetics: Artifice in *Orlando*', in *Unmanning Modernism: Gendered Re-Readings*, ed. Elizabeth Jane Harrison and Shirley Peterson, Knoxville: The University of Tennessee Press, 1997, p. 172.

48 Virginia Woolf, *Women and Fiction: The Manuscript Versions of A Room of One's Own*, ed. S.P. Rosenbaum, Oxford: Blackwell, 1992.

49 Ibid., p. 145.

50 Nigel Nicolson, *Portrait of a Marriage*, London: Weidenfeld & Nicolson, 1973, p. 212.

51 Karen Lawrence, 'Orlando's Voyage Out', *Modern Fiction Studies*, 38:1, 1992, p. 271. See also di Battista, 'To be nature's bride is the radical solution espoused by the Romantic and solitary imagination. To be wed and accept marriage as the final feminine destiny is emblematic of an authentic cultural impasse generated by the contradictions inherent in the spirit of the nineteenth century, an impasse she circumvents through the marriage to the androgynous Shel' (*Virginia Woolf's Major Novels*, p. 138).

52 Vita Sackville-West to Virginia Woolf, 11 October 1928, *The Letters of Vita Sackville-West to Virginia Woolf*, ed. Louise de Salvo and Mitchell Leaska.

53 See also Young: 'The gap between language and "reality" represents the (multiply signifying) gap between costume and the body it covers. Each costume/sex change in *Orlando* in turn stands for the ultimate indeterminacy of language', 'The Unnatural Object of Modernist Aesthetics: Artifice in Woolf's *Orlando*', p. 175.

54 Pierre Bourdieu, *The Field of Cultural Production*, p. 34, cited in Armstrong *The Radical Aesthetic*, p. 154.

55 Nancy L. Paxton, *George Eliot and Herbert Spencer: Feminism, Evolutionism, and the Reconstruction of Gender*, Princeton, NJ: Princeton University Press, 1991, p. 17.

4 The Second Wave

1 Ellen Piel Cook, *Psychological Androgyny*, Oxford: Pergammon, 1985, p. 15.

2 Ibid., p. 2.

3 Barbara Charlesworth Gelpi, 'The Politics of Androgyny', *Women's Studies* 2, 1974, p. 150.

4   A.J.L. Busst, 'The Myth of the Androgyne in the Nineteenth Century', in
    Ian Fletcher (ed.), *Romantic Mythologies*, London: Routledge & Kegan Paul,
    1967, p. 1.
5   Catharine R. Stimpson, 'The Androgyne and the Homosexual', in *Where
    the Meanings Are*, New York and London: Methuen, 1988, p. 54.
6   June Singer, *Androgyny: The Opposites Within*, Boston: Sigo Press, 1976,
    p. 11.
7   Grace Tiffany, *Erotic Beasts and Social Monsters: Shakespeare, Jonson and
    Comic Androgyny*, Newark: University of Delaware, 1985, p. 13.
8   Singer, *Androgyny*, p. 199.
9   Cook, *Psychological Androgyny*, p. 2.
10 Mary Daly, *Beyond God the Father: Towards a Philosophy of Women's
    Liberation* London: The Women's Press, 1973, p. 26.
11 Diane Long Hoeveler, *Romantic Androgyny: The Women Within*, University
    Park and London: Pennsylvania State University Press, 1990.
12 Singer *Androgyny*, p. 199.
13 Catriona MacLeod, *Embodying Ambiguity: Androgyny and Aesthetics from
    Winckelmann to Keller*, Detroit: Wayne State University Press, 1998, p. 16.
14 Carolyn Heilbrun, *Towards a Recognition of Androgyny*, New York and
    London: Harper and Row, 1973, p. 58. Woolf claimed in *A Room of One's
    Own* that whatever Coleridge meant, he did not mean that the androgynous
    mind was one 'that has any special sympathy with women'.
15 Kari Weil, *Androgyny and the Denial of Difference*, Charlottesville and
    London: University of Virginia Press, 1992, p. 149.
16 Heilbrun wanted to distance androgyny from homosexuality, bisexuality
    and hermaphroditism, but it is interesting to compare Daniel Harris's cri-
    tique of androgyny in 'Androgyny: The Sexist Myth in Disguise', special
    issue 'The Androgyny Papers', *Women's Studies* 2, 1974: 'The habit of
    demeaning men by comparing them with women, the blatant contempt
    for women which that comparison involves, Lucian's implicit equation
    between androgyny and impotence (with its corresponding apotheosis of
    male fertility), and the bias against homosexuality and lesbianism: these
    are the basic constituents of the androgynous tradition', p. 174.
17 Ibid., p. 118.
18 Ibid., p. xii.
19 Andrea Dworkin, *Woman Hating*, New York: Plume Books, p. 162.
20 Carolyn Heilbrun, 'Further Notes Toward a Recognition of Androgyny',
    Women's Studies 2, 1974, p. 144. Other contributors to the 1974 volume,
    notably Daniel Harris and Catharine Stimpson, noted the historical (and
    pejorative) associations of androgyny with homosexuality.
21 Shulamith Firestone, *The Dialectic of Sex: The Case for Feminist Revolution*,
    London: Women's Press, 1979, p. 200.
22 Daly, *Beyond God the Father*, p. 190.
23 Cynthia Secor, 'The Androgyny Papers', *Women's Studies* 2, 1974, p. 141.
24 Harris, 'Androgyny Papers: The Sexist Myth in Disguise', p. 173.
25 Camille Paglia, *The Yale Review* LXII:4, 1973, p. viii. The review is
    unsigned, but Paglia cited it in a recent correspondence in *The Chronicle
    of Higher Education* to support an argument about the longevity of her
    career as an outspoken feminist critic. 'A good illustration of my position

was my blisteringly negative review, published in the Summer 1973 issue of "The Yale Review", of Carolyn Heilbrun's feminist book, "Toward a Recognition of Androgyny." There I spoke of Heilbrun's "muddled, naively sentimental view of human nature," and I called her book "so poorly researched that it may disgrace the subject in the eyes of serious scholars."' http://chronicle.com/letters/98/06/980617041.shtml

26   Although it is worth considering Secor's criticism, that the feminised male suggested 'the perfect marriage in which the female has been acquired by the male in order to complete himself'. 'The Androgyny Papers', p. 166.

27   Heilbrun was, though, curiously adamant that androgyny was not commensurate with feminism: 'In discussing androgyny and the novel, one is under the necessary and difficult restraint of not confusing androgyny with feminism. The confusion is almost inevitable because the anti-androgynous temper against which the great novels were written is also the temper against which the fighters for women's rights raged.' Carolyun Heilbrun, *Towards a Recognition of Androgyny*, New York and London: Harper and Row, 1973, p. 58. Cook reinforced Heibrun in *Psychological Androgyny*: 'androgyny is *not* synonymous with: (a) economic or sexual emancipation, (b) the absence of any sex-role differentiation, or (c) physical hermaphroditism or bisexuality', p. 19.

28   Heilbrun, ibid., p. 127.

29   Ibid., p. x. Singer echoes this almost verbatim: 'Androgyny has the power to liberate the individual from the confines of the "appropriate".' *Androgyny: The Opposites Within*, p. 11.

30   This position would be overturned by Julia Kristeva in 'Women's Time', where the dichotomous relation of men and women was rejected precisely for being 'metaphysical' – 'the very dichotomy man/woman as an opposition between two rival entities may be understood as belonging to *metaphysics*.' And she goes on to wonder, 'What can "identity," even "sexual identity," mean in a new theoretical and scientific space where the very notion of identity is challenged?' 'Women's Time', cited in Toril Moi, *Sexual/Textual Politics*, London: Methuen, 1989, pp. 12–13.

31   Daly, *Beyond God the Father*, p. 41.

32   Paglia didn't reject androgyny, but she did suggest that it had ceased to satisfy: 'Androgyny, the promise of the Seventies, has ceased to satisfy, as each sex searches for its lost identity.' 'What a Drag: Vested Interests: Cross-Dressing and Cultural Anxiety', in *Sex, Art and American Culture*, Harmondsworth: Penguin, 1977, p. 99.

33   The village of My Lai was the scene of a massacre of over 300 Vietnamese civilians by American troops on 16 March 1968. At Kent State University, four students, Allison Krause, Jeffrey Miller, Sandra Scheuer and William Schroeder, were killed and nine other students were injured when the National Guard opened fire on a student protest demonstration against the Vietnam War, on 4 May 1970.

34   Daly, *Beyond God the Father*, p. 42.

35   Paglia suggested that 'Her definition of androgyny is so idiosyncratic as to be nearly useless. Indeed, her terminology shifts fuzzily from page to page.' *Yale Review*, p. viii. Paglia is less idiosyncratic in her impressively

wide-ranging study, but not above 'invent[ing] a special category of the androgyne' (for example, 'the Venus Barbata' to denote 'strident termagants', *Sexual Personae*, p. 291).

36 Warren appears to be citing Heilbrun: 'What is important now is that we free ourselves from the prison of gender and, before it is too late, deliver the world from the almost exclusive control of the masculine impulse.' *Towards a Recognition of Androgyny*, p. xiv. See also Daly: 'The feminist movement is potentially the source of real movement in the other revolutionary movements (such as Black Liberation and the Peace Movement), for it is the catalyst that enables men and women to break out of the prison of self-destructive dichotomies perpetuated by the institutional father.' *Beyond God the Father*, p. 190.

37 Mary Anne Warren, in Mary Vetterling-Braggin, *'Femininity', 'Masculinity', and 'Androgyny': A Modern Philosophical Discussion*, New Jersey: Littlefield, Adam and Co., 1982, p. 170.

38 Dworkin, *Woman Hating*, p. 175.

39 Daly, *Beyond God the Father*, p. 15. See also Dworkin: '[Androgyny] may be the one road to freedom open to women, men, and that emerging majority, the rest of us.' *Woman Hating*, p. 154.

40 Joyce Trebilcot, 'Two Forms of Androgynism' (1974), in Vetterling-Braggin, *'Femininity', 'Masculinity', and 'Androgyny'*, p. 165.

41 Ibid.

42 Daly, *Beyond God the Father*, p. 158.

43 Margot Hentoff, 'Growing up Androgynous', *New York Review of Books*, 9 May 1968, pp. 32–3.

44 Maria Montez made *The Siren of Atlantis* in 1948.

45 Catharine R. Stimpson, 'My O My O Myra', in Jay Parini, ed., *Gore Vidal: Writer Against the Grain*, London: André Deutsch, 1992, p. 192.

46 Heilbrun, 'Further Notes Towards a Recognition of Androgyny', p. 149.

47 Dworkin, *Woman Hating*, p. 186.

48 See Mary Anne Warren: 'Once the old stereotypes of femininity and masculinity have thoroughly broken down, and people find it bizarre to speak of rationality as masculine or intuition as feminine, the concept of psychological androgyny will have served its purpose', in Vetterling-Braggin, *'Femininity', 'Masculinity', and 'Androgyny'*, p. 182.

49 Daly, *Beyond God the Father*, pp. 105–6.

50 Cook, *Psychological Androgyny*, p. 23.

51 Ibid., p. 33.

52 MacLeod, *Embodying Ambiguity*, p. 16.

53 Heilbrun, 'Further Notes Toward a Recognition of Androgny', p. 149.

54 Gelpi, 'The Politics of Androgyny', p. 157.

55 Ibid., p. 159.

56 Harris, 'Androgyny', p. 173; Nancy Topping Bazin and Alma Freeman, 'The Androgynous Vision', *Women's Studies* 2, 1974, p. 187.

57 Cynthia Secor, 'The Androgyny Papers', Women's Studies 2, 1974, p. 163.

58 Ibid.

59 Topping Bazin and Freeman, 'The Androgynous Vision', p. 185.

60 Dworkin, *Woman Hating*, pp. 184–5.

61 Jan Morris, *Conundrum*, London: Penguin, 1997, p. 95.

62 Stimpson, 'The Androgyne and the Homosexual', p. 242.

63 'It poses no practicable alternative to contemporary society, since it is based on an imaginary, radical change in human anatomy. All it tries to do is open up an alternative viewpoint ... The most it says is, I think, something like this: if we were socially ambisexual, if men and women were completely and genuinely equal in their social roles, equal legally and economically, equal in freedom, in responsibility, and in self-esteem, then society would be a very different thing.' 'Is Gender Necessary?' p. 146.

64 Harold Bloom, ed., *Ursula K. Le Guin's The Left Hand of Darkness*, New York and Philadelphia: Chelsea House Publishers, 1987, p. 9.

65 Ursula K. Le Guin, Introduction to *The Left Hand of Darkness*, reprinted in *The Language of the Night: Essays on Fantasy and Fiction*, London: The Women's Press, 1989.

66 Ursula K. Le Guin, 'Is Gender Necessary?' in ibid., p. 137.

67 Ibid.

68 Ibid., p. 136.

69 Ibid.

70 Ibid., p. 141.

71 Le Guin acknowledged that one of the book's real flaws was the fact that we only ever see Estraven as a man; she was aware that 'the central failure in [Gethenian physiology] comes up in the frequent criticism I receive that the Gethenians seem like *men*, instead of menwomen.' Ibid., pp. 144–5.

72 Ibid., p. 144.

73 Ibid., p. 145.

74 Gelpi, 'The Politics of Androgyny', p. 153.

75 Dworkin, *Woman Hating*, p. 191

76 Ibid., p. 193.

77 In *The Dialectic of Sex* (p. 19) Firestone had argued that the goal of the feminist revolution would be the abolition of sexual difference altogether, and Piercy appears to consider that goal seriously as she casts the androgyne as a redemptive alternative to the iniquitous effects of sexual division in contemporary America.

78 Dworkin, *Woman Hating*, pp. 157–8.

79 The contrast between these uses of the word 'cyborg' merely serves to underline the ambiguity and lack of rigorous definition associated with it. To draw a parallel with androgyny, the word cyborg is used to denote a simple human-machine hybrid and also to evoke, as Haraway does, complex systems of human/technological interface, as if the one word 'androgyny' had to encompass both androgyny *and* hermaphroditism.

80 Lisa Rado, *The Modern Androgyne Imagination: A Failed Sublime*, Charlottesville and London: University of Virginia Press, 2000, p. 185.

81 Secor, 'The Androgyny Papers', p. 163. Stimpson also noted that 'If the homosexual is an outlaw of many cultures, the androgyne is their unicorn.' 'The Androgyne and the Homosexual', p. 242. In context, Stimpson was arguing against the erroneous assumption made by people that the culturally constructed categories of masculinity and femininity were natural, a mistake then compounded by advocates of androgyny

who urged a merging of masculine and feminine characteristics. Whilst the homosexual was 'real', she argued, the androgyne 'is nothing more, or less, than an idea. More accurately, the androgyne is the result of the adding together of two ideas: the idea of the feminine, the idea of the masculine', p. 242.

82 Secor, 'The Androgyny Papers', p. 163.
83 Dworkin, *Woman Hating*, p. 161.
84 Elizabeth Lane Beardsley, 'On Curing Conceptual Confusion: A Response to Mary Anne Warren', in Vetterling-Braggin, *'Femininity', 'Masculinity', and 'Androgyny'*, p. 197.
85 Cook, *Psychological Androgyny*, p. 29. Cook is referring to the work of Spence and Helmreich, and as she points out, those terms are used because the associations are typical. By 1983, Spence stated that masculinity, femininity and androgyny were 'murky, unanalyzed concepts', cited in ibid., p. 31.
86 MacLeod, *Embodying Ambiguity*, p. 16.
87 Daniel Harris, 'Androgyny: The Sexist Myth in Disguise', *Women's Studies* 2, 1974, p. 172.
88 Ibid., p. 175.
89 Showalter, *A Literature of Their Own*, p. 263.
90 Ibid., p. 264.
91 Ibid., 278.
92 Ibid.
93 Ibid., p. 280.
94 Ibid., p. 282.
95 Ibid., p. 287.
96 See also Moi, 'What feminists such as Showalter ... fail to grasp is that the traditional humanism they represent is in effect part of patriarchal ideology. At its centre is the seamlessly unified self – either individual or collective – which is commonly called "Man".' *Sexual/Textual Politics*, p. 8.
97 Ibid., p. 13.
98 Singer, *Androgyny: The Opposites Within*, p. 7.
99 Ute Kauer, 'Narration and Gender: The Role of the First-Person Narrator in Jeanette Winterson's *Written on the Body*', in *'I'm Telling You Stories': Jeanette Winterson and the Politics of Reading*, ed. Helena Grice and Tim Woods, Amsterdam: Rodopi, 1998, p. 41.
100 Chris Straayer, *Deviant Eyes, Deviant Bodies: Sexual Reorientations in Film and Video*, New York: Columbia University Press, 1996, p. 80.
101 Judith Halberstam, *Female Masculinity*, Durham, NC and London: Duke University Press, 1998, p. 57.
102 Catherine Belsey, 'Postmodern Love: Questioning the Metaphysics of Desire', *New Literary History* 25, 1994, p. 687.
103 Lisa Moore, 'Teledildonics: Virtual Lesbians in the Fiction of Jeanette Winterson', in Elizabeth Grosz and Elspeth Moore, eds, *Sexy Bodies: The Strange Carnalities of Feminism*, London: Routledge, 1995, p. 110.
104 Ibid.
105 Hélène Cixous, 'Sorties', in *The Newly Born Woman*, Minneapolis and London: Minnesota University Press, 1986, p. 84.
106 Ibid.

107 Ibid., p. 85.
108 Ibid., p. 72.
109 Morag Shiach, *Hélène Cixous: A Politics of Writing*, London: Routledge, 1991, p. 17.
110 Cixous, 'Sorties', p. 83.
111 Dworkin, *Woman Hating*, p. 187.
112 Firestone, *The Dialectic of Sex*, p. 195.
113 Kate Bornstein, *Gender Outlaw: On Men, Women and the Rest of Us*, London and New York: Routledge, 1994, p. 115.
114 *Transgender Warriors*, p. ix.
115 Ibid., p. x.
116 Jay Prosser, *Second Skins: The Body Narratives of Transsexuality*, New York: Columbia University Press, 1998, p. 182.

5 *Myra Breckinridge* and *The Passion of New Eve*

1 Purvis E. Boyette, '*Myra Breckinridge* and Imitative Form', *Modern Fiction Studies* XVII:2, 1971, p. 236.
2 William Blake's Beulah is the location of an idealised union of the sexes where sexual distinction remains intact; in Eden, sexual distinction has been forgotten. My thanks to Ed Larissy for this point.
2 Bernard F. Dick, *The Apostate Angel: A Critical Study of Gore Vidal*, New York: Random House, 1974, p. 158.
3 Ibid., p. 159.
4 Ibid., p. 157.
5 Ibid., p. 159.
6 Gore Vidal, in *Views from a Window: Conversations with Gore Vidal*, ed. Robert J. Stanton and Gore Vidal, Secanus, NJ: Lyle Stuart Inc, 1980, p. 227.
7 Cynthia Secor, 'The Androgyny Papers', *Women's Studies* 2, 1974, p. 163.
8 Catharine Stimpson, 'My O My O Myra', in Jay Parini, ed., *Gore Vidal: Writer against the Grain*, London: André Deutsch, 1992, p. 196.
9 Susan Sontag, 'Notes on "Camp"', originally published in *Against Interpretation*, the essay was subsequently reprinted in *The Susan Sontag Reader* and all page references are from the *Reader*, p. 108.
10 Ibid., p. 113.
11 Ibid., p. 114.
12 Ibid., p. 113.
13 Ibid., p. 114.
14 Ibid., p. 108.
15 Ibid.
16 Camille Paglia, in *Sexual Personae: Art and Decadence from Nefertiti to Emily Dickinson*, New Haven, CT: Yale University Press, 1990, following Nietzsche, adopted the Apollonian (culture) and Dionysian (nature) as the twin but opposing frames that structure western culture.
17 Angela Carter, 'Angela Carter's Curious Room', *Omnibus*, BBC1, 15 September 1992.
18 Johnson has noted that the narrative shape of *The Passion of New Eve* follows that of alchemical theory, beginning with Leilah, the embodiment

of Chaos; Tristessa's glass house is 'an exaggerated version of the hermetic vessel' and the chymical wedding of Sol and Luna is enacted by Tristessa and Eve. The narrative ends, she notes, with the convergence of the four elements, 'as if fashioning a cosmic diagram'. Heather Johnson, 'Unexpected Geometries: Transgressive Symbolism and the Transsexual Subject in Angela Carter's *The Passion of New Eve*', in *The Infernal Desires of Angela Carter: Fiction, Femininity, Feminism*, ed. Joseph Bristow and Trev Lynn Broughton, London: Longman, 1997, p. 169.

19 M.H. Abrams, *Natural Supernaturalism: Tradition and Revolution in Romantic Literature*, Oxford: Oxford University Press, 1971, p. 160.

20 Ibid.

21 Ibid.

22 Diane Long Hoeveler, *Romantic Androgyny: The Women Within*, University Park and London: Pennsylvania University Press, 1990, p. 11.

23 Alison Lee also points to the role of Tristessa as *femme fatale*; see 'De/En-Gendering Narrative', in *Ambiguous Discourse: Feminist Narratology and British Women Writers*, ed. Kathy Mezei, Chapel Hill: University of North Carolina Press 1996, p. 247.

24 Ibid., p. 246.

25 'And all you signified was false!' (p. 6), 'for when she was in charge of issuing her rare smiles, they came in a code that signified nothing to do with joy' (p. 7). Baudrillard, 'The Precession of Simulacra', p. 2.

26 John Haffenden, *Novelists in Interview*, London: Methuen, 1985, p. 82.

27 Angela Carter, 'Notes from the Front Line', in *Shaking a Leg: Journalism and Writings*, ed. Jenny Uglow, London: Chatto and Windus, 1997, p. 38.

28 Ibid., p. 38.

29 Ibid., p. 38.

30 Paulina Palmer, 'Gender as Performance in the Fiction of Angela Carter and Margaret Atwood', in *Contemporary Women's Fiction: Narrative Practice and Feminist Theory*, pp. 29 and 19. Carter had suggested that 'All the mythic versions of women, from the myth of the redeeming purity of the virgin to that of the healing, reconciling mother, are consolatory nonsenses; and consolatory nonsenses seem to me a fair definition of myth anyway. Mother goddesses are just as silly as a notion as father gods' (Angela Carter, *The Sadeian Woman: An Exercise in Cultural History*, London: Virago, 1979, p. 5).

31 See, for example, Albert Béguin, cited in Hoeveler, *Romantic Androgyny*: 'The myth is like every tragedy a confrontation with the real, an act of confidence in the faculties of transfiguration that man wishes to attribute to himself and his inventions', p. 13.

32 History does repeat itself: when the Children's Crusade capture Eve and Tristessa, they kill Tristessa as Eve 'had no choice but to impotently witness his distress since two soldiers pinioned me, I could not move', p. 155.

33 Carl Jung, *Psychology and Alchemy*, London: Routledge, 1953, p. 227.

34 Carter, *The Sadeian Woman*, p. 4,

35 In the Jewish Kabbalistic *Zohar*, Lilith was created equally as Adam's first wife, rather than being derived from him to complement him as his 'other' as in Genesis.

36 See, for example, Palmer: 'This identity, Carter implies, represents the "true self"; the former is dismissed as mere play-acting.' 'Gender as Performance

in the Fiction of Angela Carter and Margaret Atwood', p. 29. Linden Peach suggests of Tristessa that she was 'both an affirmation and a denial of femininity for in her masquerade as Woman she implied that femininity was a mask that could be taken off'. *Angela Carter*, p. 115.

37 Christina Britzolakis, 'Angela Carter's Fetishism', *Textual Practices* 9:3, 1995, p. 467.

38 Lyndy Abraham, *Dictionary of Alchemical Imagery*, Cambridge: Cambridge University Press, 1998.

39 Ibid. See also Johnson: 'Tristessa's glass house is an exaggerated version of the hermetic vessel as a 'spherical or circular house of glass', 'Transgressive Symbolism and the Transsexual Subject', p. 169.

40 Jung, *Psychology and Alchemy*, p. 37.

41 'The Wound in the Face', *New Society*, 1975, p. 91, reprinted in *Nothing Sacred: Selected Writings*.

42 Ibid.

43 In *'Campe-Toi!* On the Origins and Definitions of Camp', Mark Booth argues that camp and kitsch are distinct: 'Kitsch is one of camp's favourite fads and fancies.' Reprinted in *Camp: Queer Aesthetics and the Performing Subject*, ed. Fabio Cleto, Edinburgh: Edinburgh University Press, 1999, p. 70.

44 Judith Butler, *Gender Trouble: Feminism and the Subversion of Identity*, London and New York: Routledge, 1990, p. 103.

45 Merja Makinen, 'Sexual and Textual Aggression in *The Sadeian Woman* and *The Passion of New Eve*', in Bristow and Brougton, eds, *The Infernal Desires of Angela Carter*, p. 158.

46 Paulina Palmer, *Contemporary Women's Fiction: Narrative Practice and Feminist Theory*, Jackson and London: University of Mississippi Press, 1989, p. 19.

47 Paulina Palmer, 'Gender as Performance in the fiction of Angela Carter and Margaret Atwood', in *The Infernal Desires of Angela Carter: Fiction, Femininity, Feminism*, ed. Joseph Bristow and Trev Lynn Broughton, p. 30. Susan Sontag reinforced Garbo as androgyne in 'Notes on "Camp"', *The Sontag Reader*, describing 'the haunting androgynous vacancy behind the perfect beauty of Greta Garbo', p. 108.

48 See Jung: 'It is worth noting that the male unicorn is called *ch'i* and the female *lin*, so that the generic term is formed by the union of both characters (*ch'i-lin*). The unicorn is thus endowed with an androgynous quality', *Psychology and Alchemy*, p. 466. Johnson argues that 'the figure of the unicorn has also been associated with a penetrative, phallic masculine identity': 'Unexpected Geometries: Transgressive Symbolism and the Transsexual Subject in Angela Carter's *The Passion of New Eve*', p. 178.

49 Lindsay Clarke, *The Chymical Wedding*, Basingstoke and Oxford: Picador, 1990, p. 298.

50 See, for example, Britzolakis, who argues that the 'figure of Tristessa resolves itself when Tristessa and Eve are united, into the mythic figure of the Platonic androgyne'. 'Angela Carter's Fetishism', p. 467. In 'Unexpected Geometries', Johnson cites Susan Suleiman, *Subversive Intent: Gender, Politics and the Avant-Garde*, and Olga Kenyon, *Writing Women: Contemporary Women Novelists*, as examples of critics who have also read this scene as positive and redemptive. Lee, focusing on the rebirth of Eve at the end of

her narrative, argues that 'There is no return to the womb as fulfilment and no harmonious concatenation of opposites; the novel does not suggest androgyny as a satisfactory alternative.' 'De/En-Gendering Narrative', p. 246.

51 Johnson has read this positively: 'The relocation of the chimerical, the hermaphroditic, within the realm of possibility, as a source of origin and a site for pleasure, is written in the bodies of these two characters.' 'Textualising the Double-Gendered Body', p. 133.

52 Lee, 'De/En-Gendering Narrative', p. 240.

53 A similar point is made in Lindsay Clarke's *The Chymical Wedding*: Edward tells Alex that alchemical symbols are 'symbols for what cannot be said – only experienced', p. 155.

54 In alchemy, the philosopher's stone passes through four different colours: black (nigredo), white (albedo), yellow (citrinitas) and red (rubedo). Red and white, Jung says, 'are King and Queen who may celebrate their "chymical wedding" at this stage', *Psychology and Alchemy*, p. 232.

55 Abraham, *Dictionary of Alchemical Imagery*.

56 Paglia, *Sexual Personae*, p. 198.

57 Jung, *Psychology and Alchemy*, p. 293.

58 Ibid., p. 227.

59 Ibid., p. 228.

60 Johnson, 'Unexpected Geometries', p. 169.

61 Catharine Stimpson, 'The Androgyne and the Homosexual', in *Where the Meanings Are*, New York and London, Methuen, 1988, p. 242.

62 Francette Pacteau, 'The Impossible Referent: Representations of Androgyny', in Victor Burgin et al., eds, *Formations of Fantasy*, London and New York: Routledge, 1986.

6   Alchemy and *The Chymical Wedding*

1 Carl Jung, *Psychology and Alchemy*, London: Routledge, 1953, p. 37.

2 H. Stanley Redgrove, *Alchemy: Ancient and Modern*, London: William Rider & Son, second edition 1922, p. 2.

3 Lyndy Abraham, *Dictionary of Alchemical Imagery*, Cambridge: Cambridge University Press, 1998, p. 37.

4 Ibid.

5 M.H. Abrams, *Natural Supernaturalism: Tradition and Revolution in Romantic Literature*, Oxford: Oxford University Press, 1971, p. 159.

6 Jung, *Psychology and Alchemy*, p. 227.

7 Ibid., p. 37.

8 Ibid. 'Hermetic' philosophy takes its name from Hermes Trismegistos, regarded as the founder of alchemy, and probably a mythical figure.

9 Daniel Harris, 'Androgyny: The Sexist Myth in Disguise', in 'The Androgyny Papers', *Women's Studies* 2, 1974, pp. 175–6.

10 Dorn, a Renaissance alchemist, wanted to transform the four elements back into the original one.

Bibliography

Abraham, Lyndy, *Dictionary of Alchemical Imagery*, Cambridge: Cambridge University Press, 1998

Abrams, M.H., *Natural Supernaturalism: Tradition and Revolution in Romantic Literature*, Oxford: Oxford University Press, 1971

Achtelstetter, Karin, 'Virginia Woolf and Androgyny', *University of Kent at Canterbury Women's Studies Occasional Papers*.

Andersen, Wayne, 'Leonardo and the Slip of Fools,' *History of European Ideas* 18:1 1994, pp. 61–78

Andersen, Wayne, *Freud, Leonardo da Vinci, and the Vulture's Tail: A Refreshing Look at Leonardo's Sexuality*, New York: Other Press, 2001

Armstrong, Isobel, *The Radical Aesthetic*, Oxford: Blackwell, 2000

Babuscio, Jack, 'Camp and the Gay Sensibility', in *Gays and Film*, ed. Richard Dyer, London: British Film Institute, 1997, pp. 40–57

Barash, Carol, 'Virile Womanhood: Olive Schreiner's Narratives of a Master Race', in Elaine Showalter, ed., *Speaking of Gender*, New York and London: Routledge 1989, pp. 269–81

Barrett, Michèle, *Virginia Woolf: Women and Writing*, London: The Women's Press, 1979

Baudrillard, Jean, *Simulacra and Simulation*, trans. Sheila Faria Glaser, Michigan: University of Michigan Press, 1994

Bazin, Nancy Topping, *Virginia Woolf and the Androgynous Vision*, New Jersey: Rutgers University Press, 1973

Becket, Fiona, *D.H. Lawrence: the Thinker as Poet*, Basingstoke: Macmillan, 1997

Beer, Gillian, *Virginia Woolf: The Common Ground*, Edinburgh: Edinburgh University Press, 1996

Bell, Michael, *D.H. Lawrence: Language and Being*, Cambridge: Cambridge University Press, 1992

Berkman, Joyce, *The Healing Imagination of Olive Schreiner: Beyond South African Colonialism*, Massachusetts: University of Massachusetts Press, 1989

Birmele, Jutta, 'Strategies of Persuasion: The Case of *Leonardo da Vinci*', in Sander L. Gilman et al., ed., *Reading Freud's Reading*, New York and London: New York University Press, 1994, pp. 129–51

Black, Michael, *D.H. Lawrence: The Early Philosophical Works: A Commentary* Basingstoke: Macmillan, 1991

Bloch, Iwan, *The Sexual Life of Our Times in its Relations to Modern Civilization*, trans. from the sixth German edition M. Eden Paul, London: Rebman Limited, 1908

Bloom, Harold, ed., *Ursula K. Le Guin's The Left Hand of Darkness*, New York and Philadelphia: Chelsea House Publishers, 1987

Boas, George, trans., *The Hieroglyphics of Horapollo*, Princeton, NJ: Princeton University Press, 1993

Bornstein, Kate, *Gender Outlaw: On Men, Women and the Rest of Us*, London and New York: Routledge, 1994

Bourke, Joanna, *Dismembering the Male: Men's Bodies, Britain and the Great War*, London: Reaktion Books, 1996

Bowen, Elizabeth, 'Orlando by Virginia Woolf' (1960), in The *Mulberry Tree*, ed. Hermione Lee, London: Virago, 1986, pp. 131–6

Bowlby, Rachel, ed., *Orlando*, Oxford: Oxford University Press, 1992

Boxwell, D.A., '(Dis)Orienting Spectacle: The Politics of *Orlando*'s Sapphic Camp', *Twentieth Century Literature* 3:44, 1998, pp. 306–27

Boyette, Purvis E., '*Myra Breckinridge* and Imitative Form', *Modern Fiction Studies* XVII:2, 1971, pp. 229–38

Brenkman, John, 'The Other and the One: Psychoanalysis, Reading, the *Symposium*', *Yale French Studies* 55/56, 1977, pp. 396–456

Brisson, Luc, *Sexual Ambivalence: Androgyny and Hermaphroditism in Graeco-Roman Antiquity*, Berkeley: California University Press, 2002

Bristow, Joe and Trev Lynn Broughton, eds, *The Infernal Desires of Angela Carter: Fiction, Femininity, Feminism*, London and New York: London, 1997

Britzolakis, Christina, 'Angela Carter's Fetishism', *Textual Practice* 9:3, 1995, pp. 459–75

Brown, Sarah Annes, *The Metamorphoses of Ovid: From Chaucer to Ted Hughes*, London: Duckworth, 1999

Brown, Tony, ed., *Edward Carpenter and Late Victorian Radicalism*, London: Frank Cass, 1990

Bryher (Winifred Ellerman), *The Heart to Artemis: A Writer's Memoir*, London: Collins, 1963

Bryher, *Two Selves* (1923), France: Contact Publishing Co., 1966

Burdett, Carolyn, *Olive Schreiner and the Progress of Feminism: Evolution, Gender and Empire*, Basingstoke: Palgrave, 2001

Busst, A.J.L., 'The Image of the Androgyne in the Nineteenth Century', in Ian Fletcher, ed., *Romantic Mythologies*, London: Routledge and Kegan Paul, 1967, pp. 1–86

Butler, Judith, *Gender Trouble: Feminism and the Subversion of Identity*, London and New York: Routledge, 1990

Carpenter, Edward, *Love's Coming-of-Age*, Manchester: Labour Press, 1897

Carpenter, Edward, *The Intermediate Sex*, London: George Allen & Co., 1912

Carpenter, Edward, *Intermediate Types Among Primitive Folk*, London: George Allen, 1914

Carpenter, Edward, *My Days and Dreams,* London: Allen & Unwin, 1916

Carter, Angela, *The Infernal Desire Machine of Doctor Hoffman*, Harmondsworth: Penguin, 1972

Carter, Angela, *The Passion of New Eve*, London: Virago, 1977

Carter, Angela, *The Sadeian Woman: An Exercise in Cultural History*, London: Virago, 1979

Carter, Angela, *Nothing Sacred: Selected Writings*, London: Virago, 1982

Carter, Angela, *Shaking a Leg: Journalism and Writings*, ed. Jenny Uglow, London: Chatto and Windus, 1997

Castle, Terry, *Noel Coward and Radclyffe Hall: Kindred Spirits*, New York: Columbia University Press, 1996

Chauncey George, *Gay New York: Gender, Urban Culture and the Making of the Gay Male World 1890–1940*, New York: HarperCollins, 1994

Chrisman, Laura, 'Allegory, Feminist Thought and the Dreams of Olive Schreiner', in Tony Brown, ed., *Edward Carpenter and Late Victorian Radicalism*, London: Frank Cass, 1990, pp. 126–50

Cixous, Hélène and Catherine Clément, *The Newly Born Woman*, Minneapolis and London: University of Minnesota Press, 1986

Cleto, Fabio, ed., *Camp: Queer Aesthetics and the Performing Subject*, Edinburgh: Edinburgh University Press, 1999

Coleridge, Samuel Taylor, *Specimens of the Table Talk of the Late Samuel Taylor Coleridge*, Vol. II, London, 1835

Collecott, Diana, *HD and Sapphic Modernism 1910–1950*, Cambridge: Cambridge University Press, 1999

Cook, Ellen Piel, *Psychological Androgyny*, Oxford: Pergammon, 1985

Corke, Helen, *Neutral Ground: A Chronicle*, London: Arthur Baker, 1933

Daly, Mary, *Beyond God the Father: Towards a Philosophy of Women's Liberation*, London: The Women's Press, 1973

Daly, Mary, *Gyn/Ecology: The Meta-Ethics of Radical Feminism*, London: The Women's Press, 1979

Delavenay Emile, *D.H. Lawrence and Edward Carpenter: A Study in Edwardian Transition*, London: Heinemann, 1971

Dellamora, Richard, *Masculine Desire: The Sexual Politics of Victorian Aestheticism*, Chapel Hill and London: University of North Carolina Press, 1990

de Salvo, Louise and Mitchell Leaska, *The Letters of Vita Sackville-West to Virginia Woolf*, London: Hutchinson, 1984

di Battista, Maria, *Virginia Woolf's Major Novels: The Fables of Anon*, New Haven, CT and London: Yale University Press, 1980

Dick, Bernard F., *The Apostate Angel: A Critical Study of Gore Vidal*, New York: Random House, 1974

Dijkstra, Bram, 'The Androgyne in Nineteenth Century Art and Literature', *Comparative Literature* 26, 1974, pp. 62–73

Dijkstra, Bram, *Idols of Perversity: Fantasies of Feminine Evil in Fin-de-Siècle Culture*, New York and Oxford: Oxford University Press, 1986

Doan, Laura, *Fashioning Sapphism: The Origins of a Modern English Lesbian Culture*, New York: Columbia University Press, 2001

Doan, Laura and Jay Prosser, eds, *Palatable Poison Critical Perspectives on The Well of Loneliness*, New York: Columbia University Press, 2001

Doniger, Wendy, *Women, Androgynes, and Other Mythical Beasts*, Chicago and London: University of Chicago Press, 1980

Dover, Kenneth, 'Aristophanes' Speech in Plato's *Symposium*', *Journal of Hellenic Studies* 86, 1966, p. 42

Dowling, Linda, *Hellenism and Homosexuality in Victorian Oxford*, Ithaca, NY and London: Cornell University Press, 1994

Draper, R.P., ed., *D.H. Lawrence: The Critical Heritage*, London: Routledge and Kegan Paul, 1970

Dworkin, Andrea, *Woman Hating*, New York: Plume Books, 1974

Easton, Alison, ed., *Angela Carter: Contemporary Critical Essays*, Basingstoke: Macmillan, 2000

Eisenberg, Davina, *The Figure of the Dandy in Barbey d'Aurevilly's 'Le bonheur de crime'*, New York: Peter Lang, 1996

Eisner, Douglas, 'Myra Breckinridge and the Pathology of Heterosexuality', in Patricia Juliana Smith, ed., *The Queer Sixties*, New York and London: Routledge, 1999, pp. 255–70

Eliade, Mircea, *The Two and the One*, trans. J.M. Cohen, London: Harvill Press, 1965

Ellis, Havelock, *Studies in the Psychology of Sex*, Vol. II, Philadelphia: F.H. Davies third edition 1917

Ellman, Richard, *Oscar Wilde*, London: Hamish Hamilton, 1987

Epstein, Julia, *Altered Conditions: Disease, Medicine and Story Telling*, London and New York: Routledge, 1995

Eugenides, Jeffrey, *Middlesex*, London: Bloomsbury, 2002

Faithfull, Theodor J., *Bisexuality: An Essay on Extraversion and Introversion*, London: John Bale, Sons, and Danielsson, 1927

Faithfull, Theodor J., *Plato and the New Psychology*, London: John Bale, Sons, and Daniellson, 1928

Faithfull, Theodor J. *The Mystery of the Androgyne: Three Papers on the Theory and Practice of Psycho-Analysis*, London: Forum Publishing Company, 1938

Farwell, Marilyn, 'Virginia Woolf and Androgyny', *Contemporary Literature* 16, 1975, pp. 433–51

Feldman, Paul R. and Diana Scott-Kilvert, *The Journals of Mary Shelley*, Baltimore and London: Johns Hopkins University Press, 1987

Fernihough, Anne, *The Cambridge Companion to D.H. Lawrence*, Cambridge: Cambridge University Press, 2001

Firestone, Shulamith, *The Dialectic of Sex: The Case for Feminist Revolution*, London: Women's Press, 1979

Forel, August, *The Sexual Question: A Scientific, Psychological, Hygienic and Sociological Study*, New York: Physicians and Surgeons Book Company, 1908

Forster, E.M., *Maurice*, Harmondsworth: Penguin, 1985

Forster, Margaret, *Daphne du Maurier*, London: Chatto and Windus, 1993

Foucault, Michel, *The History of Sexuality: An Introduction*, trans. Robert Hurley, Harmondsworth: Penguin, 1990

Freud, Sigmund, 'The Psychogenesis of a Case of Homosexuality in a Woman', *Standard Edition*, Vol. XVIII, London: Hogarth Press, 1955

Freud, Sigmund, 'The Sexual Aberrations' (1905), in *On Sexuality*, Pelican Freud, Vol. 7, Harmondsworth: Penguin, 1987

Freud, Sigmund, 'Leonardo da Vinci and a Memory of His Childhood', in *Art and Literature*, trans. James Strachey, ed. Albert Dickson, The Penguin Freud Library, Vol. 14, London: Penguin, 1990, pp. 143–232

Friedman, Susan Stanford, *Analyzing Freud: Letters of H.D., Bryher, and Their Circle*, New York: New Directions Books, 2002

Fussell, Paul, *The Great War and Modern Memory*, Oxford: Oxford University Press, 1977

Garber, Marjorie, 'Androgyny and Its Discontents', in *Bisexuality and the Eroticism of Everyday Life*, New York: Routledge, 2000, pp. 207–36

Gibbs, Philip, *Realities of War*, London: Heinemann, 1920

Gibson, Margaret, 'Clitoral Corruption, Body Metaphors and American Doctors' Construction of Female Homosexuality 1870–1900', in Vernon A. Rosario, ed., *Science and Homosexualities*, London: Routledge, 1997, pp. 108–29

Gilbert, Sandra and Susan Gubar, *No-Man's Land: The Place of the Woman Writer in the Twentieth Century*, London and New Haven, CT: Yale University Press, 1989

Gillespie, Diane Filby, 'Virginia Woolf's Miss La Trobe: the Artist's Last Struggle against Masculine Values', *Women and Literature* 5:1, 1977, pp. 38–9

Gilman, Sander L., 'Sigmund Freud and the Sexologists: A Second Reading', in Sander L. Gilman et al., eds, *Reading Freud's Reading*, New York and London: New York University Press, 1994

Glendinning, Victoria, *Vita: The Life of V. Sackville-West*, Harmondsworth: Penguin, 1984

Greenway, Judy, 'It's What You Do with it that Counts: Interpretations of Otto Weininger', in Lucy Bland and Laura Doan, eds, *Sexology in Culture: Labelling Bodies and Desires*, Chicago: University of Chicago Press, 1998

Gualtieri, Elena, *Virginia Woolf's Essays: Sketching the Past*, Basingstoke: Macmillan, 2000

Haffenden, John, *Novelists in Interview*, London: Methuen, 1985

Halberstam, Judith, *Female Masculinity*, Durham, NC and London: Duke University Press, 1998

Hamilton, Walter, *The Symposium*, Harmondsworth: Penguin, 1951

Hardy, Thomas, *Tess of the d'Urbervilles*, London: Macmillan, 1974

Harris, Daniel, 'Androgyny: The Sexist Myth in Disguise', in special issue, ' The Androgyny Papers', *Women's Studies* 2, 1974

HD, *Notes on Thought and Vision* and *The Wise Sappho*, London: Peter Owen, 1988

Heath, Stephen, *The Sexual Fix*, London: Macmillan, 1982

Heilbrun, Carolyn, *Towards A Recognition of Androgyny*, New York and London: Harper and Row, 1973

Hentoff, Margot, 'Growing up Androgynous', *New York Review of Books*, 9 May 1968, pp. 32–3

Herrmann, Anne, *Queering the Moderns*, Basingstoke: Palgrave, 2000

Hobman, D.L., *Olive Schreiner: Her Friends and Times*, London: Watts and Co., 1955

Hoeveler, Diane Long, *Romantic Androgyny: The Women Within*, University Park and London: Pennsylvania University Press, 1990

Holmes, Diana, *Rachilde: Decadence: Gender and the Woman Writer*, Oxford and New York: Berg, 2001

Huxley, Aldous, *Point Counter Point*, London: Flamingo, 1994

Huysmans, J.K., *À Rebours*, English trans. *Against Nature*, Harmondsworth: Penguin, 1959

Hyder Clyde K., ed., *Swinburne Replies: Notes on Poems and Reviews*, Syracuse, NY: Syracuse University Press, 1966

Hynes, Samuel, *A War Imagined: The First World War and English Culture*, London: Pimlico, 1990

Johnson, Heather L., 'Unexpected Geometries: Transgressive Symbolism and the Transsexual Subject in Angela Carter's *The Passion of New Eve*', in *The Infernal Desires of Angela Carter: Fiction, Femininity, Feminism*, ed. Joseph Bristow and Trev Lynn Broughton, London: Longman, 1997, pp. 166–83

Johnson, Heather L., 'Textualising the Double-gendered Body: Forms of the Grotesque', in *The Passion of New Eve*, pp. 127–35, cited in Alison Easton, ed., *The New Case Book*, Basingstoke: Macmillan, 2000

Jones, Ellen Carol, 'Figural Desire in *Orlando*', in *Virginia Woolf: Emerging Perspectives Selected Papers from the Third Annual Conference on Virginia Woolf*, ed. Mark Hussey and Vara Neverow, New York: Pace University Press, 1994, pp. 108–14

Joukovsky, Nicholas A., ed., *The Letters of Thomas Love Peacock*, Vol. I, 1792–1827, Oxford: Clarendon Press, 2001

Jowett, Benjamin, *The Dialogues of Plato*, Vol. II, Oxford: Clarendon Press, 1875

Joyce, Michael, *The Collected Dialogues of Plato*, ed. Edith Hamilton and Huntington Cairns, Bollinger Series LXXI, Prnceton, NJ: Princeton University Press, 1963

Jung, Carl, *Psychology and Alchemy*, London: Routledge, 1953

Jung, Carl, 'Anima and Animus', in *Aspects of the Feminine*, trans. R.F.C. Hull London and New York: Ark, 1989, pp. 77–100

Kaplan, Alexandra and Mary Anne Sedney, *Psychology and Sex Roles: An Androgynous Perspective*, New York: Little, Brown, 1980

Kent, Susan Kingsley, *Making Peace: The Reconstruction of Gender in Interwar Britain*, Princeton, NJ: Princeton University Press, 1993

Kiernan, Robert F., *Gore Vidal*, New York: Frederick Ungar Publishing, 1982

Kimbrough, Robert, *Shakespeare and the Art of Humankindness* Englewood Cliffs, NJ: Humanities Press International Inc., 1990

Kincaid-Weeks, Mark, *D.H. Lawrence: Triumph to Exile* Cambridge: Cambridge University Press, 1996

Krafft-Ebing, Richard von, *Psychopathia Sexualis*, trans. Jack Hunter, New York: Creation Books, 1997

Kunzru, Hari, *The Impressionist*, London: Hamish Hamilton, 2002

Lacan, Jacques, *The Four Fundamental Concepts of Psychoanalysis*, ed. Jacques Alain Miller, trans. Alan Sheridan, Harmondsworth: Penguin, 1977

Lawrence, D.H., *Fantasia of the Unconscious*, New York: Thomas Selzer, 1922

Lawrence, D.H., *The Letters and Works of D.H. Lawrence*, Vol. II, June 1913–October 1916, ed. George J. Zytaruk and James T. Boulton, Cambridge: Cambridge University Press, 1981

Lawrence D.H., *The Study of Thomas Hardy and Other Essays*, ed. Bruce Steele, Cambridge: Cambridge University Press, 1985

Lawrence D.H. *Lady Chatterley's Lover*, London: Penguin, 1994

Lawrence D.H., *Women in Love*, London: Penguin, 1995

Lawrence D.H., *The Rainbow*, London: Penguin, 1995

Lawrence D.H., *Studies in Classic American Literature*, ed. Ezra Greenspan, Lindeth Vasey and John Worthen, Cambridge: Cambridge University Press, 2003

Lawrence, Karen, 'Orlando's Voyage Out', *Modern Fiction Studies* 38:1, 1992, pp. 253–77

Ledger, Sally and Roger Luckhurst, eds., *The Fin de Siècle: A Reader in Cultural History c. 1880-1900*, Oxford: Oxford University Press, 2000

Lee, Alison, 'De/En-Gendering Narrative', in *Ambiguous Discourse: Feminist Narratology and British Women Writers*, ed. Kathy Mezei, Chapel Hill: University of North Carolina Press, 1996, pp. 238–49

Lee, Hermione, *Virginia Woolf*, London: Chatto & Windus, 1996

Le Guin, Ursula, ed., *The Language of the Night: Essays on Fantasy and Science Fiction*, London: The Women's Press, 1989

Lind, Earl, *The Autobiography of an Androgyne*, New York: Medico-Legal Journal, 1918

Lokke, Karen Elise, 'Orlando and Incandescence: Virginia Woolf's Comic Sublime', *Modern Fiction Studies* 38:1, 1992, pp. 235–52

Mackworth, Margaret Haig (Vicountess Rhondda), *This Was My World*, London Macmillan and Co., 1933

MacLeod, Catriona, *Embodying Ambiguity: Androgyny and Aesthetics from Winckelmann to Keller*, Detroit: Wayne State University Press, 1998

MacPike, Loralee, 'Is Mary Llewellyn an Invert? The Modernist Supertext of *The Well of Loneliness*', in *Unmanning Modernism: Gendered Re-Readings*, ed. Elizabeth Jane Harrison and Shirley Peterson, Knoxville: The University of Tennessee Press, 1997, pp. 73–89

Majumdar, Robin and Allen McLaurin, *Virginia Woolf: The Critical Heritage* London: Routledge and Kegan Paul, 1975

Makinen, Merja, 'Sexual and Textual Aggression in *The Sadeian Woman* and *The Passion of New Eve*', in Joseph Bristow and Trev Lynn Broughton, eds, *The Infernal Desires of Angela Carter: Fiction, Femininity, Feminism*, London and New York: Longman, 1997

Mannin, Ethel, *Young in the Twenties: A Chapter of Autobiography*, London: Hutchinson, 1971

Marcus, Jane. '"Taking the Bull by the Udders": Sexual Difference in Virginia Woolf – a Conspiracy Theory', in Jane Marcus, ed., *Virginia Woolf and Bloomsbury: A Centenary Celebration*, Bloomington: Indiana University Press, 1987, pp. 146–69

Marcus, Jane, 'Sapphistory: The Woolf and the Well', in Karla Jay and Joanne Glasgow, eds, *Lesbian Texts and Contexts: Radical Revisions*, New York: Onlywomen Press, 1992, pp. 164-178

Marx-Aveling, Edward and Eleanor, *The Woman Question*, London: Swan Sonnenschein, 1886

Mayne, Xavier (pseud.) *The Intersexes: A History of Similisexualism As a Problem in Social Life*, [Rome]: privately printed, 1908

McNichol, Stella *Virginia Woolf and the Poetry of Fiction* London and New York: Routledge 1990

Minow-Pinkney, Makiko, *Virginia Woolf and the Problem of the Subject: Feminine Writing in the Major Novels*, Brighton: Harvester, 1987

Moi, Toril, *Sexual/Textual Politics*, London: Methuen, 1989

Moore, Lisa 'Teledildonics: Virtual Lesbians in the Fiction of Jeanette Winterson', in Elisabeth Grosz and Elspeth Moore, eds, *Sexy Bodies: The Strange Carnalities of Feminism*, London: Routledge, 1995

Morris, Jan *Conundrum*, London: Penguin, 1997

Mure, G.R.G., 'Oxford and Philosophy', *Philosophy* XII, 1937

Nichols, Beverley, *The Sweet and the Twenties*, London: Weidenfeld and Nicolson 1958

Nicolson, Nigel, *Portrait of a Marriage*, London: Weidenfeld & Nicolson, 1973

Nin, Anais, *D.H. Lawrence: An Unprofessional Study*, Chicago: Swallow Press, 1964

Notopoulos, James, *The Platonism of Shelley: A Study of Platonism and the Poetic Mind*, Durham, NC: Duke University Press, 1949

Oosterhuis, Harry, 'Richard von Krafft-Ebing's "Step-Children of Nature": Psychiatry and the Making of Homosexual Identity', in Vernon A. Rosario, ed., *Science and Homosexualities*, London: Routledge, 1997

Pacteau, Francette, 'The Impossible Referent: Representations of the Androgyne', in Victor Burgin et al. ed., *Formations of Fantasy*, London and New York: Routledge, 1986, pp. 62–84

Paglia, Camille, Review of *Towards a Recognition of Androgyny*, *Yale Review* LXII:4, 1973

Paglia, Camille, *Sexual Personae: Art and Decadence from Nefertiti to Emily Dickinson*, New Haven, CT: Yale University Press, 1990

Paglia, Camille *Sex, Art and American Culture*, Harmondsworth: Penguin, 1992

Palmer, Paulina, *Contemporary Women's Fiction: Narrative Practice and Feminist Theory*, Jackson and London: Mississippi University Press, 1989

Parkes, Adam, 'Lesbianism, History and Censorship: *The Well of Loneliness* and the Suppressed RANDINESS of Virginia Woolf's *Orlando*', *Twentieth Century Literature* 40, 1994, pp. 434–60

Pater, Walter, *The Renaissance: Studies in Art and Poetry*, Oxford: Oxford University Press, 1986

Paxton, Nancy L., *George Eliot and Herbert Spencer: Feminism, Evolutionism, and the Reconstruction of Gender*, Princeton, NJ: Princeton University Press, 1991

Peach, Linden, *Angela Carter*, Basingstoke: Macmillan, 1998

Peach, Linden, *Virginia Woolf*, Basingstoke: Macmillan, 2000

Pick, Daniel, *The War Machine: The Rationalisation of Slaughter in the Modern Age* New Haven, CT and London: Yale University Press, 1993

Piggford, George, '"Who's that Girl?": Annie Lennox, Woolf's *Orlando* and Female Camp Androgyny', *Mosaic: A Journal for the Interdisciplinary Study of Literature*, 30:3 September 1997, pp. 39–45

Praz, Mario, *The Romantic Agony*, trans. Angus Davidson, Oxford: Oxford University Press, 1933

Prosser, Jay, *Second Skins: The Body Narratives of Transsexuality*, New York: Columbia University Press, 1998

Rachilde, *Monsieur Vénus*, Cambridge: Dedalus, 1992

Rackin, Phyllis, 'Androgyny, Mimesis, and the Marriage of the Boy Heroine on the English Renaissance Stage', in Elaine Showalter, ed., *Speaking of Gender*, New York and London: Routledge, 1989, pp. 113–33

Rado, Lisa, *The Modern Androgyne Imagination: A Failed Sublime*, Charlottesville and London: University Press of Virginia, 2000

Raitt, Suzanne, *Vita and Virginia: The Work and Friendship of V. Sackville-West and Virginia Woolf*, Oxford: Oxford University Press, 1993

Redgrove, H. Stanley, *Alchemy: Ancient and Modern* (1911), London: William Rider and Son, second edition 1922

Rolfe, Frederick (Baron Corvo), *The Desire and Pursuit of the Whole: A Romance of Modern Venice* (1934), intro. A.J.A. Symons, Foreword Philip Healy, Oxford and New York: Oxford University Press, 1986

Rosario, Vernon A., ed., *Science and Homosexualities*, London: Routledge, 1997

Roth, Philip, *The Human Stain*, London: Vintage, 2001

Rowbotham, Sheila and Jeffrey Weeks, *Socialism and the New Life The Personal and Sexual Politics of Edward Carpenter and Havelock Ellis*, London: Pluto Press, 1977

Rowe, C.J., ed. and intro., *Plato: Symposium*, Warminster: Aris and Phillips, 1998

Sage, Lorna, ed., Introduction, *The Voyage Out*, Harmondsworth: Penguin, 1992

Scher, Arthur, 'Leonardo da Vinci, Sigmund Freud, and Fear of Flying', *Midwest Quarterly: A Journal of Contemporary Thought* 42:2, 2001, pp. 115–32

Schreiner, Olive, *Woman and Labour*, London: Virago, 1978

Secor, Cynthia, 'The Androgyny Papers', *Women's Studies* 2, 1974

Segal, Naomi, *Narcissus and Echo: Women in the French Récit*, Manchester: Manchester University Press, 1988

Shiach, Morag, *Hélène Cixous: A Politics of Writing*, London: Routledge, 1991

Shiach, Morag, ed., *A Room of One's Own*, Oxford: Oxford University Press, 1992

Showalter, Elaine, *A Literature of Their Own: British Women Novelists from Brontë to Lessing*, London: Virago, 1986

Singer, June, *Androgyny: The Opposites Within*, Boston: Sigo Press, 1976

Smith Angela K., *The Second Battlefield: Women, Modernism and the First World War*, Manchester: Manchester University Press, 2000

Snider, Clifton, '"A Single Self": A Jungian Interpretation of Virginia Woolf's *Orlando*', *Modern Fiction Studies* 25, 1979, pp. 263–8

Sontag, Susan, *Against Interpretation and Other Essays*, London: Eyre and Spottiswoode, 1967

Souhami, Diana, *The Trials of Radclyffe Hall*, London: Virago, 1999

Stanton, Robert J and Gore Vidal, *Views from a Window: Conversations with Gore Vidal*, New Jersey: Lyle Stuart Inc., 1980

Stape, J.H., *Orlando*, Oxford: Blackwell, 1998

Steakley James D., '*Per scientiam ad justitiam:* Magnus Hirschfeld and the Sexual Politics of Innate Homosexuality', in Vernon A. Rosario, ed., *Science and Homosexualities*, London: Routledge, 1997, pp. 133–54

Stevens, Hugh and Caroline Howlett, eds, *Modernist Sexualities*, Manchester: Manchester University Press, 2001

Stevenson, Warren, *Romanticism and the Androgynous Sublime*, London: Associated University Presses, 1996

Stimpson, Catharine R., 'The Androgyne and the Homosexual', in *Where the Meanings Are*, New York and London: Methuen, 1988

Stimpson, Catharine R., 'My O My O Myra', in Jay Parini, ed., *Gore Vidal: Writer against the Grain*, London: André Deutsch, 1992

Straayer, Chris, *Deviant Eyes, Deviant Bodies: Sexual Reorientations in Film and Video*, New York: Columbia University Press, 1996

Taylor, Greg, *Artists in the Audience: Cults, Camp and American Film Criticism*, Princeton, NJ: Princeton University Press, 1999

Taylor, Melanie, '*Orlando*, Life-writing, and Transgender Narratives', in *Modernist Sexualities*, ed. Hugh Stevens and Caroline Howlett, Manchester: Manchester University Press, 2000, pp. 202–18

Thiele, Beverley, 'Coming-of-Age: Edward Carpenter on Sex and Reproduction', in Tony Brown, ed., *Edward Carpenter and Late Victorian Radicalism*, London: Frank Cass, 1990, pp. 100–25

Tiffany, Grace, *Erotic Beasts and Social Monsters: Shakespeare, Jonson and Comic Androgyny*, Newark: University of Delaware Press, 1995

Tyrrell, William Blake, *Amazons: A Study in Athenian Mythmaking*, Baltimore: Johns Hokpins University Press, 1984

Veeder, William, *Mary Shelley and Frankenstein: The Fate of Androgyny*, Chicago: University of Chicago Press, 1986

Vetterling-Braggin, Mary, *'Femininity', 'Masculinity', and 'Androgyny': A Modern Philosophical Discussion*, New Jersey: Littlefield, Adam and Co., 1982

Weil, Kari, *Androgyny and the Denial of Difference*, Charlottesville and London: University of Virginia Press, 1992

Weininger, Otto, *Sex and Character*, London: William Heinemann, 1906

Wilkinson, Oliver Marlow, assisted by Christopher Wilkinson, *The Letters of John Cowper-Powys to Frances Gregg*, London: Cecil Woolf, 1994

Williams, Linda Ruth, *Sex in the Head: Visions of Femininity and Film in D.H. Lawrence*, Detroit: Wayne State University Press, 1993

Woolf, Virginia, *Letters*, Vol. 3, London: Chatto and Windus, 1977

Woolf, Virginia, *The Pargiters*, ed. Mitchell Leaska, London: Hogarth Press, 1978

Woolf, Virginia, *Diary*, Vol. 3, 1925–1930, Harmondsworth: Penguin, 1982

Woolf, Virginia, *Diary*, Vol. 5, 1936–1941, Harmondsworth: Penguin, 1985

Woolf, Virginia, *Collected Essays*, Vol. II London: Hogarth Press, 1987

Woolf, Virginia, *The Voyage Out* (1915), London: Hogarth Press, 1990

Woolf, Virginia, *Night and Day* (1919), London: Hogarth Press, 1990

Woolf, Virginia, *Orlando* (1928), London: Hogarth Press, 1990

Woolf, Virginia, *Women and Fiction: The Manuscript Versions of A Room of One's Own*, ed, S.P. Rosenbaum, Oxford: Blackwell, 1992

Woolf, Virginia, *A Room of One's Own* (1928), Harmondsworth: Penguin, 1993

Worthen, John, *D.H. Lawrence and the Idea of the Novel*, London and Basingstoke: Macmillan, 1979

Young, Suzanne, 'The Unnatural Object of Modernist Aesthetics: Artifice in Woolf's *Orlando*', in *Unmanning Modernism: Gendered Re-Readings*, ed. Elizabeth Jane Harrison and Shirley Peterson, Knoxville: The University of Tennessee Press, 1997, pp. 168–88

Index